VOTES FOR WOMEN! THE AMERICAN WOMAN SUFFRAGE MOVEMENT AND THE NINETEENTH AMENDMENT

Recent Titles in the Guides to Historic Events in America
Randall M. Miller, Series Editor

The Underground Railroad: A Reference Guide
Kerry Walters

Lincoln, the Rise of the Republicans, and the Coming of the Civil War: A Reference Guide
Kerry Walters

America in the Cold War: A Reference Guide
William T. Walker

Andrew Jackson and the Rise of the Democrats: A Reference Guide
Mark R. Cheathem

The Progressive Era: A Reference Guide
Francis J. Sicius

Reconstruction: A Reference Guide
Paul E. Teed and Melissa Ladd Teed

The War for American Independence: A Reference Guide
Mark Edward Lender

The Constitutional Convention of 1787: A Reference Guide
Stuart Leibiger

The Civil Rights Movement: A Reference Guide
Peter B. Levy

The Immigration and Nationality Act of 1965: A Reference Guide
Michael C. LeMay

The Watergate Crisis: A Reference Guide
Michael A. Genovese

VOTES FOR WOMEN! THE AMERICAN WOMAN SUFFRAGE MOVEMENT AND THE NINETEENTH AMENDMENT

A REFERENCE GUIDE

Marion W. Roydhouse

Guides to Historic Events in America
Randall M. Miller, Series Editor

An Imprint of ABC-CLIO, LLC
Santa Barbara, California • Denver, Colorado

Library of Congress Cataloging-in-Publication Data

Names: Roydhouse, Marion W. (Marion Winifred), 1949- author.
Title: Votes for women! : the American woman suffrage movement and the Nineteenth Amendment : a reference guide / Marion W. Roydhouse.
Description: 1 Edition. | Santa Barbara : ABC-CLIO, 2020. | Series: Guides to historic events in America | Includes bibliographical references and index.
Identifiers: LCCN 2020008672 (print) | LCCN 2020008673 (ebook) | ISBN 9781440836701 (hardcover) | ISBN 9781440836718 (ebook)
Subjects: LCSH: Women—Suffrage—United States—History. | Suffragists—United States—History. | Women's rights—United States—History. | CYAC: United States. Constitution. 19th Amendment.
Classification: LCC HQ1236.5.U6 R69 2020 (print) | LCC HQ1236.5.U6 (ebook) | DDC 305.420973—dc23
LC record available at https://lccn.loc.gov/2020008672
LC ebook record available at https://lccn.loc.gov/2020008673

ISBN: 978-1-4408-3670-1 (print)
      978-1-4408-3671-8 (ebook)

24 23 22 21 20   2 3 4 5

This book is also available as an eBook.

ABC-CLIO
An Imprint of ABC-CLIO, LLC

ABC-CLIO, LLC
147 Castilian Drive
Santa Barbara, California 93117
www.abc-clio.com

This book is printed on acid-free paper ∞

Manufactured in the United States of America

CONTENTS

Biographical Essays

Primary Documents

A photo essay appears following page 156.

SERIES FOREWORD

Perhaps no people have been more difficult to comprehend than the Americans. As J. Hector St. Jean de Crèvecoeur asked during the American Revolution, countless others have echoed ever after— "What then is this American, this new man?" What, indeed? Americans then and after have been, and remain, a people in the process of becoming. They have been, and are, a people in motion, whether coming from a distant shore, crossing the mighty Mississippi, or packing off to the suburbs, and all the while following the promise of an American dream of realizing life, liberty, and happiness. The directions of such movement have changed, and sometimes the trajectory has taken a downward arc in terms of civil war and economic depression, but always the process has continued.

Making sense of that American experience demands attention to critical moments—events—that reflected and affected American ideas and identities. Although Americans have constructed an almost linear narrative of progress from the days of George Washington to today in relating their common history, they also have marked that history by recognizing particular events as pivotal in explaining who and why they believed and acted as they did at particular times and over time. Such events have forced Americans to consider closely their true interests. They also have challenged their commitment to professed beliefs of freedom and liberty, equality and opportunity, tolerance and generosity. Whether fighting for independence or empire, drafting and implementing a frame of government, reconstructing a nation divided by civil war, struggling for basic rights and the franchise, creating a mass-mediated culture, standing up for capitalism and democracy and against communism, to name several critical developments, Americans have understood that historic events are more than just moments. They are processes of change made clear through particular events but not bound to a single moment or instance. Such thinking about the character and consequence of American history informs this new series of *Guides to Historic Events in America*.

Drawing on the latest and best literature, and bringing together narrative overviews and critical chapters of important historic events, the books in the series function as both reference guides and informed analyses to critical events that have shaped American life, culture, society, economy, and politics and fixed America's place in the world. The books do not promise a comprehensive reading and rendering of American history. Such is not yet, if ever, possible for any single work or series. Nor do they chart a single interpretive line, though they share common concerns and methods of inquiry. Each book stands alone, resting on the expertise of the author and the strength of the evidence. At the same time, taken together the books in this new series will provide a dynamic portrait of that ongoing work in progress, America itself.

Each book follows a common format, with a chronology, historical overview, topical chapters on aspects of the historical event under examination, a set of biographies of key figures, selected essential primary documents, and an annotated bibliography. As such, each book holds many uses for students, teachers, and the general public wanting and needing to know the principal issues and the pertinent arguments and evidence on significant events in American history. The combination of historical description and analysis, biographies, and primary documents also moves readers to approach each critical event from multiple perspectives and with a critical eye. Each book in its structure and content invites students and teachers, in and out of the classroom, to consider and debate the character and consequence(s) of the historic event in question. Such debate invariably will bring readers back to that most critical and never-ending question of what was/is "the American" and what does, and must, "America" mean.

Randall M. Miller
Saint Joseph's University, Philadelphia

PREFACE

Voter registration, voter identification laws, gerrymandering of Congressional districts, access to the polling booth on election day—all are questions with which we are familiar in our current political climate. Few consider women voting to be an issue for participatory democracy in today's America. Yet, it took from the founding of the nation until 1920 before women could vote in every state of the nation.

The woman suffrage movement and the civil rights movement constitute the two most important mass movements for equality and political participation in American history. The passage in 1920 of the Nineteenth Amendment, giving women the right to vote, was a momentous event, coming as it did after more than seventy years of organized effort, and signaling as it did a national commitment to a wider access to political power for women at a time when "making the world safe for democracy" had brought the question of universal suffrage and participatory democracy into a national debate.

This work looks at the process of building a historical interpretation of how women got the vote, as well as telling the story of woman suffrage through the lens of those who fought the suffrage campaigns. It also puts the question of woman suffrage in the context of the political, social, and economic changes taking place in the United States. Historians mined the deep resources provided by suffragists themselves in the massive *History of Woman Suffrage*, produced by Susan B. Anthony, Elizabeth Cady Stanton, Matilda Joslyn Gage, and Ida Husted Harper. The limits of this history have come into focus since the 1990s as biographies and regional histories have added to the layers of meaning needed to understand the nature of the movement as a whole.

Core questions are addressed in the chapters that follow: How did outsiders to the political system become part of the political structure? Why would politicians increase the number of people to whom they were accountable? Why were some states more fertile ground for campaigning than others? Enfranchisement of women was a process of state-by-state battles as well as national campaigns. Women and men undertook long, difficult, and often discouraging campaigns for access to local, state, and federal participation in the mechanics of the democratic process. *Votes for Women! The American Woman Suffrage Movement and the Nineteenth Amendment* explores these political issues.

Other questions call for viewing the woman suffrage movement through the lens of social history. What would create the seismic shift in cultural attitudes needed to win the vote? How would deeply held religious beliefs be modified? Women in the nineteenth century were hemmed in by social conventions that prohibited public speaking and public roles. How, then, did women create large, effective organizations that conducted massive political campaigns and eventually triumphed over these deeply entrenched conventions.

This volume examines the process of the movement and the doubling of the electorate not as a triumphalist and inevitable march to woman suffrage but as a movement that faced enormous barriers, was perceived as threatening the very core of accepted beliefs, and waxed and waned over the years before 1920. It is a tale full of strong protagonists and brilliant organizers who were intellectually innovative and yet reflective of the great divides of race, class, and religion existing throughout the nation.

As a schoolgirl in New Zealand in the 1950s and 1960s, the fact that we were the first nation where women voted was a source of pride. Women won the vote in New Zealand in 1893, but the myth created around that event had men "giving" women the vote, without any effort on the women's part. This was not true, but, like other myths surrounding woman suffrage, this one stuck tenaciously. I can remember no other discussion of women in New Zealand history. Actually, the subject of New Zealand history was still in its youth, and examination of the role of women settling this particular frontier was in its infancy. Only when I came to North Carolina and was guided by Anne Firor Scott into a new world of women's history did I realize how important the right to vote was for women.

Writing this book has been an intellectual adventure that allowed me to leave the world of higher education administration and return to women's history. I am indebted to the many historians whose efforts have informed my research; much of their work is cited in this book.

This journey could not have been accomplished without the help of a great many people.

The staff at Jefferson University's East Falls campus library, particularly Dee Linke and Meg Leister, kept my long list of interloan requests flowing. I owe Randall Miller, the series editor and a friend, more than I can ever repay. His support, guidance, and patience have been endless, his scholarship has helped me avoid many an embarrassing error, and his editing skills molded the final version into a worthwhile contribution to a part of American history that needs more investigation. Adele Lindenmeyr is a model historian and also the best of friends who gave me needed bolstering as we shared life and our work over breakfasts. To employ a much used cliché, I could not have finished this book without the support of my family. My daughter, Kate, who was writing her dissertation allowed me to share the daily agonies of research and writing, and my son Tom kept the household going doing every errand, collecting piles of interloan books, cooking and cleaning. Once my husband Peter retired, he became the chief cook and much more. Peter suffered through too many anecdotes about fascinating women and he read and reread the manuscript, being the best editor, while a somewhat argumentative one. He is also the best companion and partner that I could ever have imagined.

Introduction— Women Vote: The Brief Episode of New Jersey

"The rights of women are no longer strange sounds to an American ear."[1]

Elias Boudinot (1793)

"The *petticoat faction's* a dangerous thing."[2]

John Conduit (1807)

The struggle for votes for women did not begin, as is sometimes thought, at Seneca Falls in 1848; it began at the very founding of the nation. Women voted in New Jersey in the early years of the Republic but had that right removed in 1807. Representative John Conduit was nearly defeated by the weight of women's votes in the elections of 1797. His subsequent opposition to women voting was driven by his opinion that the "petticoat faction" was a "dangerous thing" and led to the legislation of 1807, which ended the brief period of woman suffrage. It was politically expedient for the Jeffersonian Republicans, like Conduit, once they were in power, to remove women from the electorate, along with free blacks, though women had been courted as voters by both parties, Federalists and Republicans, when their votes were advantageous in close-fought elections. The Representative behind the 1807 bill to eliminate all but "free, white, male, citizens," argued that the state constitution referred to "all inhabitants," and this could mean white men, white women, single and married, free blacks, men and women, "unfree" blacks, men and women, and aliens. Surely "no-one could suppose" that this was the intent of the constitutional delegates in 1776. He proposed to disfranchise women and free black men and women. The 1807 bill was couched as a means of eliminating blatant fraud at the polls rather than a specific attack on women voters or free black male voters.[3]

For this brief moment in American history, women were assumed to be citizens who were part of the body politic, who had rights as citizens that included the right to vote. The Continental Congress directed all thirteen states to draw up their own constitutions in 1776. New Jersey promptly did so, producing one of the most liberal provisions of who should have the right of voting; the law provided that "all inhabitants of this colony of full age, who are worth fifty pounds . . ., shall be entitled to vote for Representatives in Council and Assembly; and also for all other public officers, that shall be elected by the people of the County at large."[4] Later legislation reinforced the interpretation that all inhabitants meant women, with reference to "he or she" in residence qualifications. In 1787, instructions about how the ballot should be given to election officials also used "he or she" in reference to voters. Single women and widows with enough property could vote. At first, there is little evidence that more than a handful of women voted, but as two parties emerged in highly contested electoral battles after 1790, women were courted as voters, and more did so.

The limitation to widows and single women was rooted in the British legal system, much of which was incorporated wholesale in American law. The British legal system defined married women as legally "dead," meaning that any rights and obligations they had were subsumed by husbands. This legal fiction described married women as "feme covert," or the married state as "coverture," to distinguish them from a "feme sole" who could own property and conduct business. Once married, a woman could not own property, or sign legal documents, she needed her husband's consent to get an education, and if he allowed her to earn money, she had to hand over wages to her spouse. Of all these curbs on individual rights, the most hated was that a mother did not have any legal right to her children. Access to more education as a means of being independent, and eradicating coverture, piece by piece, were the first goals of women's rights activists as they organized in the 1840s.[5]

New Jersey politics in the 1790s and the first decade of the 1800s were notoriously corrupt, and elections became increasingly hard fought as "the Junto" (the Federalists) and the increasingly powerful Jeffersonian

Republicans competed for control of the state. During the celebration of the Fourth of July in 1793, a close friend of Federalist Alexander Hamilton, native New Jerseyan Elias Boudinot, delivered a ringing speech extolling the blessings of the new country that could be enjoyed by all, including women, for the "rights of women are no longer strange sounds to an American ear."[6] Other Federalists connected natural rights with women, and there were some public comments on the worth of Englishwoman Mary Wollstonecraft's radical theories on woman's rights and the need for education to support "independence" when needed.[7] Newspapers included stories of women who devoured the newspapers for political news, of women writing political essays, and of women sending letters to be published.

Not everyone was convinced. William Pennington of Newark, provoked by a loss in 1802 which he attributed to women's votes, introduced a bill to eliminate all but free white males from electoral rolls. The bill was patently unconstitutional because the state constitution could not be amended by legislation alone, and when it was clear that the Republicans did not have the votes to pass the bill, it was withdrawn, but the incident was a sign of things to come. Both parties began to calculate the significance of the women's vote—one Federalist writer estimated ten thousand women were eligible, but the evidence doesn't reveal how many actually voted. In 1803, some 150 votes by Federalist women for a senatorial seat indicate that the numbers were not insignificant. In the meantime, the Republicans also courted women's votes; in 1800, another Fourth of July speech included reference to "Our daughters are the same relation to us as our sons; we owe them the same duties; they have the same science, and are equally competent to their attainments."[8] The same year, men lifted toasts to "The fair daughters of Columbia" who voted for Thomas Jefferson and Aaron Burr.

As the balance between Federalist and Republican parties grew even, and as both parties concluded that the other party had more women supporters, the enthusiasm for both women and black voters waned. These voters, it was believed, could not be relied upon in the growing party system where voters were no longer individuals but members of a party. The tide turned against women. In 1806 and 1807, factionalism within the Republican Party resulted in a particularly fraud-ridden election over the placement of a new courthouse, either in Newark or Elizabeth-town.

A county-wide referendum in Essex County was riddled with stuffed ballots and barely concealed efforts to vote more than once. The voter turnout in Elizabeth was 290 percent, with reports of women and men impersonating women among those who voted more than once.[9] "Women vied with men, and in some instances surpassed them, in illegal voting," wrote one commentator, recalling the election years later.

The result was that the Republicans healed their internal divisions and supported a bill to "eliminate corruption" in elections. Eliminating corruption turned out to mean that removing women and free blacks and reducing the electorate to free, white, male citizens would solve the problem. This time there was no significant objection to the fact that this legislation de facto amended the state constitution. Under the guise of improving the young democracy, the right to vote in New Jersey was based upon property holding and gender, and given that by 1807 the amount of property needed was small, the electorate was effectively reduced to free, white, male citizens.

New Jersey's constitution writers were working in a climate of revolutionary ardor. They were men who absorbed the theories of the English, Scottish, and French Enlightenment philosophers who rejected the "divine right" given by God to monarchs who supported authoritarian regimes, and the British system that Patriots were fighting against. John Locke argued that women were able to reason as men did; only their lack of knowledge (therefore their lack of education) prevented them from being equal to men. This and other questions of women's abilities were debated, but few denied that women did not have "natural rights." It was just unclear what those natural rights meant when it came to forming a democratic government.[10]

The question of women's ability or right to be part of those who voted for congressional representatives did come up for discussion during the Constitutional Convention in 1787. James Wilson of Pennsylvania wrote a draft proposal outlining who should be included as electors in each state. Representation, Wilson wrote, should be "in proportion to the whole number of white & other free Citizens & inhabitants of every age sex and condition including those bound to servitude for a term of years and three fifths of all other persons not comprehended in the forgoing description, except Indians not paying taxes, in each State." But this draft went to the Convention's Committee on Style who took their pens up to edit. In the final version, the word "sex" was removed from the list of electors. Women were not part of the body of those who were deemed the body politic.[11]

The failure of men to continue woman suffrage in New Jersey and, as historian Linda Kerber has observed, the limitation of the electorate and "restricting women's politicization was one of a series of conservative choices that Americans made in the postwar years as they avoided the full implications of their own revolutionary radicalism."[12] Women themselves had to fight for the right to have political influence. Those excluded from voting, male and female African Americans and white women, became a continual source of political and social agitation well into the twentieth century. Enfranchising male and female African Americans and white women took generations of conflict, and the issue was not settled until both the passage of the Nineteenth Amendment and then the Civil Rights Movement of the 1960s, and not even then. Voting restrictions are still a subject of dispute.[13]

Few historians recognized New Jersey's first constitution as intentionally including women, and few people remembered that women voted there for a short period. Many decades later, historians who knew women voted dismissed it as an aberration, a mistake by those writing the New Jersey constitution. One of those who did not forget was the abolitionist and suffragist, Lucy Stone, who refused to pay real estate taxes for her Orange, New Jersey, property in 1857. "Women," she informed the tax collector, "suffer taxation without representation and yet have no representation, which is not only unjust to one half the adult population but is contrary to our theory of government." Lucy Stone lectured New Jersey audiences on the history of woman suffrage in New Jersey, calling for the removal of the words "male" and "white" from the New Jersey constitution. She reminded a committee of the state legislature that New Jersey had once led the way with its suffrage laws.[14] Here, she said, was a way to restore New Jersey's leadership in creating the kind of democracy envisioned by the Founding Fathers—with the consent of the governed, including the consent of half the population that were women.

This book travels the journey from New Jersey's first woman voters onward to the birth of a woman's rights movement and the emergence of a suffrage movement in the 1850s and 1860s. After the Civil War and the passage of the Fourteenth and Fifteenth Amendments, which included the word "male" for the first time in the U.S. Constitution, women who had expected to be included with freedmen as voters turned to organizing again. Woman suffrage, by itself, rather than as a part of a series of woman's rights issues, became an organized movement, and indeed a mass movement.

The intent of this examination of the long process of getting woman suffrage and the passage of the Nineteenth Amendment is to show how women organized to put pressure on the country's political system to allow women entrance into the body politic and into the political arenas of the states and the federal government. Electoral politics and gender ideology were central to the decades-long struggle. The mass movement created over the nineteenth century and swelling more in the early twentieth century included women from every state, from every walk of life, highly educated and barely educated, immigrants and those who traced their family roots to the early colonies, women who had access to powerful politicians, and those who knew only the ward leader in political machine–run cities such as New York, Chicago, Boston, and Philadelphia.

The vote seems a usual and necessary part of a participatory democracy, and a prized part of being a citizen. But it turns out that politics are not an abstract thing, but intertwined with changing cultural and moral values, as well as "pure" politics. That the fight for votes for women took over seventy years, from a woman's rights convention held in Seneca Falls in 1848, usually seen as the formal start, until the ratification of the Nineteenth Amendment by the thirty-sixth state to do so, Tennessee, in August 1920, seems peculiar now, to say the least. Even after the Nineteenth Amendment was added to the U.S. Constitution, some writers and later some historians thought the impact of the Amendment was minuscule, because common wisdom had it that women were voting as their husbands or fathers told them. It is now commonly known that women did vote without male guidance and fought on in the decades after 1920 for entrance into the rooms of power within political parties. Knowing the long history of the woman suffrage fight illuminates the current battles over registration, the number of polling places, gerrymandering to ensure the victory of one party over another, and other barriers to universal suffrage that still exist.

NOTES

1. Elias Boudinot, quoted in Judith Apter Klinghoffer and Lois Elkis, "'The Petticoat Electors': Women's Suffrage in New Jersey, 1776–1807," *Journal of the Early Republic* 12, no. 2 (Summer 1992): 174.

2. John Conduit, quoted in Klinghoffer and Elkis, "The Petticoat Electors," 177.

3. Klinghoffer and Elkis, "The Petticoat Electors," 177.

4. Jan Ellen Lewis, "Rethinking Women's Suffrage in New Jersey, 1776–1807," *Rutgers Law Review* 63, no. 3 (August 8, 2011): 101–19; Edward Raymond Turner, "Women's Suffrage in New Jersey, 1790–1807," *Smith College Studies in History* 1, no. 4 (July 1916): 165–87.

5. Linda K. Kerber, *Women of the Republic: Intellect and Ideology in Revolutionary America* (Chapel Hill, NC: University of North Carolina Press, 2000), 139–55.

6. Klinghoffer and Elkis, "The Petticoat Electors," 174.

7. Mary Wollstonecraft (1759–1797) was an English author whose work, *A Vindication of the Rights of Woman*, published in 1792, is still a core reading for women's history. See Rosemarie Zagarri, *Revolutionary Backlash: Women and Politics in the Early American Republic* (Philadelphia: University of Pennsylvania Press, 2007), 40–43.

8. Klinghoffer and Elkis, "The Petticoat Electors," 177–9; Zagarri, *Revolutionary Backlash*, 30–37.

9. Lewis, "Rethinking Women's Suffrage in New Jersey, 1776–1807," 101–19.

10. Scottish Enlightenment thinking saw women as having dual obligations; first, they had obligations and duties which were to husbands and family, and only secondarily did they have membership in the state. Zagarri, *Revolutionary Backlash*, 174–80; Kerber, *Women of the Republic*, 15–32.

11. Lewis, "Rethinking Women's Suffrage in New Jersey, 1776–1807," 101–79.

12. Kerber, *Women of the Republic*, 287.

13. Alexander Keyssar, *The Right to Vote: The Contested History of Democracy in the United States* (New York, NY: Basic Books, 2000); Alan J. Lichtman, *The Embattled Vote in America: From the Founding to the Present* (Cambridge, MA: Harvard University Press, 2018).

14. Sally G. McMillen, *Lucy Stone: An Unapologetic Life* (New York, NY: Oxford University Press, 2015), 244.

CHRONOLOGY: WOMAN SUFFRAGE

1776	New Jersey women, aged twenty-one and over, who are single or widowed, can vote if they fulfill residency and property requirements.
1792	Publication in London of Mary Wollstonecraft's *A Vindication of the Rights of Woman*.
1807	New Jersey legislature rescinds women's right to vote.
1833	Oberlin College founded. African American men are admitted in 1835 and women beginning in 1837. Suffragists Lucy Stone and Antoinette Brown (Blackwell) graduate in 1847.
1836	Married Women's Property Act introduced in the New York state legislature.
	Angelina Grimke publishes *Appeal to the Christian Women of the South*, attacking slavery. Angelina and sister Sarah speak to mixed ("promiscuous") audiences of men and women.
1837	First National Anti-Slavery Society Convention of American Women held in New York. Nearly 200 women representing twenty female antislavery groups attended.
1839	Mississippi passes the first Married Woman's Property Act.
1840	
May	The American Anti-Slavery Association splits over the question of women speaking, voting, or holding office.

June 12–23	The World's Anti-Slavery Convention is held in London. Female delegates are told they will not be seated. Lucretia Mott meets Elizabeth Cady Stanton for the first time.
1846	Six women from Jefferson County, New York, petition delegates to the state constitutional convention demanding political rights.

1848

	New York passes the Married Women's Property Act.
July 19–20	Seneca Falls Convention meets in the Wesleyan Chapel in Seneca Falls, New York. Participants sign "The Declaration of Rights and Sentiments" inspired by the Declaration of Independence.

1850

	Sojourner Truth, itinerant preacher, suffragist, abolitionist, and ex-slave, publishes her autobiography, *The Narrative of Sojourner Truth*.
October 23–24	First National Woman's Rights Convention held in Worcester, Massachusetts. One thousand people attended.

1851

May 28–29	Sojourner Truth delivers her "Ain't I a Woman?" speech at a Women's Rights Convention in Akron, Ohio.
October 15–16	Second National Woman's Rights Convention held in Worcester, Massachusetts.

1852

September 8–10	Third National Woman's Rights Convention held in Syracuse, New York. Matilda Joslyn Gage and Susan B. Anthony enter the movement.
	Amelia Bloomer publishes a sketch of "Turkish dress" in the journal *The Lily*; they become known as "bloomers."

1853

Antoinette L. Brown (later Blackwell) becomes first ordained female minister of a recognized denomination at the First Congregational Church in Wayne County, New York.

October 6–8   Fourth National Woman's Rights Convention held in Cleveland, Ohio.

1854

Mary Ann Shadd Cary is the first black woman to publish a newspaper, *The Provincial Freeman*, in Windsor, Ontario.

October 18   Fifth National Woman's Rights Convention held in Philadelphia, Pennsylvania.

1855

May 1   Lucy Stone marries Henry Blackwell. Stone keeps her own name, and together they read a protest against marriage laws. A married woman who retains her own name is now labeled a "Lucy Stoner."

October 17–18   Sixth National Woman's Rights Convention held in Cincinnati, Ohio.

1856

November 15–26   Seventh National Woman's Rights Convention held in New York City.

1861   Civil War begins; U.S. Sanitary Commission established with funds raised by Union women.

1862   Julia Ward Howe publishes "Battle Hymn of the Republic."

1863   The Woman's National Loyal League is formed by Elizabeth Cady Stanton and Susan B. Anthony to support the war effort and end slavery.

1865

December 6	Thirteenth Amendment of the U.S. Constitution is ratified, abolishing slavery.
	Great Britain: John Stuart Mill, campaigning for Parliament in Britain, includes votes for women in his election campaign. Start of U.K. suffrage organizations.

1866

May 10	American Equal Rights Association (AERA) founded. Lucretia Mott, Elizabeth Cady Stanton, Lucy Stone, Susan B. Anthony, Frederick Douglass, and Henry Blackwell are founders of the AERA, which is to be an organization for all races and genders, dedicated to universal suffrage and the rights of women and freed slaves.

1868

January	Anthony and Stanton publish the first edition of *The Revolution*, with the slogan "Men, their rights and nothing more; women, their rights and nothing less." The paper closes in 1872.
July 28	Fourteenth Amendment to the Constitution is ratified, which guarantees full rights of citizenship to "all persons born or naturalized in the United States." For the first time, the word "male" is used to define "citizens" and "voters."
November	Isabella Beecher Hooker organizes the New England Suffrage Association.
November 19	In Vineland, New Jersey, 172 women, both black and white, cast ballots in a separate box during the presidential election, inspiring similar demonstrations in following years.
December 7	Senator S. C. Pomeroy of Kansas introduces the first resolution for a federal woman's suffrage amendment in Congress.

1869

	Wyoming territorial legislature passes woman suffrage.

March	Federal woman's suffrage amendment is introduced as a Joint Resolution to both Houses of Congress by Rep. George W. Julian of Indiana.
May 15	The National Woman Suffrage Association (NWSA), based in New York City, founded by Elizabeth Cady Stanton and Susan B. Anthony to achieve the vote by federal amendment.
November 18	The American Woman Suffrage Association (AWSA) is formed by Lucy Stone, Henry Blackwell, Julia Ward Howe, and others.
	Francis Minor publishes pamphlet presenting the "New Departure" argument that under the Fourteenth Amendment women are citizens and can, therefore, vote.

1870

	Utah territorial legislature passes woman suffrage.
	The *Woman's Journal* founded—edited by Mary Livermore, Lucy Stone, and Henry Blackwell of the AWSA.
March 30	Fifteenth Amendment certified, granting suffrage without regard to "race, color, or previous condition of servitude."

1871

January 11	Victoria Woodhull addresses the House Judiciary Committee, arguing women's right to vote is covered by the Fourteenth amendment because women are citizens.

1872

October 15	Virginia Minor tries to vote in Missouri and is refused. Civil suit brought by Francis Minor and Virginia Minor.
November 5	Susan B. Anthony votes with fifteen other women in Rochester. Two weeks later they are arrested.

1873

April 15   *Bradwell v. Illinois*: U.S. Supreme Court rules that Myra
                Bradwell's rights have not been denied because Illinois
                refused her the right to practice law on the grounds
                that she was a married woman.

June 17   Susan B. Anthony is tried for voting illegally in Canandaigua, New York, and is convicted on the grounds
                that the Fourteenth Amendment did not protect her
                right to vote. She refuses to pay the $100 fine.

December 23   The Woman's Christian Temperance Union (WCTU)
                is founded in Hillsboro, Ohio. Led by Annie Wittenmyer, it becomes the largest woman's organization in
                the nation. Francis Willard becomes president in 1876.

1874   *Minor v. Happersett*: U.S. Supreme Court rules that
                Fourteenth Amendment does not protect a woman's
                right to vote. Court rules that women as citizens do not
                have the same rights as men. Individual states have the
                right to decide which citizens could vote.

1876

July 4   Anthony and Matilda Joslyn Gage disrupt the Centennial Program at Independence Hall, Philadelphia,
                during the 1876 Centennial Exhibition. Anthony
                presents the "Declaration of Rights of the Women of
                the United States" to President Pro Tempore of the
                U.S. Senate, Thomas Ferry.

1878

January 10   Senator Aaron A. Sargent of California introduces
                a Joint Resolution that will eventually become the
                Nineteenth Amendment (also called the "Susan B.
                Anthony Amendment").

1880   Mary Ann Shad Cary organizes the Colored Women's
                Progressive Franchise Association in Washington, DC,
                an auxiliary to the predominantly white NWSA.

1881

Elizabeth Cady Stanton, Susan B. Anthony, and Matilda Joslyn Gage publish the first volume of *The History of Woman Suffrage*. There will be six volumes published by 1922.

October   WCTU, led by Frances Willard, endorses woman suffrage.

1882   U.S. Senate and House of Representatives appoint select committees on woman suffrage—both report out favorably for woman suffrage.

1883   Washington territorial legislature passes full voting rights for women.

1884   Belva Ann Lockwood becomes the first woman candidate to be nominated by a significant party (the National Equal Rights Party) to run for President of the United States.

1887

January 25   The first vote on woman suffrage is taken in the Senate, where it is defeated 34–16, with twenty-five members absent.

Congress rescinds women's suffrage in Utah. Territorial Supreme Court repeals woman suffrage in Washington Territory.

1890

The NWSA and the AWSA merge to form the National American Woman Suffrage Association (NAWSA). Elizabeth Cady Stanton is elected president.

The General Federation of Women's Clubs is founded.

1892

African American leader Josephine St. Pierre Ruffin founds the Woman's Era Club in Boston.

Ida B. Wells launches her national antilynching campaign after the murder of three black businessmen in Memphis, Tennessee.

Elizabeth Cady Stanton delivers the "Solitude of Self" speech and leaves NAWSA.

1893

Colorado is the first state to pass a state referendum on woman suffrage.

New Zealand becomes the first country to give women the vote.

October 18   Lucy Stone dies.

Hannah Greenbaum Solomon founds the National Council of Jewish Women at the Columbian Exposition in Chicago.

1894

Clara Cressingham, Carrie C. Holly, and Frances S. Klock are elected to the Colorado House of Representatives, becoming the first women to serve in a state legislature.

Josephine St. Pierre Ruffin founds and edits the *Boston Woman's Era*, dedicated to publishing works of "representative colored women."

1895

New York State Association Opposed to the Extension of the Suffrage to Women formed.

Massachusetts Association Opposed to the Further Extension of Suffrage to Women is launched.

Elizabeth Cady Stanton, with contributions from twenty-five women, publishes *The Woman's Bible*, which challenges interpretation of the scriptures that claims that women should be subservient to man. NAWSA distances itself from Stanton despite objections from Susan B. Anthony.

1896

Utah admitted to statehood with woman suffrage.

Idaho referendum passes votes for women.

The National Federation of Afro-American Women and the National League of Colored Women merge to form the National Association of Colored Women (NACW). The first president is Mary Church Terrell.

1897   The National Union of Women's Suffrage Societies (NUWSS) formed in Britain to bring together women's suffrage groups. Millicent Garrett Fawcett becomes the president.

1900   Susan B. Anthony resigns as president of NAWSA and nominates Carrie Chapman Catt, who succeeds her.

1901   College Equal Suffrage League is founded by Maud Wood Park in Massachusetts.

1902

October 26   Elizabeth Cady Stanton dies.

1903

National Women's Trade Union League (NWTUL) is founded.

NAWSA holds convention in New Orleans and supports a states' rights approach to membership which endorses segregated membership.

Women's Social and Political Union (WSPU) is founded in Britain by Emmeline Pankhurst. It will be the "militant" wing of the British movement.

1904

Carrie Chapman Catt resigns as NAWSA president. Anna Howard Shaw elected.

The International Alliance of Women founded in Berlin to promote woman suffrage and equality.

1906

March 13   Susan B. Anthony dies.

1907   Harriot Stanton Blatch forms the Equality League of
                  Self-Supporting Women (later called the Women's
                  Political Union) in New York.

1908   National College Women's Suffrage League is formed
                  with M. Carey Thomas as president.

1909   The National Association for the Advancement of
                  Colored People (NAACP) is formed. It will be a voice
                  for equal rights for African American women.

1910

                  Washington State referendum passes women's suffrage
                  referendum.
                  First major women's suffrage parade is held in New
                  York City. The parade, led by Harriot Stanton Blatch
                  and Maud Malone, marches down Fifth Avenue.
                  NAWSA establishes Congressional Committee as liai-
                  son group to lobby Congress.
                  New York Men's League for Woman Suffrage holds its
                  first meeting.

1911

                  California referendum passes women suffrage.
                  New methods of publicity and public campaigning
                  adopted.

March 25   A fire at the Triangle Shirtwaist factory, in New York,
                  kills 146 workers.

November   Josephine Jewell Dodge establishes the National Asso-
                  ciation Opposed to Woman Suffrage (NAOWS).

1912

                  Theodore Roosevelt and Progressive (the "Bull
                  Moose") Party support woman suffrage.

	Militant "suffragettes" in Britain escalate tactics and undertake terrorist acts against property: mass window breaking, setting fire to empty buildings and post boxes, and cutting telegraph and telephone wires.
January	Kansas referendum on woman suffrage passes with a large majority.
November	Arizona referendum approves women suffrage amendment with two-to-one majority.
December	Alice Paul is appointed chair of the NAWSA Congressional Committee. Joined by Lucy Burns, Crystal Eastman, and Dora Lewis.

1913

	Alaska territorial legislature votes for woman suffrage.
March 3	Alice Paul and Lucy Burns organize suffrage parade in Washington, DC, the day before Woodrow Wilson's inauguration. Around eight thousand people parade, attracting national attention when the marchers are attacked by the crowds.
April	Alice Paul and Lucy Burns found the Congressional Union (CU), later known as the National Woman's Party (NWP).
June 26	The Illinois state legislature votes for "presidential suffrage," which will be copied in other states as an alternative to state constitutional amendments via referendum.
	Ida. B. Wells-Barnett founds the Alpha Suffrage Club in Chicago.
November	The Southern States Woman Suffrage Conference is formed by Kate Gordon to lobby state legislatures for suffrage for white women's votes. The Conference supports states' rights and opposes federal amendment.
November 15	CU begins publication of *The Suffragist*. In December, the journal declares that the CU will hold the party in power responsible for the success of a federal amendment.

1914

Montana referendum passes woman suffrage.

Nevada referendum passes woman suffrage.

Shafroth-Palmer Amendment presented to Congress: will require states to hold referenda on suffrage if 8 percent of voters petition for it. Undermines Susan B. Anthony Amendment campaign and is later withdrawn.

National Federation of Women's Clubs endorses woman suffrage.

Frank Leslie bequeaths two million dollars to Carrie Chapman Catt, but family contests the will. Catt receives around $1 million for woman suffrage campaigns.

December 8   During President Wilson's address in Congress, five militant suffragists unfurl a banner that reads "Mr. President, What Will You Do for Woman Suffrage."

President Wilson declares that woman suffrage should be decided by the states.

1915

Woman suffrage amendments defeated in New York, Pennsylvania, Massachusetts, and New Jersey.

Jane Addams, Fannie Garrison Villard, and Crystal Eastman organize the Woman's Peace Party.

Alpha Suffrage Club and Ida B. Wells are pivotal to the election of Oscar Priest as Chicago alderman.

June 5–7   The NWP is formed for women who already have the vote. NWP Joins with CU in 1917.

September   Sara Bard Field travels across country from San Francisco to Washington, stopping on the way to speak and gather more signatures for suffrage petition which eventually carries 550,000 names.

December   Carrie Chapman Catt is elected President of the NAWSA.

1916

April–May   "The Suffrage Special" with twenty-three CU members leaves Washington, DC, on a five-week train tour of the West to gather support.

August   Thirty-six NAWSA state chapters endorse Carrie Catt's "Winning Plan." The plan sets out a unified national campaign combining federal and state campaigns, and primary election campaigns in the South.

1917

New York passes woman suffrage by constitutional referendum.

North Dakota secures presidential suffrage by legislative enactment.

Nebraska secures presidential suffrage by legislative enactment.

Rhode Island secures presidential suffrage by legislative enactment.

Arkansas secures primary suffrage by legislative enactment.

January 10   NWP pickets appear in front of White House holding up two banners—"Mr President, What Will You Do For Woman Suffrage" and "How Long Must Women Wait for Liberty?" Women remain there regardless of the weather. The protesters are named the "Silent Sentinels."

April 2   Jeannette Rankin of Montana is seated in the U.S. House of Representatives, the first woman to be elected to Congress. She votes against entering the war.

April 6   United States enters World War I. Known at the time as the "Great War."

April 20   Anna Howard Shaw named by President Wilson to found and head the Woman's Committee of the Council of National Defense. Carrie Chapman Catt joins the Committee's work.

September 24   U.S. House Committee on Woman Suffrage formed.

October	Arrested while protesting and imprisoned in Occoquan Workhouse, Lucy Burns circulates a petition that demands better conditions for the suffragists. Every woman who signs the petition is removed from Occoquan and placed in solitary confinement.
October 16–22	Alice Paul and other members of the NWP arrested while picketing. Paul sentenced to seven months in Occoquan Workhouse. The suffragists demand to be treated as political prisoners, not criminals.
November 5	Alice Paul and Rose Winslow begin a hunger strike. After a week, they are subjected to force-feeding three times a day for three weeks. Paul is separated from the other prisoners and placed in a psychiatric ward with the intention of having her committed involuntarily.
November 15	Imprisoned militant suffragists in Occoquan Workhouse endure the "night of terror" when guards use brutal force to put the women in their cells. The next day sixteen women go on a hunger strike.

1918

	Great Britain: Representation of the People Act gives the vote to women over age thirty if they are householders, wives of householders, occupiers of property with annual rent of five pounds, or graduates of British universities.
	Texas allows women participation in primaries.
	South Dakota passes woman suffrage after six prior defeats.
	Michigan passes woman suffrage.
	Oklahoma passes woman suffrage.
January 9	President Wilson states public support of the federal woman suffrage amendment for the first time.
January 10	House votes 274–136, precisely two-thirds, in favor of woman suffrage amendment.
March 4	District of Columbia Court of Appeals declares that the 1917 arresting and sentencing of picketers was invalid.

September 30	President Wilson addresses the Senate and argues for the passage of the federal woman suffrage amendment as a war measure.
September 30	Senate fails to give the necessary two-thirds vote to the federal woman suffrage amendment.
November 11	World War I ends.

1919

	Indiana presidential suffrage, passed in 1917 but rendered questionable by court decision, passed again with only six dissenting votes.
	Seven states pass presidential suffrage:

    Maine
    Missouri
    Iowa
    Minnesota
    Ohio
    Wisconsin
    Tennessee

January 6	In an urn directly in line with the White House front door, the NWP lights a perpetual "watch-fire for freedom"—burns words of Wilson's speeches on democracy.
March 24	Carrie Chapman Catt proposes formation of a League of Women Voters to "finish the fight" at the fiftieth Anniversary Jubilee Convention of the NAWSA in St Louis.
May 21	House passes woman suffrage, 304–89, a margin of forty-two over the needed two-thirds. Opponents block action in the Senate for another two weeks, delaying ratification as most legislatures had adjourned for the year.
June 4	Senate passes Nineteenth Amendment with two votes to spare, 56–25. Sent to the states for ratification.
	New Zealand, Australia, Finland, Norway, Denmark, Iceland, Russia, Austria, Canada, Germany, Hungary, Latvia, Lithuania, Poland, United Kingdom, Belgium, Kenya, Luxembourg, Netherlands, and Rhodesia already have woman suffrage in 1919.

1920

	Women's Joint Congressional Committee founded.
	League of Women Voters founded as "mighty experiment."
February	Victory Convention of the NAWSA in Chicago. Thirty-three states ratify.
August 18	Tennessee becomes the thirty-sixth state to ratify the Nineteenth Amendment.
August 26	The Nineteenth Amendment is signed into law by Secretary of State Bainbridge Colby. Women can vote in states where they are not blocked from voting by literacy tests, poll taxes, and other means.

1921

| November 23 | Sheppard-Towner Act passes, providing funding for mothers and infants. |

1923

| July | Alice Paul proposes the Equal Rights Amendment (ERA) to Congress at the seventy-fifth anniversary of the Seneca Falls Convention. The ERA asks that "men and women shall have equal rights throughout the United States and every place subject to its jurisdiction." |

1926

| November | A group of African American women are beaten by election officials in Birmingham, Alabama, when they attempt to register to vote. |

1928

| July 2 | British Parliament passes legislation to allow all men and women over the age of twenty-one to vote. |

1965

| January 3 | Patsy Takemoto Mink becomes the first woman of color elected to Congress and represents Hawaii in the House for nearly twenty-six years. |

August 6	The Voting Rights Act is signed into law by President Lyndon Baines Johnson, forbidding states to impose various discriminatory restrictions on voters.

1968

June 18	Shirley Chisholm is the first African American woman elected to Congress, representing New York.
1972	The ERA passes both houses of Congress and goes to the states for ratification, with a deadline of 1979. The deadline was extended until 1982, but the amendment was not ratified. The ERA passed in thirty-seven of the thirty-eight states needed for ratification.
2018	Record breaking 126 women are elected to the U.S. Congress at the mid-term elections. One hundred two women are elected to the House of Representatives, including forty-three women of color. Twenty-four women are elected to the Senate, including four women of color.

CHAPTER 1

A WORLD OF HOPE: ABOLITION AND WOMAN'S RIGHTS, 1807–1861*

AN AGE OF REFORM

Nearly six feet tall, with magnificent straight bearing, and with great presence, Sojourner Truth could rivet an audience to their seats and could face down a mob.[1] Born in the 1790s into a Dutch-speaking, slaveholding family in the Hudson Valley, and named by them, Isabella Van Wagenen, as soon as she was a free woman, renamed herself Sojourner Truth, began her career as an abolitionist speaker, and sold copies of her autobiography to tell her own story and make money. Truth was not just an abolitionist; she was one of the women who launched woman's rights conventions which were the beginning of the suffrage movement. In 1848, Seneca Falls, in upstate New York, was the site of the first convention to gather people to discuss only woman's rights, and then a first "National" convention was held in Worcester, Massachusetts, in October 1850. Sojourner Truth was on the platform with Frederick Douglass and other dignitaries at meetings in Worcester and then Akron. Together they reminded the overwhelmingly white audience that enslaved women should be an essential part of the fight for equal rights for women.

---

* In the eighteenth and nineteenth centuries writers referred to woman's rights and the woman's movement. Only in the twentieth century did it change to the plural—women's movement and women's rights.

A year later in Akron, Ohio, in 1851, Sojourner Truth made a speech that became her most famous piece of oratory, lasting in significance in history alongside the Declaration of Sentiments the Seneca Falls convention had issued in 1848. Truth's speech became legendary, catching the imagination of generations of women. Her biographer, Nell Irvin Painter, referred to Truth's status as one of the two (with Harriet Tubman) most famous black women in history and reminds us that when most Americans thought of slaves as male and women as white, Truth embodied a fact that still bears repeating; "Among the blacks are women; among the women, there are blacks."[2]

The speech was captured by a reporter from the Salem *Anti-Slavery Bugle*. With a voice like "rolling thunder," Truth spoke:

> I want to say a few words about this matter. I am woman's rights. I have as much muscle as any man, and can do as much work as any man. I have plowed and reaped and husked and chopped and mowed, and can any man do more than that! I have heard much about the sexes being equal; I can carry as much as any man, and can eat as much too, if I can get it. I am as strong as any man that is now. As for intellect, all I can say is, if a woman have a pint and man a quart—why can't she have her little pint full? You need not be afraid to give us our rights for fear we will take too much,—for we can't take more than our pint'll hold. The poor men seem to be all in confusion, and don't know what to do. Why children, if you have woman's rights, give it to her and you will feel better. You will have your own rights, and they won't be so much trouble . . . man is in a tight place, the poor slave is on him, woman is coming on him, he is surely between a hawk and a buzzard.[3]

Sojourner Truth's smashing of the shibboleths of the conventional wisdom on properly behaved and physically delicate women revealed the way that contemporary views of proper behavior applied only to white, middle-class, and comfortably off women. Sojourner Truth forced her audience to link woman's rights and abolition, and reminded them that woman's rights meant the rights of both black and white women. Truth's speech also highlighted the conflict between a vision of women at the center of their households, who did not participate in the economy outside their family home except by proxy, and the reality for the working women, black and white, who had to earn a living to support their family.

Historians are intrigued by the puzzles posed by people's behavior. What inspired one person into a life of reform and not another with a similar background? They look beyond institutions and public reform struggles to see how one man or one woman took the steps that made them to see the world around them as flawed. What made this person decide to take action themselves and endure the condemnation of their families, their church congregation, or others who otherwise mattered to them? Glimpses into the paths taken by those who built the woman's movement and the suffrage movement can illuminate the historian's attempt to reveal the wider world in which they lived and the social, cultural, and economic shifts that fostered the changes over time that formed the suffrage movement. Changes in American life in the 1830s, 1840s, and 1850s laid the underpinnings of an organized woman's movement. Sojourner Truth's passage to woman's rights is distinctive to only a few women, but her conviction that women deserved equality was not.

Historians have also diverged in their interpretations of the routes women took to woman's rights conventions and into the suffrage movement. Some trace women's growing sense of disquiet with the roles assigned to them and their subsequent involvement in reform and particularly in woman's rights to the narrowing of white middle-class women's lives forced by the domestic ideology that took hold during the 1830s and after. Others have pointed to the number of activist women who were Quakers, Unitarians, and Universalists, rather than members of Protestant churches. Whether women who went through conversion in the sweep of evangelical fervor that peaked in the 1830s were more likely than others to join reform organizations and then the woman's rights movement is another question asked by historians.[4] Two changes that historians largely agree upon are the rise of a domestic ideology, and with it the division of public and private life, and the huge impact of the Second Great Awakening that began in Connecticut in the 1790s and grew to a crest across much of the United States in the 1830s.

The common wisdom of essential biological differences between men and women escalated into a powerful ideology of differing gender roles over the 1830s and 1840s. This "Cult of True Womanhood," as historian Barbara Welter termed it, was rooted in a view of women as not only biologically but also intellectually different from men and that each sex belonged to a "separate sphere" where their influence could be best put to work to create a righteous world. For women, that sphere was the world of the family and the domestic household, which extended into church and charitable work. According to the logic of the "true woman" presented in women's advice books and women's magazines, a woman's selflessness, moral purity, religious conviction, and piousness could influence the greater social order.[5] The precise nature of this domestic sphere, whose boundaries have proved to be more porous than unyielding, has been the subject of historical debate, but the general notion of a separate world of women holds its usefulness in examining the rise of a woman's rights movement, and particularly the opposition to the woman's rights crusades. Only a middle-class family could sustain such a vision of women's roles. It was not possible for textile workers working long hours for little pay in the mills of Lowell or for slave woman whose families could be sold away at any time. An implied precept of this domestic ideal was that a woman's place was not in politics or business; if women were to have a voice in politics, it would be through their husbands and male relatives.

This ideology took a deep hold on the nation's psyche and combined with new religious fervor. As a great religious revival swept the nation, women took up benevolent and charitable work in an endeavor to make a more perfect world; they created and ran orphanages and homes for the aged and widows, they raised money for direct relief—food, fuel, and clothing, and they supported temperance efforts. The increasing proportion of women to men in Protestant churches combined with the message of perfectionism drew women to benevolent work and some to reform and woman's rights. Protestant ministers were eager supporters of benevolent voluntarism, although somewhat wary of women's role in their churches. Northern women also became abolitionists, seeking to eliminate one of the most glaring examples of sin in the antebellum world.

Americans were optimistic about creating a new world and set about making that new world more perfect than the one they were living in. Reforms of all kinds became a major defining force; mankind could conquer sin by sheer force of individual will. The sins of intemperance, slavery, prostitution—all could be addressed in this "Perfectionist" or "Ultraist" view of one's moral duty. Women tried to stop prostitution, built schools and homes for orphans, endeavored to raise the morals of the poor, and created utopian communities to provide a model for a better way to live.

As a great evangelical crusade rolled across the country, taking deep hold in the 1830s, the free-thinkers, religious skeptics, and deists of the

Revolutionary years were forced to defend themselves against the new, more emotional, religiosity produced by the prolonged evangelical revivals called the "Second Great Awakening," to distinguish it from the Great Awakening of the 1730s and 1740s. Charles Grandison Finney, the Second Great Awakening's most effective and most famous, most flamboyant preacher and legendary orator, was over six feet tall, with piercing eyes and unruly eyebrows. He held audiences spellbound for hours on end during extended revival meetings that could last days. Men and women were led to salvation and dedicated themselves to eradicating individual sins and creating a more perfect world which would lead the way to the millennium (the Second Coming).

In the 1830s, Charles Finney became a professor at the newly established Oberlin College in Ohio, the first college to admit African American men in 1835 and then four women, who enrolled in 1837. Leading abolitionists, and particularly abolitionist women—Lucy Stone, Antoinette Brown—attended Oberlin as did Wendell Phillips who became both an abolitionist leader and woman's rights supporter. William Lloyd Garrison, who was an Oberlin supporter, did the same. Oberlin graduates were molded by the Great Awakening, and some of its women graduates interpreted the domestic sphere as having elastic boundaries as they did what they knew was "God's work."

RADICAL THINKERS: A SOURCE OF WOMAN'S RIGHTS OPINIONS

Whether educated at home, self-educated, or given some formal schooling at an academy, women in the postrevolutionary period became more literate, particularly in the northeast. A small number of articulate women produced essays, books, and journals, which were distributed and shared up and down the East Coast and to inland settlements. Here was the fuel for women who wanted to listen to lectures or read newspapers and essays on woman's rights, despite the opposition of the majority of male clergy and much public outrage at women who stepped across the boundaries of the household and suitable behavior.

English author Mary Wollstonecraft was the earliest and most widely read intellectual source on women's status and limited rights. *A Vindication of the Rights of Woman*, published in 1792, argued that if women were ever to be granted full rights, they needed to be educated and able to support themselves as independent individuals. Wollstonecraft's work was an instant hit; publisher Matthew Carey in Philadelphia printed fifteen hundred copies and quickly had to reprint more. Judith Sargent Murray, an American-born theorist, produced essays arguing for women's ability to participate in civil society. Women, Murray claimed, had all the attributes for political citizenship.[6] In 1798, Murray published her collected columns and essays, *The Gleaner*, in which she examined the need for a new nation to have intelligent (and educated) women, claiming that a woman's brain was not inherently inferior. Woman's rights were a topic of discussion in private salons and gatherings among urban elites and wealthier rural families.

Traveling lecturers were another way of self-education and spreading radical ideas. Fanny Wright, a Scottish-born woman's rights advocate, sailed for America in the summer of 1818. An admirer of the American Revolution, she toured the country and then wrote a series of laudatory letters that were published as *Views of Society and Manners in America*. After a failed utopian experiment to free slaves and a lecture tour, Wright's reputation suffered as she became known for believing in free love, attacked the hypocrisy of a religion that condoned slavery, and argued for equal rights for women. Public speaking and pursuit of equality for women roused deep antipathies that manifested in a link between sexual license and reforming women exemplified by Fanny Wright. Conservative clergy labeled Fanny Wright "The Red Harlot," a "procuress of atheism and infidelity," making her a symbol for all that was wrong with free thinking.[7] "Wrightism" became an epithet used to attack women abolitionists and women's rights speakers.

The first African American woman to give public lectures on woman's rights, free-born Maria Miller Stewart, encountered even deeper opposition. Her speaking career lasted only three years, from 1830 to 1833, because Stewart felt it fruitless to continue in the face of such antipathy, which denied her message any chance of success.

Despite this opposition, women persisted in raising the question of woman's rights. The roots of a woman's movement were just reaching into the fertile soil of optimism for humankind's improvement that was engendered by the natural rights principles of the Enlightenment, which still informed nineteenth-century thinking, and the perfectionist thrust of the Second Great Awakening.

ANTISLAVERY AND THE EMERGENCE OF A WOMAN'S RIGHTS MOVEMENT

The wave of evangelism spurred the radical antislavery movement in the 1830s. William Lloyd Garrison founded the American Anti-Slavery Society (AASS) in 1833 with the goal of immediate freedom for slaves, who must be given the "same privileges as persons of white complexion," and no compensation for slave owners.[8] Philadelphia women Lucretia Mott, Lydia White, Esther Moore, and Sidney Ann Lewis were with the sixty-four men at the AASS organizing convention in Philadelphia. Paid agents circulated antislavery literature and petitions and recruited new members. Women became traveling agents, and some of these women, particularly Abby Kelley and Lucy Stone, added woman's rights to their speaking repertoire in the 1840s.

By 1836, there were nearly one thousand state and local antislavery societies. When women's auxiliaries were attacked as unseemly, antislavery women fought back by defending themselves in print, often in William Lloyd Garrison's newspaper *The Liberator*. They argued in letter after letter that they were simply doing God's work. As "True Women," they declared, they were following the Biblical injunctions to participate in charitable work and to work for moral change.

A racially integrated group of fourteen women in Philadelphia organized a notably successful female abolition society, the Philadelphia Female Anti-Slavery Society, founded in 1833. Lucretia Coffin Mott—a Quaker preacher and an abolitionist already famous for her interest in Indian rights, as well as the equality of women—was a founder.[9] Several free black women—Charlotte Forten, her daughters Margaretta and Sarah, and Harriet Forten Purvis—joined Lucretia Mott. Charlotte's husband, James Forten, and Robert Purvis, Harriet's husband, were among Philadelphia's wealthiest black families. The Forten women, along with Sarah Mapps Douglass, Grace Bustill Douglass, and others were committed to "racial uplift."[10] These abolition associations were the starting point for woman suffrage support for some of the women.

In the 1830s, Philadelphia greeted two white women who fled South Carolina, rejecting the slave system that supported their family income. Daughters of a wealthy slave-owner and Chief Justice of the South Carolina Supreme Court, Angelina and Sarah Grimké grew up in Charleston and on the family's up-country plantation. Both sisters eventually fled

Charleston because they were no longer willing to live with the institution of slavery. In Philadelphia, in 1835, Angelina wrote a letter to William Lloyd Garrison relating her life story and sympathy with abolition; Garrison published the letter, bringing instant fame to both sisters. They traveled across the Northeast giving accounts of the horrors of slavery, which caused an uproar in the South. They were attacked by hostile crowds in the North both for their abolitionism and violation of female propriety by speaking in public. Angelina wrote "An Appeal for the Christian Women of the South," which when published by the AASS was burned as treasonous in the South, and Charleston's leaders warned the sisters not to return.

Between 1836 and 1839, the sisters worked as the first female agents of the AASS, initially speaking only to women. Soon husbands wanted to attend, and Angelina was speaking to both men and women in "promiscuous" crowds. Few people hearing Angelina could fail to be moved by her speeches, delivered in a musical voice with passion. "I stand before you as a southerner, exiled from the land of my birth by the sound of the lash and the piteous cry of the slave. I stand before you as a repentant slaveholder," began one of her speeches.[11]

All too soon the Grimké sisters joined Fanny Wright and Mary Wollstonecraft as bywords for unwomanly behavior. A group of Congregational ministers issued a "Pastoral Letter" in 1837 attacking Angelina for unwomanly behavior.[12] Sarah wrote a pamphlet in response, *Letters on the Equality of the Sexes, and the Condition of Women*, which was widely praised and widely berated. It was a manifesto for equality and woman's rights. Angelina made her last public speech at the newly opened Pennsylvania Hall for Free Discussion on May 16, 1838. The hall was filled to overflowing, and antiabolitionist mobs milled outside. As speeches went on, the crowd in the hall became violent, forcing the speakers to stop and flee the mêlée. The next day the building was burned to the ground by proslavery crowds. The two sisters, and Angelina's new husband, Theodore Weld, retreated to New Jersey. Her successor as an agent for the AASS, Quaker Abby Kelley, trod the same path from abolition to woman's rights.[13] Over the following years, Abby Kelley helped grow what historian Julie Roy Jeffrey concludes was a "Great Silent Army of Abolitionism" in rural areas and small towns who took on the idea that it was outlandish for women to take part in public reform work.[14]

Abby Kelley led abolitionist women in gathering signatures for an antislavery petition to Congress. Using the right to petition, abolitionist women acquired organizational skills and a tough skin. Because the right to petition for redress of wrongs was well-rooted in British and American law, as abolitionists grew in number and slavery became more and more divisive, petitioning became a major strategy to force the attention of the U.S. Congress. Organizing petition campaigns became a key strategy for temperance reform and later woman suffrage, as well as antislavery.[15]

Responding to the deluge of antislavery petitions sent to the U.S. Congress in the 1830s asking for the end of slavery in the District of Columbia and other antislavery measures, southern Representative Henry Wise of Virginia rose to declare that politics was the province of man and that "woman in the parlor, woman in her proper sphere, is the ornament and comfort of man; but out of the parlor, out of her sphere, if there is a devil on earth, when she is a devil, woman is a devil incarnate!"[16] Congress moved to silence such women by refusing to accept the antislavery petitions. Henry Wise's sentiments on woman's roles echoed over the generations and even to the last suffrage battle in Tennessee in 1920.

DISSENSION IN THE ABOLITIONIST MOVEMENT

Early in 1840, the AASS split after a rancorous discussion of the place of women in the organization, and over the question of direct action and political participation rather than "moral suasion" to educate the American people on the deep wrong that slavery presented. The precipitating event was that William Lloyd Garrison had put forward AASS agent Abby Kelley for the AASS executive committee. Henry Stanton and James Birney led the opposition, forming the American and Foreign Anti-Slavery Society (AFASS), which did not allow women as voting members and intended to work within the political system.

Soon after the split all the abolitionists responded to a call to the "World's Anti-Slavery Convention," in London. In early May 1840, abolitionist delegates arrived in London finding themselves in the midst of controversy. It had not occurred to the English organizers that women might arrive expecting to be seated as formal delegates. Lucretia Mott, with pardonable sarcasm, wrote later that the male organizers were sure that the women would be honored to simply sit and listen to the convention debates as spectators. A long debate ensued on the "woman" question. Mary Grew from Philadelphia must have cringed to hear her father speak against women being seated, saying it was the "ordinance of Almighty God."[17] Boston patrician Wendell Phillips leaped to speak on the women's behalf.[18] Phillips was ably seconded by Unitarian George Bradburn, a "tall, thick-set man with a voice like thunder, standing head and shoulders above," who held forth against attacks on women's right to speak based on biblical interpretation, declaring "that if they could prove to him that the Bible taught the entire subjection of one-half of the race to the other, he should consider that the best thing he could do for humanity would be to bring together every Bible in the universe and make a bonfire of them."[19] From the start of the woman's rights movement there were men who were eager allies.

One can imagine how the Freemason's Hall rang with loud objections from some of the clergymen present. The women lost, fated to observe from the gallery. William Lloyd Garrison, arriving some days later, refused to sit on the floor of the "segregated" convention. He was repeatedly urged to speak, but he held fast. Black activist Charles Lenox Remond and two other men also joined the women.

Fathers and daughters were not the only ones divided by the "woman question." Elizabeth Cady Stanton, daughter of well-off Judge Daniel Cady from upstate New York, was there, not as a delegate, but on her honeymoon, as the newly married wife of noted abolitionist organizer, Henry B. Stanton. For Elizabeth, much of the "slavery question" was new to her, despite her family's antislavery connections. She had met abolitionists and fleeing slaves during her many visits to her wealthy abolitionist, philanthropist, and reforming cousin, Gerrit Smith.[20] Elizabeth Cady Stanton quickly became friendly with the Garrisonian women, who explained to her that marriage did not mean the burying of her own intellectual self in the views of her husband. One of Elizabeth Cady Stanton's biographers' comments that Henry may never have known what hit him once his young wife took up woman's rights.[21]

For Elizabeth, this London sojourn was a turning point as she reveled in Lucretia Mott's conversation, writing in her memoirs that the two women discussed holding a woman's rights convention at home in the United States. Elizabeth Cady Stanton's new friendships began a revolution in her life—her public career in woman's rights began in London.[22] The other American women delegates were also battle-scarred as abolition-ists and reformers in a way that Elizabeth Cady Stanton, with her lim-ited exposure to reform, could not understand. For Stanton, the issue was woman's equality foremost, and antislavery second. In fact, abolition was almost peripheral in Stanton's public life. She was a new kind of woman's rights activist, without strong roots in either temperance or abolition.

Elizabeth Cady Stanton went back to Boston and then to Seneca Falls in 1847. Seneca Falls was in the middle of the heavily evangelical part of upstate New York, near the bustling economic center of Rochester. Roch-ester was also the home of black abolitionist Frederick Douglass. Abby Kelley's antislavery campaigns in Seneca Falls in 1843 had thrown local church congregations into disarray with her forceful antislavery message. Kelley also gave woman's rights speeches—the town was well acquainted with the "woman question." Lucy Stone was giving speeches on woman's rights across New York and westward into Ohio in the same decade.

A petition from six farm women in New York to the 1846 New York state constitutional convention asking for woman suffrage, examined as evidence of a wider discussion of woman's rights and woman suffrage that went on in New York, has been incisively examined by historian Lori Ginzberg. Ginzberg sees the ideas that people might have discussed over dinner or at night by candlelight as prelude to the actions taken by these women, who could be described as "ordinary," who were doing something that was unusual, and in many ways extraordinary.

These women remain relatively opaque to us. These were the kind of women who disappear from historical record. Yet, these women demanded the vote, using the political right of petition, and writing that because governments "derive their just powers from the consent of the governed," natural rights demanded that New York's women be enfranchised. It was a question, they made clear, of natural rights, simple equality as citizens. Their petition was ignored, but it showed that the question of woman suffrage was not as unusual before the Seneca Falls meeting of 1848 as most histories have it; rather, that famous meeting in Seneca Falls perhaps reflected a level of discussion of woman suffrage that made the adoption of the resolution in support of woman suffrage at Seneca Falls less shocking than Elizabeth Cady Stanton knew at the time.

Seneca Falls is known today for the "second tea party that shook the world" and that led to a woman's rights convention and "struck what now seems a mighty spark," comments Lori Ginzberg.[23] In 1848, Seneca Falls seemed too isolated and too small, for Elizabeth Cady Stanton, used as she was to the comforts of servants and a household often full of visitors. At home with three small boys, often alone while Henry Stanton traveled, she "suffered from mental hunger, which, like an empty stomach, is very depressing. I had books, but no stimulating companionship. . . . An invitation to afternoon tea with Lucretia Mott in nearby Waterloo came as a much-welcomed interruption."[24] Jane and Mary Hunt hosted the tea, joined by Mary Ann McClintock and her daughter Elizabeth McClintock.

Hunt family lore remembered that in the afternoon Richard Hunt joined the women gathered in the parlor and challenged them to do more than talk, but "do something." Conventions, public gatherings with an array of speakers, were a model for reformers that all the women knew. The women decided that they must call a meeting while Lucretia Mott—as a famous speaker—was available to draw a crowd. The only gathering spot open to such a meeting was the Wesleyan Chapel in Seneca Falls, recently founded as a Methodist congregation open to all reformers. After some anxious discussion as to their goals, one of the women read out the Declaration of Independence with heavy sarcasm and with emphasis on the rights of "man," and so the seeds of the Seneca Falls "Declaration of Rights and Sentiments" were sown.

The first part of the declaration was comparatively easy to construct, replacing the single word "men" with the phrase "men and women." But the second section, echoing the list of grievances in the Declaration of Independence, was harder to write. Elizabeth Cady Stanton felt strongly that they should include in the grievances that men had "never permitted her to exercise her inalienable right to the elective franchise."

Here Stanton stood alone. Lucretia and James Mott as Quakers believed that any involvement in secular politics was to be avoided. Henry Stanton involved with the Free-Soil Party and Martin Van Buren's run for the presidency was convinced that the time was not right for woman suffrage. Indeed, Henry left Seneca Falls to give more political speeches on the eve of the convention, not before exclaiming that "you will turn the proceedings into a farce."[25] Probably seeing the suffrage grievance as the meeting began, Lucretia famously said "Lizzie, thou will make the convention ridiculous."[26] Even so, Elizabeth Cady Stanton held fast.

Despite the later myths stemming from Elizabeth Cady Stanton's own retelling of the convention, none of the organizers were complete novices in terms of public speaking or of arranging meetings. But they were doing something new; they were not calling a meeting that would include a number of reform causes. Elizabeth Cady Stanton steadfastly ignored Lucretia Mott's questions about including speakers on Indian rights or abolition. Stanton was able to hold her position that this was to be a convention about woman's rights only.

The morning of Wednesday, July 19, was clear and warm, and the day promised to be hot, as Elizabeth Cady Stanton, her visiting sibling Harriet Cady Eaton, and young Daniel Eaton set forth for the Wesleyan Chapel. They arrived to find a group gathered outside facing locked doors. Daniel was hoisted over a windowsill and promptly solved the problem, and everyone moved ahead into the building. The first day was intended for women only, but as whole families arrived, James Mott, Frederick Douglass, and some forty men were there the first day. The gathered men and women took apart the Declaration of Rights and Sentiments, usually just referred to as the Declaration of Sentiments, piece by piece.

"We hold these truths to be self-evident" reads Jefferson's Declaration. The Declaration of Sentiments changed the next phrase to "that all men and women are created equal." The section ends with the call that women must "demand the equal station to which they are entitled. The history of mankind is a history of repeated injuries and usurpations on the part of man toward woman, having in direct object the establishment of an absolute tyranny over her." The call for equality and the cry of tyranny of man over woman ends with "to prove this, let facts be submitted to a candid world," again repeating Jefferson.

The eighteen grievances that follow focus first on women's legal status and then the limits put on women's ability to be educated and join professions. Next comes Stanton's "he has never permitted her to exercise her inalienable right to the elective franchise." This complaint was the most controversial of the convention and beyond. As a result, went on the grievances, women have had to suffer from legislation in which they had no say. "He has compelled her to submit to laws, in the formation of which she had no voice," despite the fact that "ignorant and degraded men—both natives and foreigners" have rights withheld from women.

This whiff of nativism and condescension among suffragists would become stronger in the latter half of the nineteenth century.

Women's inferior legal status when married is then laid bare. Women's Declaration declared that "he has made her, if married . . . civilly dead" and prevented women from controlling their own wages, while also levying taxes on women's property, should she have any. Divorce laws are "wholly regardless of the happiness of women" because guardianship of children is given to men with the "false supposition of the supremacy of man." Men are able to "deprive women of liberty," they can "administer chastisement," and force women to "promise obedience," which pointed to the legal situation where a husband (in a reference to slavery that will be used by woman's rights advocates) is "to all intents and purposes, her master."

Worlds are closed to women because men have "monopolized nearly all the profitable employments" and paid women less for those jobs they could secure. Reflecting a burgeoning middle-class worldview, the grievances next point to the situation where theology, medicine, and law were closed to women. Women were also prevented from getting a college education, asserted the Declaration, although that situation was already changing by 1848, for Oberlin College admitted women on an almost equal footing, Mount Holyoke College for women was founded in 1837, and Otterbein College (1847) admitted both men and women.

In sum, men have "usurped the prerogative of Jehovah himself," excluding women from the ministry, enforcing subordinate positions in churches, and creating a "different code of morals for men and women." All this combined to "destroy her confidence in her own powers, to lessen her self-respect, and to make her willing to lead a dependent and abject life." Women "do feel themselves aggrieved, oppressed, and fraudulently deprived of their most sacred rights."

It is hard to overstate the significance of the Declaration of Sentiments in the history of feminism. It is the most important feminist statement to emerge from the woman suffrage movement. It still resonates with us, particularly because the echoing of the Declaration of Independence makes it feel familiar, and yet it is distinctly different. Historian Sally McMillen sums up the impact of the Declaration of Sentiments, writing that it captured the spirit of a generation. Another historian, Lori Ginzberg, labels the Declaration a foundational text in American democratic ideals in a "format that was both familiar and breathtaking, mainstream and radical, and that left many listeners wondering why they had not said these things first or as well." Further, comments Ginzberg, "adopting the language of the Declaration of Independence was an inspired move; it made the document instantly recognizable and because of that, repeatable. It also underscored Stanton's and McClintock's conviction that the rights they demanded fit squarely within the nation's traditions of equality and rebellion."[27]

The only resolution that sparked real debate, that women needed the vote, engendered extended discussion, much of it unfavorable. Frederick Douglass came to Elizabeth Cady Stanton's aid. He could not, he said, claim the vote for himself if he would not allow women the same right. Frederick Douglass later remembered with some pride his defense of this franchise resolution. The women and men in the church pews, fanning themselves in the late afternoon heat, proved willing to endorse the call for the franchise.

Asking for woman suffrage was indeed the most radical of the demands, or to view it in another way, the one demand that was new to many. Seneca Falls became the glorious start to the women's movement in the myth of the origins of the suffrage movement created by Elizabeth Cady Stanton and Susan B. Anthony.[28] Elizabeth would remember it as "the greatest movement for human liberty recorded on the pages of history— a demand for freedom for one- half the entire race."[29] The convention went on to a second day, where it was open to all in the community, and then the Seneca Falls convention was over and had been a great success. Within weeks a second convention, a larger and more diverse audience, including more Quakers who stayed in woman's rights reform, was held in Rochester. Elizabeth Cady Stanton and Elizabeth McClintock were initially outraged that a woman, Abby Bush, was elected to preside, but were reconciled to the idea. Abby Bush's presiding over the meeting was another step forward in the march to woman's rights and woman suffrage. Women could manage organizations alone.

BIRTH OF WOMAN'S RIGHTS CONVENTIONS

Seneca Falls marked the beginning of a series of conventions held across the Northeast and Midwest. These conventions were organized in the same informal fashion where several women formed an organizing group and conducted all the necessary planning. As a means of spreading the word, the convention allowed for meetings to be held over all the regions where woman's rights talks had been part of the abolitionist carpet-bag of topics, particularly where the Grimké sisters, Abby Kelly, and Lucy Stone had traveled as agents of the AASS.

These woman's rights conventions took place in a country slipping toward turmoil over the continuation of slavery in the South and the threat of expansion of slavery westward. Political turmoil was also widespread in Europe, where revolutionary movements threatened monarchies and conservative regimes. Woman's rights were part of reform agendas for some European revolutionary groups, which meant that the woman question was alive on both sides of the Atlantic.

In the 1850s, woman's rights conventions, with their speeches published and newspaper coverage, were the basic means of conveying the woman's rights causes to the antebellum public. They were the source of growing interest in the cause of woman's equality and woman's rights. Historian Nancy Isenberg argues for the vital role of these conventions in the 1850s, noting that they brought to public notice three main "revolutionary goals" for women: the right to have rights, the right to be citizens with political standing, and the right to equal treatment under the law.[30] Woman's rights conventions were rooted in the well-known right of people to assemble, the right of the people to address the government by petition, and the models of other gatherings by other reform groups; abolition and temperance were the closest models. Conventions had secretaries who took careful notes, and the minutes were published, as were speeches. Newspapers sent reporters, and men and women at the conventions wrote letters and articles for publication in both sympathetic and antagonistic newspapers.

Lucy Stone, and after 1852 together with Susan B. Anthony, led the organization of woman's rights conventions before the Civil War. Elizabeth Cady Stanton, staying in Seneca Falls to raise her increasing brood of children, provided speeches and essays and kept up a flow of correspondence with the growing network of woman's rights women. The three women's combined personalities and organizational abilities defined the organized woman's movement over the next forty years, through the division of the movement in 1869 and until the death of Lucy Stone in 1893.

Lucy Stone called the meeting in May 1850, where in a dingy room in Boston, a few people gathered to discuss a "national" woman's rights convention rather than those attracting people from one state or town. A small committee of seven women was formed, including Lucy Stone and writer Paulina Wright Davis. This group, with others coming and going, created the only national organizing committee in existence during the 1850s. Davis wrote the "call" or invitation to a national convention in Worcester, Massachusetts, for October 1850. Eighty-nine women and men signed the call in a list that reads as a who's who of the abolition and woman's rights movement. The call laid out issues for discussion: women's education, women's need for opportunities in the professions and all workplaces, women's political and legal needs, and woman's rights as an individual and a citizen. This was the broad agenda for woman's rights conventions for the decade.

Lucy Stone, the force behind this national convention, rose to national fame as an abolitionist speaker and agent of the AASS in the 1840s. Born in 1818 at "Coy's Hill," a moderately profitable farm in western Massachusetts, Lucy Stone was the eighth of nine children born to her abolitionist parents. Her father was a fairly successful farmer and tanner, and a hard drinker who was quick to anger. Perhaps not surprisingly her mother was a temperance supporter. Her father was adamant that education was wasted on women and refused to pay for more education for Lucy beyond that available near home. Saving enough money herself to attend Oberlin College in 1843, Stone then became a voracious scholar, reading widely, happily debating with fellow students, and forging a lifelong friendship with Antoinette Brown, a theology student who became her sister-in-law. When abolitionist Abby Kelley Foster and husband Stephen Foster visited Oberlin, both Stone and Brown made their first steps toward a life in abolition. Stone returned home to Massachusetts to teach, where she met William Lloyd Garrison and launched her career as a traveling lecturer for the Massachusetts Anti-Slavery Society. She moved into the ranks of the most famous orators of the era. Lucy Stone was tiny, bouncy, and charming, with a magical voice; she was deceptively like the current ideal of womanhood. Philosopher Ralph Waldo Emerson wrote, "Eloquence was dog-cheap in those days. . . . Even so, Stone stood out." One impressed reporter wrote, "I have never, anywhere, heard a speaker whose style of eloquence I more admired: the pride of her acquaintances, the idol of the crowd, wherever she goes, the people en masse turn out to hear Lucy Stone." Stone used plain prose, the speech of everyday life, when most orators of the time used a "high falutin" theatrical style. Her ability to convey that she was a gently raised women overwhelmed some of the antipathy raised by her subject matter—abolition and woman's rights. Stone negotiated to speak on woman's rights during the week and on anti-slavery on the weekends when the crowds were larger.[31]

In 1852, Stone went to Seneca Falls to stay with Elizabeth Cady Stanton for the first time. There she met Susan B. Anthony and Amelia Bloomer and promptly had her own Bloomer costume made. Stone now traveled the country in the short skirt and trousers for as long as she could endure the public shaming; wearing the skirt and trousers on the street caused groups of boys to congregate and follow her chanting ditties. "Hordes of boys pursue me and destroy all comfort," she complained, unable to sight-see in new towns. Lucretia Mott's daughters refused to be seen on the street with her in Philadelphia for the embarrassment and fuss it caused.

In 1855, at the height of her speaking career Stone agreed to marry Henry (Harry) Blackwell, an abolitionist who had been courting her for nearly three years. Stone had feared the loss of control over her life and income that marriage would bring. Henry Blackwell renounced any control of Lucy's property or income and together they wrote an attack on marriage laws which Thomas Wentworth Higginson, the presiding minister at the wedding, a fellow abolitionist and woman's rights advocate, endorsed and published. The marriage made headlines. Lucy also refused to take Blackwell's name, fighting convention for the rest of her life, particularly because her single name went unrecognized in legal actions, despite public shock and condemnation. Women who kept their own surnames were now known as "Lucy Stoners."

Egalitarian marriages were relatively common among abolitionists and in the woman's rights movement. Historian Blanche Hersh observes that "an impressive number of these (feminist) women chose to marry men who were also feminists; these couples shaped their marriages into new patterns, created egalitarian unions based on autonomy and shared responsibilities that would still be radical today." These couples refused to accept woman's "proper sphere" and managed to share responsibilities to allow women to be mothers, wives, and reformers.[32]

Susan B. Anthony was noticeably irritated when Lucy Stone married. Ida Husted Harper, Anthony's biographer, noted that "in 1855, to Miss Anthony's great regret, Lucy Stone and Antoinette Brown were married. . . . She [Anthony] was not opposed to marriage per se but she felt that such women as Lucy Stone and Antoinette Brown might make a sacrifice and consecrate themselves to the great needs of the world which were demanding the services of the ablest women."[33] In 1857, both Lucy Stone and Antoinette Brown Blackwell were pregnant. Susan was unhappy about organizing a national convention alone.

Born in 1820 to Daniel and Lucy Read Anthony, Susan was raised in a Quaker, abolitionist, and temperance family. Like Lucy Stone, Anthony's was a family whose economic fortunes waxed and waned, unlike the well-to-do comfort of Elizabeth Cady Stanton's home. Daniel Anthony moved the family in search of income, ending up in 1846 on a small farm near Rochester. Susan started teaching. At home in the fall of 1848, her family regaled her with the wonderful speeches they had heard at the woman's rights convention in Rochester. Susan initially scoffed, telling her father that he "was getting a good deal ahead of the times," but she was intrigued.

Anthony met Elizabeth Cady Stanton and began their lifelong friendship when she went to Seneca Falls in 1851 to hear the English Member of Parliament and world-famous abolitionist, George Thompson, who with William Lloyd Garrison was staying at the Stanton house. Soon she began her own reform career as a temperance speaker. Anthony traveled New York state organizing temperance meetings, raising petitions on married women's rights, and beginning her lifetime habit of staying at the Stanton house in between journeys. She and Stanton also began a lifetime partnership as the two women together produced letters, essays, speeches, and articles on woman's rights and suffrage. In 1856, Anthony became a traveling antislavery agent. Stanton felt that theirs was a perfect coalition. In working together, "we did better work than either could alone . . . she supplied the facts and statistics, I the philosophy and rhetoric, and, together, we have made arguments that have stood unshaken through the storms of long years."[34]

Anthony became an extraordinary organizer, a single-minded leader, but one with a comparative lack of speaking ability. Her plain looks, made plainer by the dull colors of her Quaker dresses, did little to show us in photographs what contemporaries described as a warm and generous person. Newspapers treated her with more ridicule and more vitriol than other woman's rights leaders, and she was widely caricatured, her critics probably spurred on by her status as a single woman. The *New York World* wrote "Susan is lean, cadaverous and intellectual, with the proportions of a file and the voice of a hurdy-gurdy."[35] One can only imagine the private hurt that Anthony endured.

Woman's Rights Convention Creates a Separate Movement

In Worcester, Massachusetts, in October 1850, for the first "national" meeting, every seat in the hall was taken, with the aisles and the platform filled with people who stood for the morning, afternoon, or evening sessions. Douglass' paper described Brinley Hall as "crowded with as intelligent, orderly, and interested a class of people as we ever saw assembled," speaking with such skill that he was inspired with "a fresh hope of humanity."

Paulina Wright Davis gave the opening speech arguing that men and women should not place blame for the wrongs suffered by women and instead focus on the goal to draw more people to the cause. Lucretia Mott immediately stood to counter Davis, speaking bluntly. Blame for wrongs should be placed clearly and loudly where women were prevented from control of their property or deprived of their rights, said Mott. Women, must demand their rights, not ask to be given them.

Frederick Douglas, Wendell Phillips, and Sojourner Truth together made sure that the gathering remembered the fate of enslaved women. A unanimously adopted resolution said that, "the cause we are met to advocate, the claims for Woman of all her natural and civil rights, binds us to remember million and a half wronged and foully outraged, of all Women; and in every effort at improvement of our civilization, we will bear, in our heart of hearts, the memory of trampled womanhood of the plantation, and omit no effort to raise it to a share in the rights we claim for ourselves."[36] This conjoining of racial oppression and woman's rights became a point of contention later on, but for the moment the movement was still so connected with abolition that the causes could be seen as connected.

The Worcester convention was covered widely in the newspapers. Some applauded, while others were vitriolic in their opposition to interracial gatherings and to the idea of woman suffrage. The headline in the *New York Herald* read "Woman's Rights Convention. Awful Combination of Socialism, Abolitionism, and Infidelity. The Pantalettes Striking for the Pantaloons. Bible and Constitution Repudiated." The delegates were easy to distinguish from the spectators "by their peculiar cast of countenance, which even among the ladies was generally gloomy and warlike. It was a convocation calculated to strike terror into the heart of the stoutest man." Abby Kelly Foster was "tall and thin, with an eye wild and resolute," and Lucretia Mott "all bone, gristle, and resolution," while Frederick Douglas, "quite a lion," was there with "several dark colored sisters [who]were visible in the corners."[37] "This was a dangerous group," concluded the *Herald*. Woman's rights advocates were tarred with the brush of radical reform, extremism, and attacks on established religious beliefs. Women were trying to "wear the breeches" in contravention to proper women's behavior.

There were some abolitionists and woman's rights reformers who thought woman's rights and abolition as causes should be separated. Jane Grey Swisshelm used her newspaper, *Pittsburgh Saturday Visiter*, to say so. "The convention was not called to discuss the rights of color; and we think it was altogether irrelevant and unwise to introduce the question."[38] There never was any unified position on immediate goals or action during any of these 1850s conventions. Lively dissension was the norm. Nonetheless the movement grew.

The 1850 National Woman's Rights convention in Worcester set the stage for future gatherings in organization and structure but it also revealed the growing problems facing black women activists. Black women found that during the 1850s, as the woman's movement widened its reach, they faced more racial prejudice within the white female community and criticism within their own communities. In 1855 Frederick Douglass signaled a change in attitude toward black women's rights, telling the Rochester Ladies Anti-Slavery Society that abolitionism had taken on too many issues, that "the battle of Woman's Rights should be fought on its own ground; as it is the slave's cause, already too heavy laden, had to bear up under this new addition."[39] Black women in reaction to this shift organized their own societies for racial uplift, which were also the conduits for woman's rights discussion.

In November 1856, the yearly national woman's rights convention was held in New York City, at the huge Broadway Tabernacle, in the same week as temperance and other reform meetings. Woman's rights had reached the stage that it was one of the great numbers of national reform organizations. For the first time, opponents were plentiful and vociferous. Mobs of men bent on disrupting the women's meeting appeared in large numbers. While Lucy Stone was speaking, someone hissed. Stone, with plenty of experience in disruption, retorted that the words of God were the same whether they came from the mouth of a woman or a man. Quiet for a while, the crowd re-erupted with laughter when Stone said men and women must be equals. The next day the hissing and booing overwhelmed all the speakers. Men clapped, yelled, whistled, and threw whatever came to hand.

Local, state, and national conventions were the most spectacular way of reaching new audiences, but other means of spreading the message became an effective way of reaching more and more women. Newspapers and journals spread the woman's rights cause to those who could afford them. Publications were handed from household to household, not simply read once and discarded. Speeches and reports from woman's rights conventions, newspaper columns in daily papers, and antislavery newspapers and journals all focused attention on the woman question. During the 1850s, newspapers and journals written and edited by women, aimed at an audience of women, came on to the market. Some were ephemeral; newspapers and journals were expensive to start up and often failed for lack of readership. Yet gradually, inch by inch, woman's rights were a subject for wide discussion across the Northeast and Midwest.

In addition to looking to local newspapers for reprints of articles and reports patched together from other sources, people in small towns and farming communities relied upon traveling speakers for news and education. Speaking tours of woman's rights advocates now reached a wide audience. The business of the lyceum, or traveling lecturer, blossomed in the 1850s. Wendell Phillips (himself very wealthy) said that a reformer needed to be free of earning a living, and Elizabeth Cady Stanton repeated Phillips's opinion. Yet, such sweeping judgments didn't reflect the reality of the lives of many women on the road who needed to earn a living.

Southern white women, those who were part of the slave-owning families, did create women's charitable and reform organizations on a smaller scale than did northern women. These elite women also had opinions on slavery, political issues, and political party conflict but had a harder road to getting them heard, than did northern women. Historian Elizabeth Varon looked closely at antebellum Virginia and concluded that southern white women were not totally excluded from the political system as many have assumed. In Virginia, the Whig Party campaigns of 1840 included women in public political rituals—party rallies, processions, and conventions. Women turned out to rallies; some made speeches, wrote pamphlets, and were appealed to as needed for a "new ideal of feminine civic duty." Such activism laid the groundwork for women's support for sectionalism in the 1850s, support for the Confederate army during the war, and support for the beginnings of woman's rights organization in the South in the postwar era. Sallie A. (Brock) Putnam of Richmond, in remembering the 1861 secession convention, wrote, "Every woman was to some extent a politician."[40] A woman's rights movement, organized in any formal way, did not appear in the antebellum South. Lucy Stone toured Kentucky, curtailing her topics to women's issues, but she was almost alone in doing so.

In the 1850s, the woman's rights movement contained a wide range (if not multitudes) of opinions on woman's equality. There was never agreement about what changes were the most important to fight for and what changes might get enough political support. Increasingly, there were battles over what were suitable topics. Elizabeth Cady Stanton caused a great uproar in 1860 in New York when she insisted on giving a speech on the need for looser divorce laws for women; she did so over the objections of Lucy Stone who feared that this topic was so explosive it would raise the mobs and be used as an example of the extreme radicalism of the women's conventions.

Stanton's speech electrified some, horrified many, and caused chaos. In her wonderfully written speeches, Elizabeth always conjured up images that could not fail to move those who heard them. In New York, she was at her best as she held the hall audience spellbound as she argued that marriage benefited men only. Wives had no choice but the accept the laws that bound them to their inequality. "Call that sacred, where woman, the mother of the race . . . consents to live in legalized prostitution! . . . held there by no tie but the iron chain of the law. . . . Call that sacred, where innocent children, trembling with fear, fly to the corners and dark places of the house, to hide themselves from the wrath of drunken, brutal fathers." The audience interrupting with its hearty applause, Stanton ended with a ringing attack on the religious argument that marriage was indissoluble. Antoinette Brown Blackwell took the floor and defended marriage as a religious institution that could not be dissolved. Wendell Phillips tried to table the whole issue to dampen the divisive debate. Was divorce a problem for both men and women, as Wendell Phillips and Stone believed, and therefore not strictly a question of woman's rights? Or was the position of women whose husbands were violent, or "drunkards," or who confined their wives to asylums with no legal recourse the result of legal inequalities that applied only to women? Debate and divisive arguments over what social and political reforms were reasonable or necessary for the woman's rights movement to fight for continued during and after the 1850s.

On the eve of the Civil War, woman's rights was still a minority cause, but its leaders and sympathizers included powerful and well-known men, from abolitionist to politicians. Wealthy Boston abolitionist Francis Jackson gave $5,000 anonymously with Stone, Anthony, and Phillips as trustees, and later the women shared in a $50,000 fund set up by Charles Hovey to support antislavery efforts as well as woman's rights. The woman's rights convention at Seneca Falls, in Rochester, the national convention in Worcester, all fostered woman's rights conventions in towns and cities in the Northeast and growing Midwest. From the women who attended these conventions came the leadership and enduring members of the woman's rights movement. These women also formed the foundation of the suffrage movement which organized formally after the Civil War.

NOTES

1. Mary Washington, *Sojourner Truth's America* (Urbana: University of Illinois Press, 2009), 111.

2. Nell Irvin Painter, *Sojourner Truth: A Life, a Symbol* (New York, NY: W. W. Norton, 2007), 4.

3. Marius Robinson, *Salem Anti-Slavery Bugle*, June 21, 1851, n.p. in Painter, *Sojourner Truth*, 125–6.

4. Nancy A. Hewitt, "Feminist Friends: Agrarian Quakers and the Emergence of Woman's Rights in America," *Feminist Studies* 12, no. 1 (1986): 27–49; Nancy A. Hewitt, *Radical Friend: Amy Kirby Post and Her Activist Worlds* (Chapel Hill: University of North Carolina Press, 2018); Anne M. Boylan, *The Origins of Women's Activism: New York and Boston, 1797–1840* (Chapel Hill: University

of North Carolina Press, 2002); Carol Smith Rosenberg, "The Female World of Love and Ritual: Relations between Women in Nineteenth-Century America," *Signs* 1 (1975): 1–29; Nancy F. Cott, *The Bonds of Womanhood: "Woman's Sphere" in New England, 1780–1835* (New Haven, CT: Yale University Press, 1977); Eleanor Flexner, *Century of Struggle: The Woman's Rights Movement in the United States* (Cambridge, MA: Belknap Press of Harvard University Press, [1959] 1996).

5. Barbara Welter, "The Cult of True Womanhood: 1820–1860," *American Quarterly* 18, no. 2 (Summer 1966): 151–74; Barbara Welter, *Dimity Convictions: The American Woman in the Nineteenth Century* (Athens: Ohio University Press, 1976).

6. Teresa Anne Murphy, *Citizenship and the Origins of Women's History in the United States* (Philadelphia: University of Pennsylvania Press, 2013), 59; Sheila L. Skemp, *First Lady of Letters: Judith Sargent Murray and the Struggle for Female Independence* (Philadelphia: University of Pennsylvania Press, 2009).

7. Lori D. Ginzberg, "'The Hearts of Your Readers Will Shudder': Fanny Wright, Infidelity, and American Freethought," *American Quarterly* 46, no. 2 (1994): 195–226.

8. Dorothy Sterling, *Ahead of Her Time: Abby Kelley and the Politics of Anti-Slavery* (New York, NY: W. W. Norton, 1991), 32.

9. Mott and her husband James were Hicksite Quakers. Hicksites were those who had formed a splinter group in 1827, who believed in "nonresistance."

10. Julie Winch, *A Gentleman of Color: The Life of James Forten* (Oxford: Oxford University Press, 2003); Shirley J. Yee, *Black Women Abolitionists: A Study in Activism, 1828–1860* (Knoxville: University of Tennessee Press, 1993); Emma Lapsansky, "Friends, Wives, and Strivings: Networks and Community Values among Philadelphia Afroamerican Elites," *Pennsylvania Magazine of History and Biography* 108 (January 1984): 3–24.

11. Gerda Lerner, *The Grimké Sisters from South Carolina: Rebels against Slavery* (New York, NY: Shocken Books, 1971), 9.

12. The "Pastoral Letter" of the General Association of Massachusetts Congregational Churches was read out in churches and attacked the temerity of women not following the directives of their pastor. See Beth A. Salerno, *How Did Local Antislavery Women Form National Networks in the Antebellum United States?* (Binghamton: State University of New York at Binghamton, 2007).

13. Sterling, *Ahead of Her Time*, 71. Angelina, Theodore, and Sarah retired to New Jersey to allow Theodore's voice to recover and the sisters to recover from the strain of their years of travel and lecturing. The sisters were determined to show that they could live exemplary lives as housewives to refute the miserable

attacks they had endured. With Theodore Weld, the two women produced the influential book, *Slavery As It Is*, compiled from interviews and southern newspapers, which Harriet Beecher Stowe used as a basis for her novel *Uncle Tom's Cabin*.

14. Julie Roy Jeffrey, *The Great Silent Army of Abolitionism: Ordinary Women in the Antislavery Movement* (Chapel Hill: University of North Carolina Press, 1998).

15. Susan Zaeske, *Signatures of Citizenship: Petitioning, Antislavery, & Women's Political Identity* (Chapel Hill: University of North Carolina Press, 2003).

16. Zaeske, Signatures of Citizenship, 128.

17. Ira V. Brown, *Mary Grew: Abolitionist and Feminist: 1813–1896* (Selinsgrove, PA: Susquehanna University Press, 1991), 27.

18. Sally G. McMillen, *Seneca Falls and the Origins of the Women's Rights Movement* (New York, NY: Oxford University Press, 2008), 73.

19. Elizabeth Cady Stanton, *Eighty Years and More: Reminiscences, 1815–1897* (1898; repr., New York, NY: Schocken Books, 1971).

20. Gerrit Smith was implicated in John Brown's raid on Harper's Ferry. Elizabeth Cady Stanton was well connected to both New York state politicians and abolitionists.

21. Lori D. Ginzberg, *Elizabeth Cady Stanton: An American Life* (New York, NY: Hill and Wang, 2009), 87.

22. Judith Wellman, *The Road to Seneca Falls: Elizabeth Cady Stanton and the First Woman's Rights Convention* (Urbana: University of Illinois Press, 2004), 63.

23. Jacob Katz Cogan and Lori D. Ginzberg, "1846 Petition for Woman's Suffrage, New York State Constitutional Convention," *Signs* 22, no. 2 (1997): 427–39; Lori D. Ginzberg, *Untidy Origins: A Story of Woman's Rights in Antebellum New York* (Chapel Hill: University of North Carolina Press, 2005).

24. Stanton, *Eighty Years and More*, 147.

25. Wellman, *The Road to Seneca Falls*, 193.

26. Wellman, *The Road to Seneca Falls*, 195.

27. Ginzberg, *Elizabeth Cady Stanton*, 58.

28. Lisa Tetrault, *The Myth of Seneca Falls: Memory and the Women's Suffrage Movement, 1848–1898* (Chapel Hill: University of North Carolina Press, 2014).

29. McMillen, *Seneca Falls*, 102.

30. Nancy Isenberg, *Sex and Citizenship in Antebellum America: Gender and American Culture* (Chapel Hill: University of North Carolina Press, 1998), 21.

31. Andrea M. Kerr, *Lucy Stone: Speaking Out for Equality* (New Brunswick, NJ: Rutgers University Press, 1992), 50–51.

32. Blanche Glassman Hersh, *The Slavery of Sex: Feminist-Abolitionists in America* (Urbana: University of Illinois Press, 1978), 218–51; Blanche Glass-

man Hersh, " 'Am I Not a Woman and a Sister?': Abolitionist Beginnings of Nineteenth-Century Feminism." In *Antislavery Reconsidered*, ed. Lewis Perry and Michael Feldman (Baton Rouge: Louisiana State Press, 1979), 252–83.

33. Ida Husted Harper, *Life and Work of Susan B. Anthony* (North Stratford, NH: Ayer Co., [1898] 1998), 128–9.

34. Stanton, *Eighty Years and More*, 166.

35. Alma Lutz, *Susan B. Anthony: Rebel, Crusader, Humanitarian* (Boston, MA: Beacon Press, 1959), 52.

36. Washington, *Sojourner Truth's America*, 205.

37. *New York Herald*, "Woman's Rights Convention," October 25, 1850, in John McClymer, *How Do Contemporary Newspaper Accounts of the 1850 Worcester Woman's Rights Convention Enhance Our Understanding of the Issues Debated at That Meeting?* https:womhist.alexanderstreet.com.

38. Sylvia D. Hoffert, *Jane Grey Swisshelm an Unconventional Life, 1815–1884* (Chapel Hill: University of North Carolina Press, 2014), 143–4.

39. Martha Jones comments, "For black activists there was little optimism to go around in the 1850s." Martha S. Jones, *All Bound Up Together: The Woman Question in African American Public Culture, 1830–1900* (Chapel Hill: University of North Carolina Press, 2007), 88–101.

40. Anne Firor Scott, *The Southern Lady: From Pedestal to Politics, 1830–1930* (Chicago: University of Chicago Press, 1970); Elizabeth R. Varon, *We Mean to Be Counted: White Women & Politics in Antebellum Virginia* (Chapel Hill: University of North Carolina Press, 1998), 154.

CHAPTER 2

THE CIVIL WAR AND THE GREAT SCHISM, 1861–1870

WOMEN AND WARTIME

And so, the war began. Men enlisted, and the huge and lumbering organization required to arm, feed, clothe and transport men, horses, and supplies moved slowly into action. By war's end, a staggering 90 percent of the eligible white men in the Confederacy and over half of the adult male population in the North had joined the military. Estimates of the number dead vary widely; the latest, best estimate of soldiers who died from battle, wounds, and disease is roughly 750,000.[1] Death and illness were common for families at the time, but the battlefield deaths and the destruction of swaths of the South were unprecedented in the lives of men and women who suffered through the war.

Women who before the war had organized for benevolent charity organizations and moral reform, antislavery, and woman's rights quickly shifted their energies during the war to meet the needs of their men and their "nation," while also assuming responsibilities for maintaining the homefront and their own homesteads. In both the Union and the Confederacy, black and white women treated men in field hospitals and hospital camps hurriedly built to house growing numbers of wounded. Women organized local relief societies, sewed uniforms, and gathered supplies and food. In the North, women's organizations tried to support an army as nurses and suppliers of all manner of fare, wares, and reading material, but many military officers initially responded with a notable lack of enthusiasm, not wanting to deal with women volunteers. Yet, women persisted, not waiting for official sanction. Within two weeks of the onset of fighting, women had formed twenty thousand aid societies.[2] In parts of the

Confederacy slave-owning women suddenly had to expand their work to the running of plantations and managing field hands. Almost everywhere in the South, families were drawn into war-related work and disruptions of war, while parts of the Union remained relatively unaffected.

Volunteer work was not the only way in which women affected the home front. Working women moved from household work or factory work into new jobs in a wartime economy. White working-class women took up new work in munitions factories, continued old work as seamstresses in new factory "arsenals" producing the jackets, trousers, underwear, and shirts for the armies, and faced new dangers making bullets and bombs. Rural free black and white farm women, left without husbands and sons, had to manage the land. Both black and white women worked as cooks and washerwomen for the armies. Women became army nurses, despite fierce opposition from army officers. Some women were spies; some fought as soldiers. Women sometimes scoured the battlefields for missing men, they pursued pensions when widowed, and looked after invalid soldiers once they were brought home.[3] Women organized support for war widows and orphans, ran soldiers' hospitals, and more.

Women who were abolitionists, woman's rights advocates, and members of moral reform societies or charity associations now formed the core of volunteer war aid organizations. The war led to new volunteer work and new fields for professional women. Elizabeth Blackwell, pioneering medical doctor, sister of suffragist Henry Blackwell, and friend of Florence Nightingale, began training women to be army nurses in New York as soon as the war began. By the end of April, she and Louisa Lee Schuyler gathered four thousand women at a meeting in New York, where they founded the Women's Central Association of Relief (WCAR). Blackwell tried to get the U.S. War Department to create a national version of the New York association.

Faced with the problem of lack of supplies and medical support available to Union troops, and looking to the British Sanitary Commission with its "scientific approach" to war support as a model, the war department accepted the services of the U.S. Sanitary Commission (USSC), a private organization originally formed to supply medical and other supplies to the camps. Despite opposition by male administrators at the Sanitary Commission, doctors Elizabeth and Emily Blackwell, mental health reformer Dorothea Dix, Red Cross founder Clara Barton, Mary Livermore of the Chicago branch of the USSC, and many other women were vital to the running of army hospitals, training army nurses, and overseeing effective supply chains for medical support. By the end of the war, over three thousand women served as paid nurses. As a part of support efforts, the USSC held huge fundraising events, called "fairs," which were largely organized and run by women. The Chicago Fair raised a staggering $80,000, more than anyone thought possible.[4]

In sum, the war brought profound change. In places where there had been women's reform societies, temperance associations, and antislavery groups the war created new realms for public work. Where such organizations had not existed before the war, women learned organizing and managing skills to meet local and national needs. The wartime demands drew women into national affairs and a strong sense of civic duty. The Civil War created a new generation of northern white, middle-class, women suffrage leaders with organizational experience rooted in the war, not radical abolitionism.

At war's end, many of these energetic women did not return to their prewar life; instead, they formed the backbone of new women's associations. They organized women's clubs, joined the swelling numbers of Woman's Christian Temperance Union (WCTU) branches, ran orphanages, staffed medical clinics, and by the end of the century led a myriad of progressive reform efforts. Northern women in the postwar decades went to the new women's colleges like Vassar College, founded in 1861, Smith College (1871), or Wellesley College in suburban Boston (1875). Women from all these organizations and higher education became woman's suffrage campaigners.

New recruits for woman's rights, and later for suffrage, were different from antebellum activists. They were not all radicals, or abolitionist agents, or viewed as extremists. They were women who enjoyed public work in wartime and began to see the limits put upon the work that women could do. These were almost all middle-class women who swelled the numbers of "moderate" rather than "ultraist" women reformers. Together with antebellum leaders, they transformed the loosely organized woman's rights conventions into an organized suffragist movement.

Southern women did not take the same path. The economic destruction of the Confederacy combined with the deaths of husbands and wage-earners forced survivors of the war to focus all their energies into plain survival. Women in the South had formed benevolent associations and charitable organizations, but none of these grew into reform organizations as they had in the North before the Civil War. During the postwar decades, Southern women formed war memorial associations and women's clubs, alongside other charitable work, but did not develop suffrage organizations until the 1890s at the earliest, with most organized after 1900.[5]

THE PATH OF WOMAN'S RIGHTS AFTER 1860

The opening of the war proved difficult for Lucy Stone, Susan B. Anthony, and Elizabeth Cady Stanton. While almost all woman's rights advocates turned toward supporting the armies and halted woman's rights campaigning, the three women who had emerged as leaders of the organized women's movement had differing reactions to the onset of war. Lucy Stone was a pacifist and spent the start of the war at home, coping with her family needs and her own fragile health. Susan B. Anthony was unwilling to halt woman's rights agitation but could not get Elizabeth Cady Stanton to agree. Elizabeth and Henry Stanton agreed that they should follow the lead of the antislavery societies and halt woman's rights conventions. Neither Elizabeth nor Susan wanted to join those who were sewing, raising money, or nursing. Elizabeth was convinced that with the emancipation of slaves, which must come from a northern victory, women would also be emancipated and win suffrage. It would be a new era for democracy, and democratic reforms would be part of the new world.

Elizabeth Cady Stanton, at forty-five, was ready to loosen the strings tying her to the household. She sold the Seneca Falls house and moved the family to New York City. Ready to lead the way to women's greater equality. She acquired further political acumen, all the while expanding her reach as a writer, thinker, and speaker. Full, as always, of self-confidence, she was deeply embroiled in the political scene. Her brother-in-law, Samuel Wilkeson, was chief Washington correspondent for the *New York Tribune* and the source of much inside political knowledge. She had influential friends, including *Tribune* owner Horace Greeley, who made room for her letters, essays, and news columns in his widely read paper. Henry Stanton secured a patronage position as deputy collector of the New York Custom House in 1861 as a reward for loyalty to Lincoln and the Republican Party.

Susan B. Anthony was not as sanguine about the future and felt for the rest of her life that the momentum lost by ceasing agitation contributed to the failure of woman suffrage during Reconstruction. In 1862, when the New York legislature repealed most of the 1860 gains, one legislator poured salt on the wound, saying, "strange that you women, so watchful and so regardful of your rights should have allowed the repeal of those important sections, without strenuous opposition." Anthony was sure that ceasing woman's rights conventions was a mistake.

WOMAN'S LOYAL NATIONAL LEAGUE

In 1863, a way forward, combining patriotic war work with women's rights work, evolved in the busy minds of the indomitable pair. Anthony and Stanton issued a call for a national meeting of women supporting the war effort. The Woman's Loyal National League (WLNL) was born in early May 1863 when a large crowd crammed into the pews at the Church of the Puritans in New York. Skilled women orators and leaders gathered again; Ernestine Rose, Lucy Stone, Angelina Grimké Weld, Susan B. Anthony, and Elizabeth Cady Stanton proposed an organization to fight for immediate full emancipation and equal suffrage. Lucy Stone, at her rousing best, called for a wide mission of war support and women's equality. But delegates from Ohio and the Midwest expected only discussion of war work. Emily Hoyt of Madison, Wisconsin, made it clear that she wanted war work "kept sacred from Anti-Slavery, Woman's Rights, Temperance, and everything else, good though they may be."[6] In the end, Lucy Stone's words swayed enough of the assembled women and a resolution passed, which declared that the women present believed that both "citizens of African descent" and women needed political and civil rights. Elizabeth Cady Stanton took the lead of the WLNL, a sign of her rising national influence.

The WLNL was a purely women's organization, new in its size and national scope. The WLNL, with membership limited to women and with leadership by Stanton and Anthony, provided a model for their own woman suffrage organization in 1869. Black women were certainly eligible for membership, but there is little evidence that any joined; this was almost totally a white endeavor. Despite its wider aspirations, the WLNL's only significant success was in gathering signatures for massive petitions in support of emancipation that were sent to Senator Charles Sumner to lay before Congress. The whiff of feminism surrounding the league hindered those working to get signatures for the emancipation petitions. Even so, the number signing swelled quickly, and by the end of the summer of 1864, the total number of signers had reached perhaps four hundred thousand. Senator Charles Sumner credited the petitions with securing the passage of the Thirteenth Amendment.

The WLNL women gained more than organizational experience. "They discussed political issues from the traditionally masculine sphere while at the same time appealing to women through the rhetoric of true womanhood," writes Wendy Hamand Venet.[7] The values of true womanhood, with women's superior moral character, were now being used as a reason for women's participation in politics, in addition to the argument that women deserved the vote by virtue of being human and citizens. The WLNL did not get fulsome praise. The *New York Times* and Greeley's *Tribune* editorialized support, but it was lukewarm. The connection between women's war work and woman's rights issues did not appeal in the current national mood. Women's aid work was praised, not woman's rights.

For Elizabeth Cady Stanton, politics had always been her world, from life in her father's household to Henry Stanton's involvement with the Republican Party. But politics was a rough and corrupt game, particularly in New York, and it led her to a healthy suspicion of the Republican Party and a cynicism that other woman's rights leaders did not have. As the campaign for Lincoln's re-election began in 1864, Henry Stanton and his son Neil were accused of corruption and lost their patronage jobs. It is highly likely that Abraham Lincoln, in return for support in the close race, agreed to give the patronage to political strongman Thurlow Weed. Henry Stanton's political career was destroyed.[8] Elizabeth picked up the burden of providing much of the family income by taking to the lecture circuit. She never forgot that the Republican Party failed her family.

With Lincoln's re-election, Radical Republicans increased pressure for full emancipation. The Thirteenth Amendment, freeing all people in bondage, passed Congress in January of 1865. William Lloyd Garrison declared that there was no longer any need for the American Anti-Slavery Society (AASS) and resigned as its president. Others leaped to disagree. "Slavery is not abolished until the black man has the ballot," said

Frederick Douglass. African American antislavery agent Frances Ellen Watkins Harper called for the AASS to create a "level playing field." Anna Dickinson, the young, white speaker who had just risen to fame preaching emancipation and Union victory and was the darling of the nation, "thundered against dissolution," writes historian Margaret Washington.[9] The result was that Wendell Phillips took over from Garrison as leader of the AASS and continued its work. This had profound effects on the woman's movement as it was Wendell Phillips who held the purse strings of funds that had been given to abolitionists and women both.

The question absorbing politicians and the nation was not woman's rights but the fate of emancipated slaves. Wendell Phillips and Frederick Douglass and the AASS fought to secure civil rights for freed slaves as well as the vote. Lucretia Mott believed that woman suffrage could be included with the black male vote, telling Phillips that she believed that the "negro's hour was decidedly the time for woman to slip in."[10] Those women who had been abolitionist leaders saw no reason that both black and white women should not be enfranchised along with black men. Their hard work for emancipation and the support of abolitionist leaders for woman's rights seemed to support their expectations.

Elizabeth Cady Stanton and Wendell Phillips argued over the question. Stanton, ever one to delight in putting forward provocative proposals, was rarely willing to compromise, says biographer Elisabeth Griffith, and her attitude and approach proved a problem in political negotiations and negotiation over woman suffrage.[11] Wendell Phillips, taking a moderate approach, thought black male suffrage needed a wide consensus. This might mean woman suffrage could not be included. There were general expectations by both men and women that woman suffrage would be considered as Republicans introduced measures to protect war gains. In Congress, the woman's cause had strong supporters. In New York, in 1866, renowned preacher Henry Ward Beecher declared that "black men's and all women's rights are one and the same."[12] It did seem for a few months that universal suffrage might happen. Then Lincoln's assassination changed the political landscape.

Hopes for universal or equal suffrage sank once the expectation faded that President Andrew Johnson would uphold Radical Reconstruction. Johnson, a racist and sympathetic to the Confederate cause, promoted the quick reentry of Southern states into the Union, demanding only white male suffrage in the months after Lincoln's assassination before Congress returned.

At this point, events in the South changed the course of Reconstruction. Violence, murder, and rape across the South and the legal suppression of black rights called Black Codes (which virtually replicated slavery) raised concerns over the fate of freedmen and freedwomen. In the middle of 1866, a mob in Memphis fired at recently disarmed black soldiers, burned freedmen's schools, and killed forty-six African Americans. In New Orleans, black and white Republicans were killed. Radical Republicans feared a coalition of northern and southern Democrats could take control of the Congress if black men were not secure in their political rights. Antislavery men tested the political winds after Lincoln's assassination and concluded that two radical causes could not be carried through Congress in the current climate.

Those who opposed black male suffrage brought up woman suffrage to doom black male suffrage. Proposals for woman suffrage made legislation much more politically risky. The blunt weapon of racism combined with the threat of woman suffrage was used to taint both causes as equally "ridiculous" and "unthinkable."

In May 1865, Wendell Phillips dealt the blow that shattered all hopes of woman suffrage. Phillips announced support for an amendment that would prevent the removal of civil rights "on account of race, color or condition." He politely added that he hoped to add "sex" later, but now was not the time. "This hour belongs to the negroes. As Abraham Lincoln said: 'One war at a time.' So I say one question at a time. This hour belongs to the negro."[13] Women's rights were moved to the back shelf.

Lucy Stone, alarmed and angry, demanded of Abby Kelley Foster, how could "you and Phillips, & Garrison, and the brave workers, who for thirty years have said 'let justice be done, if the heavens fall,' now smitten by a strange blindness, believe that the nation's peril can be averted if it can be induced to accept the poor half loaf of justice for the Negro, poisoned by its lack of justice for every woman of in the land."[14] Stanton and Anthony were equally furious. Others were unsure of the right response. Should women wait for their turn? Should they campaign against an amendment that proposed only black male suffrage and not equal or universal suffrage?

During the winter of 1865 and 1866, Stanton and Anthony tried in vain to persuade Wendell Phillips to shift his position. Phillips, as trustee to the two remaining abolition and woman's rights funds, also withheld badly needed money from the women. The Hovey Fund and the Jackson Fund were legacies left for both antislavery and woman's rights. Phillips justified his actions by referring to the "negro's hour." The push for women's rights was seriously pinched by lack of access to funds.

The Fourteenth Amendment passed through Congress in April, May, and June of 1866. This Amendment dashed any hopes that were left by inserting the word "male" into the Constitution for the first time.[15] Senator Charles Sumner told Lucy Stone, somewhat cynically, that he had written draft after draft trying to include equal suffrage, but just could not manage to do so! To this huge blow, Stanton responded angrily; with the word "male" inserted in the Constitution, "it will take us a century at least to get it out." It would take over fifty years until women got a woman suffrage amendment ratified, and as historian Christine Stansell notes, it would be one hundred years before the Supreme Court applied the Fourteenth Amendment's equal protection guarantee to women.[16]

Activist women had to decide whether to support the ratification of the Fourteenth Amendment. Despite her concerns that black men would not recognize black women's independence, Sojourner Truth decided that black men needed political rights so badly that women would have to wait. After some wavering, Lucy Stone joined her. Susan B. Anthony and Elizabeth Cady Stanton did not. The Fourteenth Amendment was ratified by the states and sent to Secretary of State William Seward to be certified in July 1868.

AMERICAN EQUAL RIGHTS ASSOCIATION

The WLNL was defunct as the war ended. In May of 1866 at a woman's rights meeting a new organization was formed to fight for universal suffrage as Stanton and Anthony tried to forge a coalition between anti-slavery groups and woman's rights organizations. The result was the short-lived American Equal Rights Association (AERA). Mott, Stanton, Anthony, and Douglass signed a memorial to Congress that read, "Woman and the colored man are loyal, patriotic, property holding, tax paying, liberty-loving citizens; and we cannot believe that sex or complexion should be any ground for civil or political degradation."[17] Frederick Douglass was willing to support women and the AERA; even as he made it clear that the freedmen's needs were primary, he did not oppose women also campaigning for suffrage.

Sojourner Truth supported the new organization, although she was not at the first two meetings of AERA in 1866. Frances Ellen Watkins Harper was and expressed the growing cynicism of some black women as to the depth of white women's support for black women. Historian Nell Painter describes her as a "formidable figure," a poet and suffragist, who worked with the Underground Railroad and lectured for the Maine Anti-Slavery Society in the 1850s, then toured the South after the Civil War working for black civil rights, temperance, education, and racial uplift. Harper spoke out on the prejudice of white women's assumption that suffrage meant the same thing to all women, "I tell you that if there is any class of people who need to be lifted out of their airy nothings and selfishness, it is the white women of America," said Harper. Historian Nell Painter comments acerbically that it is not surprising that this was too strong for Elizabeth Cady Stanton and Susan B. Anthony, who erased these comments from Harper from the history of woman suffrage as they compiled it in the *History of Woman Suffrage* (HWS).[18]

To Harper, woman suffrage was a white woman's cause, unless white women showed her otherwise. Other black women leaders who had been abolitionists and worked with white women abolitionists were less blunt but had the same goal of black women's rights as they worked for the AERA. Sarah Remond and Hattie Purvis gave speeches at the convention, and Purvis served on the executive committee and the finance committee and was recording secretary. Hattie Purvis spent the rest of her life working with Susan B. Anthony, one of the few African Americans to do so.[19]

That white women lacked any awareness of race barriers was reinforced for all these women when Elizabeth Cady Stanton, at the AERA meeting in 1867, began calling for limited suffrage and educational qualifications. Sojourner Truth responded with outrage. Black restaurateur George Downing asked Stanton directly if she would oppose black male suffrage if women were not also included in the proposed Fifteenth Amendment. Stanton replied, "I would not trust him [the black man] with my rights; degraded, oppressed himself, he would be more despotic than even our Saxon rulers are. I desire that we go into the kingdom together; for individual and national safety demand that not another man be enfranchised without the woman by his side."[20] Without woman suffrage, "only the highest type of manhood" should vote.[21] Stanton's words put on record the racist rhetoric and class-bound attitudes that marred Stanton's position on suffrage in the next decades. Anthony and Stanton abandoned their twenty-year battle for black rights.

It is hard for present-day readers to understand or justify this descent into racial stereotypes. Once Elizabeth Cady Stanton abandoned the cause of universal suffrage for "limited suffrage" or "educated suffrage," she alienated black reformers and ended ties with black women and white women who were committed to racial justice. Though Stanton began this path of limited suffrage, other suffragists took to the same road, laying the way for generations who wanted to restrict woman suffrage, in one way or another. This strain of class and race prejudice emerged over and over again throughout the suffrage campaigns from this point on.

As 1867 ended, Stanton and Anthony had alienated editor Horace Greeley by insulting him at the New York state constitutional convention thus losing a prime newspaper outlet, without getting woman suffrage in New York state. They had turned away from old allies and long-held convictions on black civil rights and black suffrage. Their last chance that year of a victory for woman suffrage seemed to be in Kansas, where the campaign for woman suffrage was continuing, however weakly, but faced the short time available before the November elections.

KANSAS, WOMAN SUFFRAGE, AND GEORGE FRANCIS TRAIN

Meanwhile, earlier in the year, Lucy Stone had returned to New York to find a letter from Kansas. A Republican Party leader in Kansas, Sam Wood, pleaded for woman suffrage workers to come and speak at an "Impartial Suffrage" convention in Topeka. In Kansas, two amendments were laid before the voters for the November 1867 elections: one for black suffrage and another for woman suffrage. Wood appealed for help from the AERA.

There was no money to pay for speakers, no money for travel, and only a tiny amount for salary for Anthony from Wendell Phillips, who controlled all the available funds. Despite this, Lucy Stone and Henry Blackwell set off together for Kansas paying their own expenses. Kansas attracted wide national interest as it was the first serious Reconstruction era state battleground for the woman suffrage. When Stone and Blackwell arrived, they found themselves embroiled in a factional battle within the state Republican party ranks. Unaware at first of the exact nature of Kansas politics and initially cheerful, Stone and Blackwell, carrying 250 lbs. of suffrage literature, set out to tour Kansas. Henry Blackwell wrote lively descriptions of the campaign trail. It was exhausting work as were all the woman suffrage campaigns.

> We climb hills and dash down ravines, ford creeks, and ferry over rivers, rattle across limestone ledges, struggle through muddy bottoms, fight the high winds on the high rolling upland prairies, and address the most astonishing (and astonished) audiences in the most extraordinary places.[22]

Republicans in Kansas, as it turned out, were not all fully behind the woman suffrage amendment. As would be the case in other times and places, proposals for woman suffrage were linked to black suffrage as a way of defeating black suffrage. Taken together both kinds of suffrage could be painted as laughable, just too ridiculous to contemplate. Despite intensive touring, Stone and Blackwell soon judged the woman suffrage amendment doomed, wrote to Stanton and Anthony of their disappointment, and returned eastward.

Unwilling to give up, Anthony and Stanton themselves set out to take up the woman suffrage campaign. In a significant political mistake for the wider cause, when Republicans failed them, they turned to the Democrats during the last weeks of the Kansas campaign, welcoming help from the wealthy, eccentric, flamboyant, and fabled Democrat, George Francis Train. Train was a virulent racist, a great political opportunist, and a spectacular campaigner in his opera capes, lavender gloves, and his comedic campaign songs. Train warmed up the audience, appealing to the worst of racist antipathies: "woman first, and negro last, is my programme."

Stanton and Anthony had not grasped the internal workings of Kansas politics. Kansas failed to produce a victory for woman suffrage; instead it added to growing divisions between suffragists. Stanton and Anthony's campaign in Kansas increased their isolation from former abolitionist allies and much of the woman's movement of the 1850s. Neither Stanton nor Anthony understood the damage that Train caused, believing instead that they had chosen a pragmatic solution. Lucy Stone, Wendell

Phillips, and Frederick Douglass begged Anthony to shed Train as an ally. Anthony and Stanton were undeterred. "He appealed most effectively to the chivalry of the intelligent Irish men, and the prejudices of the ignorant; conjuring them not to take the word "white" out of their constitution unless they did the word "male" also; not to lift the negroes above the heads of their own mothers, sisters, and daughters. The result was a respectable democratic vote in favor of woman suffrage," wrote Elizabeth after the election. Both women were convinced that George Train had increased the vote for woman suffrage.[23]

To make things worse, an AERA advertisement announcing Train's lectures in Kansas included Lucy Stone's name, unbeknownst to her, implying that Stone supported Train and his racist venom. Stone was outraged when Anthony only gave her a lukewarm apology. It was the start of the long-running conflict and personal antipathy between the two women that shaped the fate of the woman suffrage movement into the 1890s.

In Boston in 1868, disquieted over George Train, conservative suffragist Caroline Severance, together with Julia Ward Howe, the wealthy society figure and writer of the "Battle Hymn of the Republic," invited Lucy Stone to join in founding a separate group from the AERA, the New England Woman Suffrage Association (NEWSA). From this Boston group came the leaders of the American Woman Suffrage Association (AWSA), founded later by Lucy Stone and Henry Blackwell. Howe represented the new Civil War recruit, with roots in a wealthier stratum of society than most of the antebellum woman's rights advocates. Until this time, writes her biographer, Elaine Showalter, Howe saw woman's rights women as unwomanly harridans. Howe was converted after hearing Lucy Stone talk on woman's rights. Howe recalled that Stone turned out to be "sweet faced and silver-voiced, the very embodiment of Goethe's 'eternal feminine.'"[24] Howe became a leading suffragist.

Deepening the divisions in the old alliance for woman's rights, Stanton and Anthony arrived back in New York and took up George Train's offer to fund a newspaper, *The Revolution*, with the masthead—"Men Their Rights and Nothing More—Women Their Rights and Nothing Less." At the start, it was mostly an organ for Train's presidential aspirations, but when Train ended up in an Irish prison for supporting Irish independence, Stanton and Anthony were left with free reins to focus on woman suffrage and all the topics Stanton personally cared about—the plight of working women, Tammany Hall corruption, prison conditions, labor conflict, marriage, and divorce. They were also left with a huge debt from losses incurred by *The Revolution*.

THE FIFTEENTH AMENDMENT

Radical Republicans realized that if Southern states chose to take lowered representation in Congress, they could eliminate black male voters. The solution was another amendment to solidify the right of black men to vote. The Fifteenth Amendment, debated on the floor of Congress in February 1869, contained the following language in Section 1: "The right of citizens of the United States to vote shall not be denied or abridged by the United States or by any State on account of race, color, or previous condition of servitude." Furious again at the failure, once more, of those who had supported woman suffrage to include a guarantee of women's right to the franchise in a constitutional amendment, Stanton and Anthony opposed the Fifteenth Amendment and campaigned against it, to no avail. The Fifteenth Amendment confirmed the fate of woman suffrage. It was not going to come without another amendment for woman suffrage alone.

Throughout 1868, Stanton and Anthony had used increasingly incendiary language on the topic of the black male vote and Congress' failure to include woman suffrage. Stanton's editorials referred to black men as a threat, including the unambiguous code words for rape—"outrages to womanhood." Condemnation of "Patrick, Sambo, Hans, and Yung Tung" as unworthy of voting before white, educated women again appeared. Stanton and Anthony couched their language in terms of a battle between men and women, although they did not actually mean all women, but that subset of white educated women that reflected their own status.

Lucy Stone tried to keep the woman's rights movement together by supporting the Fifteenth Amendment in the hope of support for a rapidly following Sixteenth Amendment. Frederick Douglass, William Lloyd Garrison, and Stephen Foster agreed with Stone; they were not going to abandon woman suffrage but argued that the black man needed immediate protection. The result for woman's rights advocates was that they had to choose sides. They could go with Stanton and Anthony and oppose the amendment, or they could support black male suffrage and put their hopes for woman suffrage in a Sixteenth Amendment.

Like white suffragists, black suffragists were divided; Mary Ann Shadd Cary, for example, was opposed to the Fifteenth Amendment and willing to fight on for universal suffrage. Some male antislavery leaders held to the woman's cause. Black leader Robert Purvis did, even as his sons supported the Fifteenth Amendment. Charles Lennox Remond said he was not ready to gain the vote without his wife or daughters also being enfranchised. These two were in a very small minority.

Once more, women would have to wait. Many were somewhat buoyed by the woman suffrage proposal presented by Senator George Julian in March 1869, but their hopes were soon crushed when the proposal was buried in committee.[25] The Fifteenth Amendment wended its way through Congress, passing both houses of Congress in February 1869. Historian Louise Michele Newman describes Elizabeth Cady Stanton's reaction as revealing palpable pain and anger when she said that if the Fifteenth Amendment were ratified "women will then know with what power she has to contend. It will be male versus female the land over. All manhood will vote not because of intelligence, patriotism, property or white skin, but because it is male, not female."[26] Stanton was clear in her mind that this was now a battle between men and women.

The result of the passage of the Fourteenth and Fifteenth Amendments was that property and race were no longer direct means of limiting male suffrage, making gender the major differential in defining who could vote.[27] Residence, character, age, and other limitations were still used by states to limit suffrage, but as these differed state by state, it was the explicit universal definition that women were not included as "inhabitants," or "persons," that was the new barrier that women had to breach. The question of what precisely were the rights of a citizen remained.

THE GREAT SCHISM

The Fifteenth Amendment had another consequence, a split in the woman's movement. From this split emerged an organized suffrage movement. The AERA did not survive; its May 1869 meeting was the organization's last, and is remembered for signaling the start of what became known as the "Great Schism" in the woman's rights movement. The uproar at that meeting revealed the unbridgeable fissures in the old abolitionist and woman's rights coalition. Adding to the deepening chasms were worsening personal conflicts, particularly between Susan B. Anthony and Lucy Stone. On May 12, two thousand people filled the seats of the massive Steinway Hall—the largest auditorium in Manhattan. Speaker after speaker rose to address the crowd as it became abundantly clear that former allies were now thoroughly angered by Stanton's rhetoric of race and "educated" suffrage. Despite efforts from Lucy Stone to moderate and reach a compromise, Stanton and Anthony sailed ahead, totally unwilling to negotiate.

Stephen Foster and Frederick Douglass came to this meeting primed to attack Stanton and Anthony because of their alliance with Train and other racist Democrats. Foster led claiming that Stanton had repudiated the goals and values of the AERA by writing in *The Revolution* for "educated suffrage" and rejecting universal suffrage. Foster continued that, if Anthony was willing to defend George Francis Train with his "ridicule of the negro and opposition to enfranchisement," then he, Foster, must leave the AERA and take his Massachusetts members with him. Douglass followed suit, denouncing Stanton's description of black men as "Sambo." Anthony refused to apologize, showing no inclination to find middle ground; suffrage must go first "to the most intelligent." Lucy Stone asserted, "If one has the right to say that you cannot read and therefore cannot vote, then it may be said that you are a woman and therefore cannot vote. We are lost . . . if we argue for one class."[28]

Elizabeth Cady Stanton lost her patience; "although much twaddle has emanated from the male tongue and pen on this subject, no man has yet made a fair, logical argument on the other side. . . . They resort to ridicule and petty objections." Congress, with the passage of the Fourteenth and Fifteenth Amendments, has "placed our free institutions in the care and keeping of every type of manhood, in the hands of ignorance and vice, ignoring their own wives and mothers, all the elevating and purifying influences of the most virtuous, humane and educated half of the American people."[29] Stanton went on further:

> In common justice woman's consent should be asked when millions of ignorant foreigners are to be introduced into the body politic to legislate for her. It might be a question with an educated American woman whether she would trust her interests in the hands of ignorant Chinamen . . . the ignorant German . . . the ignorant African . . . in whose eyes woman is simply the being of man's lust . . . with the mothers of the race crouching at your

feet, while iron-heeled peasants, serfs, and slaves, exalted by your hands, tread our inalienable rights into the dust? While all men, everywhere, are rejoicing in newfound liberties, shall woman alone be denied the rights, privileges, and immunities of citizenship? Woman suffrage is needed to bring a "new evangel of womanhood, to exalt power, virtue, morality, true religion, to lift man up into the higher realms of love, purity, and thought."

There is power in Stanton's rhetoric, but it reveals a deep-seated ethnic and racial prejudice that will be a recurring theme in parts of the white woman's suffrage movement. Black women disappeared from the equation in Stanton's writings and speeches, with only occasional exceptions.[30] Stanton was also appealing to the domestic ideology of woman's difference rather than her long-held argument for the vote on the basis of simple justice.

The AERA meeting dissolved in acrimony. Men and women who were fighting for equal rights for African Americans rejected Stanton and Anthony and their supporters. Significantly for the deep rupture in the woman's movement, the majority of the audience stood with Stone, Douglass, Foster, and Phillips.

In evaluating this shift in Stanton's thinking, historian and biographer Lori Ginzberg lays out a critical assessment concluding "the desperation or priorities of African American women failed to divert her from her own focus on abstract principles and rights," and Stanton "kept her eye firmly on those rights that had been denied her, which she framed in terms of the 'broader question' of universal rights." The result was that "mere mention of the Reconstruction-era schism and of the choices Elizabeth Cady Stanton made could raise the ire of activists, and their children, for decades to come; it still rankles historians."[31] Historian Faye Dudden observes, with acuity, that if we consider the context of the wider society, "the founding mothers of suffrage feminism were not racially enlightened. On the contrary, they engaged in plenty of racial stereotyping and racialist thinking. Even as radical outsiders, they inevitably partook of the social attitudes and scientific arguments of their day. Held up to our standards, no white individual of the nineteenth century, with the possible exception of John Brown, would escape censure entirely."[32]

Historian Ellen DuBois argues from a different stance, concluding that Stanton's refusal to give up on woman's rights when deserted by former allies was actually a strong feminist position, with Stanton taking a principled stance against those who said women must wait. Stanton had believed that Reconstruction could lead to a better republic, with no "invidious distinctions among citizens" and had hoped it was time to "bury the woman and the negro in the citizen," meaning that black men and (black and white) women could be defined in the same group—as citizens with the vote. When that vision was destroyed, she saw fighting for woman suffrage as her only option. Freed from the old abolition alliance, Stanton, Anthony, and their followers sought to build a truly woman's movement. But at the same time they held to a limited version of woman suffrage instead of having universal suffrage as a goal.

TWO ORGANIZATIONS WITH ONE GOAL: THE GREAT SCHISM IN ACTION

Stanton and Anthony left the AERA meeting furious at what they saw as a betrayal of years of work and furious at those who, like Lucy Stone, were willing to wait for another amendment. By Saturday evening, following the AERA meeting, most people had left the city. Stanton and Anthony remained, and called together a meeting at the Cooper Union that almost surely deliberately excluded Lucy Stone and Henry Blackwell, although Stanton and Anthony stoutly denied this. Anthony led the meeting and organized a new group, the National Woman Suffrage Association (NWSA), known as the National.

Historian Ellen DuBois argues that the National was a new kind of organization; it was the first national feminist organization. Women created this organization and directed its policies and tactics Born in New York, it was a woman's association, declared the founders, and its goal was first of all woman suffrage with other woman's rights issues second. Women needed to vote; equal rights would follow with the vote secured. There was a lengthy debate as to whether men should be allowed to be members, if not officers, with those who favored men's inclusion barely in the majority. Men could belong, but not hold office. NWSA was also to have a loose membership structure. Anyone could join NAWSA as an individual, and any member could attend national conventions. This lack of hierarchy and sprawling organizational structure allowed Anthony, Stanton, and the national leadership great control over decision-making because there were no state organizations as intermediaries between members and the national organization.

When they heard about the clandestine Saturday night meeting, Lucy Stone, Henry Blackwell, and Julia Ward Howe were furious at what they saw as a move by Anthony and Stanton to take control of the whole woman's movement. Rallying her allies in Boston and across the Northeast and Midwest, Stone advertised a national meeting to be held in Cleveland to create a "national" suffrage association, which would, the publicity said, be "more comprehensive and more widely representative" than "existing organizations."[33]

In November 1869, a large auditorium filled to the edges with around 1,000 men and women. Lucy Stone chaired the meeting, hoping to head off discussion of the Fifteenth Amendment. Julia Ward Howe and Mary Livermore, both the new kind of suffragist emerging from the war and both nationally known women whose fame rested on war work, were appointed to leadership positions. In contrast to the NWSA, the AWSA, known as the American, continued the antebellum woman's movement tradition with men and women on an equal footing in the organization. From the start, male allies, from Frederick Douglass to Theodore Weld, Wendell Phillips to Henry Blackwell, had been supporters of the earlier woman's movement. At the Cleveland gathering, Thomas Wentworth Higginson and then William Lloyd Garrison spoke in support of woman suffrage, followed by Henry Ward Beecher, one of the nation's foremost preachers and part of the influential Beecher family. Henry Ward Beecher was then elected president of the AWSA.

In the AWSA, women and men each held half of the positions in leadership and on committees. The organizational structure was hierarchical; in contrast to NWSA, local societies sent delegates to the state organizations and states sent delegates to national conventions. There was, then, a national network through which communication could flow easily, and at conventions, the different regions would all be represented. The AWSA leaders planned an efficient lobbying machine to enable them to organize quickly and efficiently if action was needed.

Mary Livermore brought her newspaper *The Agitator* to Boston, and with Lucy Stone and Henry Blackwell, created a new paper, the *Woman's Journal*, the voice of the American. Blackwell wrote an editorial for its first edition in January 1870, explaining that the AWSA would restrict its focus to woman suffrage. This approach, he wrote, would bring in more people to the suffrage cause because the American would be free from controversial and separating issues, and it would therefore allow reformers to come together who came from various (often conflicting) causes. The American intended to continue the antebellum strategy of campaigning state by state. In 1869 Wyoming had just passed votes for women and Utah was looking positive.

Black women joined the American in larger numbers than those joining the National. Among them were Caroline Remond Putman, of the famous abolitionist family, who had founded the Massachusetts Woman Suffrage Association, and Josephine St. Pierre Ruffin, later a central spokeswoman for black women's organizations. These women found a more welcoming climate with Lucy Stone, Julia Ward Howe, Henry Ward Beecher, and the Boston-based suffragists than with the National.

Stone, Blackwell, and the AWSA leadership proceeded to pointedly ignore the existence of the NWSA, covering it only sporadically in the *Woman's Journal*, to the intense annoyance of both Stanton and Anthony. Lucy Stone referred to NWSA as "Miss Anthony's association." The ill feeling between Stone and Anthony surfaced in public when Anthony attended the second AWSA convention, rising to ask why AWSA did not campaign for issues other than suffrage? Why not divorce laws, or property rights? Attacking Stone personally, she claimed that the *Woman's Journal* should not ignore woman's need for greater freedom in marriage since one of its editors (Lucy Stone) "refused to submit to the legal form of marriage." Anthony was referring to Stone and Blackwell's protest at the time of their wedding at the legal constraints imposed on women by marriage. The audience sat stunned, shocked at Anthony's rudeness. Thomas Wentworth Higginson rose quickly to speak, saying that as he was the minister who had presided at Lucy and Henry's wedding, he knew that Lucy Stone was indeed properly married, her marriage "pure and true." Anthony later apologized—but it did little to heal the wounds already inflicted. Personal antipathy between the two women increased over the decade, even as people on both sides attempted conciliation. This antagonism helped keep the two associations apart until 1890.

Indeed, unification efforts began almost immediately. Frederick Douglas and Lucretia Mott called for union after the first AWSA meeting. Midwesterners, who knew less of the personal conflicts, could not understand the need for two organizations, and they too called for union. Theodore Tilton, a prominent newspaper editor and woman's rights advocate, called for a joint meeting in New York where he would preside and mediate. Anthony, by then traveling out West, was furious. AWSA leaders also opposed any meeting led by Tilton.

Anthony, when she found many of the Western women she was meeting in her travels were in favor of unification, wrote back home telling one of the editors of *The Revolution*, Pillsbury Parker, to attend the Tilton meeting. The AWSA then had to send representatives, unhappy but afraid of what might transpire without them. Tilton put forward his plan, with the basis for a unification agreement and a new consolidated organization to be support for a federal woman suffrage amendment. There would be no hierarchical organization and an annual convention to be held only in New York.

Obviously, Stanton and Anthony and the National's organizational structure and interests were being favored. The New York focus threatened the American leadership, so the American delegates walked out. By doing so, they appeared to be the ones making unification impossible, which was exactly what Anthony had hoped. NWSA emerged as the conciliating voice. Tilton himself didn't actually want a joint new organization but wanted to lead his own new woman suffrage organization. After some negotiation, Tilton's Union Woman Suffrage Association merged with NWSA; both sought the passage of a Sixteenth Amendment for woman suffrage. A very rocky coalition lasted into 1871, when Tilton's own divorce scandal erupted, his newspaper failed, and he was forced to withdraw from the woman suffrage movement.[34]

With all unification attempts failing, the woman suffrage movement now grew with Boston and New York as two fulcrums. The AWSA and the NWSA built separate suffrage networks, created local and state societies, paid traveling agents when there were enough funds, and held separate national conventions. Across the country, both organizations sought and found support, recruiting from the same audience of generally white, middle- and upper-middle-class women.

NOTES

1. J. David Hacker, "A Census Based Count of the Civil War Dead," *Civil War History* 57, no. 4 (2011): 307–48. See also, Nicholas Marshall, "The Great

Exaggeration: Death and the Civil War," *Journal of the Civil War Era* 4, no. 1 (March 2014): 3–27.

2. Anne Firor Scott, *Natural Allies: Women's Associations in American History* (Urbana: University of Illinois Press, 1991), 58–77. See also, Judith Ann Giesberg and Randall M. Miller, eds., *Women and the American Civil War: North-South Counterpoints* (Kent, OH: Kent State University Press, 2018); and Stephanie McCurry, *Women's War: Fighting and Surviving the American Civil War* (Cambridge, MA: Belknap Press of Harvard University Press, 2019).

3. Judith Ann Giesberg has written a moving description of the impact of the war; see Judith Ann Giesberg, *Army at Home: Women and the Civil War on the Northern Home Front* (Chapel Hill: University of North Carolina Press, 2012). See also, Giesberg and Miller, *Women and the American Civil War*; Lee Ann Whites, *Gender Matters: Civil War, Reconstruction, and the Making of the New South* (New York, NY: Palgrave Macmillan, 2005); Nina Silber, *Daughters of the Union: Northern Women Fight the Civil War* (Cambridge, MA: Harvard University Press, 2005); and Drew Gilpin Faust, *Mothers of Invention: Women of the Slaveholding South in the American Civil War* (Chapel Hill: University of North Carolina Press, 1996).

4. Giesberg, *Army at Home*, 232.

5. Anastatia Sims, *The Power of Femininity in the New South: Women's Organizations and Politics in North Carolina, 1880–1930* (Columbia: University of South Carolina Press, 1997), 6–53.

6. Genevieve G. McBride, *On Wisconsin Women: Working for Their Rights from Settlement to Suffrage* (Madison: University of Wisconsin Press, 1993), 31.

7. Mary Hamand Venet, *Neither Ballots nor Bullets: Women Abolitionists and the Civil War* (Charlottesville: University Press of Virginia, 1991). See also, Rebecca R. Edwards, *Angels in the Machinery: Gender in American Party Politics from the Civil War to the Progressive Era* (New York, NY: Oxford University Press, 1997); Faye E. Dudden, *Fighting Chance: The Struggle Over Woman Suffrage and Black Suffrage in Reconstruction America* (New York, NY: Oxford University Press, 2011); and Laura E. Free, *Suffrage Reconstructed: Gender, Race, and Voting Rights in the Civil War Era* (Ithaca, NY: Cornell University Press, 2015).

8. Henry Stanton had been a magnificent orator, a man who had faced down violent mobs and led the abolition movement. Now nearing 60 years old, he became a full-time journalist in Manhattan and faded as a central figure in Republican politics.

9. Margaret Washington, *Sojourner Truth's America* (Urbana: University of Illinois Press, 2009), 335.

10. Carol Faulkner, *Lucretia Mott's Heresy: Abolition and Women's Rights in Nineteenth-Century America* (Philadelphia: University of Pennsylvania Press, 2011), 187.

11. Elisabeth Griffith, *In Her Own Right: The Life of Elizabeth Cady Stanton* (New York, NY: Oxford University Press, 1984), 119.

12. Lori D. Ginzberg, *Elizabeth Cady Stanton: An American Life* (New York, NY: Hill and Wang, 2009), 119.

13. Free, *Suffrage Reconstructed*, 53.

14. Andrea M. Kerr, *Lucy Stone: Speaking Out for Equality* (New Brunswick, NJ: Rutgers University Press), 121–2.

15. The Fourteenth Amendment read as follows:

Section 1. All persons born or naturalized in the United States, and subject to the jurisdiction thereof, are citizens of the United States and of the state wherein they reside. No state shall make or enforce any law which shall abridge the privileges or immunities of citizens of the United States; nor shall any state deprive any person of life, liberty, or property, without due process of law; nor deny to any person within its jurisdiction the equal protection of the laws.

Section 2. Representatives shall be apportioned among the several states according to their respective numbers, counting the whole number of persons in each state, excluding Indians not taxed. But when the right to vote at any election for the choice of electors for President and Vice President of the United States, Representatives in Congress, the executive and judicial officers of a state, or the members of the legislature thereof, is denied to any of the male inhabitants of such state, being twenty-one years of age and citizens of the United States, or in any way abridged, except for participation in rebellion, or other crime, the basis of representation therein shall be reduced in the proportion which the number of such male citizens shall bear to the whole number of male citizens twenty-one years of age in such state.

16. Christine Stansell, *The Feminist Promise: 1792 to the Present* (New York, NY: Modern Library, 2011), 86.

17. Faulkner, *Lucretia Mott's Heresy*, 187.

18. Nell Irvin Painter, *Sojourner Truth: A Life, a Symbol* (New York, NY: W. W. Norton, 2007), 223–6.

19. Rosalyn Terborg-Penn, *African American Women in the Struggle for the Vote, 1850–1920* (Bloomington: Indiana University Press, 1998), 26.

20. Barbara Hilkert Andolsen, *"Daughters of Jefferson, Daughters of Bootblacks": Racism and American Feminism* (Macon, GA: Mercer University Press, 1986), 7.

21. Painter, *Sojourner Truth*, 228.

22. Kerr, *Lucy Stone*, 12.

23. Patricia G. Holland, "George Francis Train and the Woman Suffrage Movement, 1867–70," *Books at Iowa*, no. 46 (1987): 8–29, https://doi.org/10.17077/0006-7474.1135.

24. Elaine Showalter, *The Civil Wars of Julia Ward Howe: A Biography* (New York, NY: Simon & Schuster, 2016), 187.

25. Kerr, *Lucy Stone*, 136.

26. Louise Michele Newman, *White Women's Rights: The Racial Origins of Feminism in the United States* (New York, NY: Oxford University Press, 1999), 5–6.

27. Ellen Carol DuBois and Richard Cándida Smith, *Elizabeth Cady Stanton, Feminist as Thinker: A Reader in Documents and Essays* (New York: New York University Press, 2007), 115.

28. Kerr, *Lucy Stone*, 139–40.

29. Stansell, *The Feminist Promise*, 190.

30. Andolsen, *"Daughters of Jefferson, Daughters of Bootblacks,"* 11.

31. Ginzberg, *Elizabeth Cady Stanton*, 127–30.

32. Dudden, *Fighting Chance*, 194–5.

33. Lisa Tetrault, *The Myth of Seneca Falls: Memory and the Women's Suffrage Movement, 1848–1898* (Chapel Hill: University of North Carolina Press, 2014), 33.

34. Tetrault, *The Myth of Seneca Falls*, 36.

CHAPTER 3

THE NEW DEPARTURE AND THE RIGHTS OF CITIZENS, 1870–1880

"We claim a right, based on citizenship."

Francis Minor[1]

"I have a new life, new hope that our battle is to be short, sharp and decisive under this 14th & 15th Amendment clause—it is unanswerable."

Susan B. Anthony, 1871[2]

As a child, Abigail Scott walked beside a covered wagon from Kentucky over the Oregon Trail in 1852, when one of the greatest westward migrations took place. Abigail's mother did not want to leave home, telling her husband that the children had never seen a train, why did they have to leave just as the frontier around them was filling up? Like so many others who endured the terrible hardships of this journey, the toll on the Scott family was enormous. Her mother, already weakened by malaria, died of cholera, which was epidemic that year on the trail. Oxen were unable to find food, and fever, illness, and death claimed many among Abigail's traveling party.[3] Her father's wagons were washed away down a river when a driver lost control of the oxen; they had sold all their belongings, and the $2,000 dollars securely wrapped and stowed was to fund their start in Oregon. The money was lost with the wagon. The penniless family arrived in the Willamette Valley to be greeted by relatives.

Two of the Scott children became nationally known, a fact that some attributed to the hardships of their earlier lives. Harvey Scott became editor of the Republican newspaper *The Oregonian*. He opposed woman suffrage but supported Abigail at points when she needed funds for travel. In 1870, now married, Abigail Scott Duniway began her career in woman suffrage, ultimately becoming Oregon's most famous suffragist. In 1871, Elizabeth Cady Stanton and Susan B. Anthony took their first trip to the West, meeting Duniway in the process. Duniway lived through the various stages of settlement, from Indian wars in Puget Sound to the arrival of the transcontinental railroad. Having endured the Oregon Trail and hardscrabble farm life, nothing daunted her as she traveled Oregon for suffrage: not rain, mud, or miserable conditions in the rudely constructed houses where she stayed. Determined to travel back east and meet eastern suffrage leaders, Duniway wangled a free train pass for part of the journey and lectured her way for the rest of the way, arriving in Philadelphia for the great Centennial Exhibition in Philadelphia in 1876. Over the following years, she continued traveling relentlessly. The availability of trains and steamship travel made possible the networks of suffragists who now exchanged information and coordinated campaigns.

By 1869 and the Great Schism of the suffrage movement, woman suffrage was no longer unthinkable or outrageous, no longer an impossible goal. Crowds were still rowdy in opposition and political opponents remained voluble, but the battlefields had shifted. The woman's rights movement transformed from small and energetic groups of radical woman's rights advocates into an organized woman suffrage movement, focused first on getting votes for women. Shifting tactics when necessary, adding pragmatic arguments when needed, the divided woman's movement created two national suffrage organizations. Both groups grew, all the while competing with each other. The two suffrage organizations—National Woman Suffrage Association (NWSA; the National) and American Woman Suffrage Association (AWSA; the American)—vied for members from the same pool of women and disagreed on strategy. In 1890, when a new generation was ready to lead, the two organizations united.

Suffragists were not immune to the profound changes taking place during the Gilded Age. The world the abolitionists knew growing up was no longer in existence. The suffrage movement operated during the decades after Reconstruction within a climate of increasing nativism and deadly racism. Native-born white Americans were made anxious by the rapidity of change and thought that existing moral standards were under threat by immigrants. Change was indeed massive, with great social, political, and economic upheavals shaping a country that reached from the Atlantic to the Pacific, with ambitions beyond that. After Radical Reconstruction, many people, including suffragists, believed that the influx of African American male voters was also a threat to political stability. The numbers of immigrants who became voters (in some states "alien" men could vote before they became naturalized citizens) also threatened to alter the party balance. Increasingly powerful political machines in New York, Chicago, Boston, Philadelphia, St. Louis, and other growing cities, needing to control their voting population to operate effectively, also shaped the national as well as the local political situation. Expanding the electorate amidst great change meant insecurity for politicians—always a threat to party interests. The national political climate shifted toward limiting the vote, not expanding it, during these increasingly conservative decades. Gone was the spirit of reform that characterized Radical Reconstruction.

Given this climate, it is not so surprising that restrictive immigration laws were passed: first the 1882 Chinese Exclusion Act, then a prohibition of "forced labor" immigration by the Alien Contract Labor laws of 1885 and 1887, followed by other exclusionary laws. Native-born white Americans turned to Social Darwinist theory to claim a hierarchy of "races." Northern Europeans, particularly "Anglo Saxons," were believed to be at the peak of intellectual and cultural development of all humans on Earth. Other groups, from Eastern Europeans to Africans and Asians, were the less developed of the species. Taking up this Social Darwinism, many white suffragists turned to racial arguments and endorsed limited suffrage.

May 12, 1869, was the date of the last AERA meeting and the start of the "Great Schism" of the suffrage movement. At the same time, out west, the symbolic joining together of the nation by transcontinental railroads took place. On May 10, 1869, at Promontory Point, Utah, Leland Stanford, wealthy industrialist and former California governor, drove in a ceremonial gold spike, watched by hundreds of laborers, engineers, and railroad officials. Now his Central Pacific Railroad, from California, joined the Union Pacific Railroad, coming from Iowa. A transcontinental railroad was reality. The railroads soon populated frontier territories by bringing new farmers and ranchers and the businesses needed to serve them. Railroads moved people, goods, and news faster, and made collaborations between western reformers and eastern suffragists easier. An infrastructure was being created that fostered a mass suffrage movement. Suffrage lecturers who had endured muddy tracks and badly sprung wagons would now wait at train stations, consulting timetables as they rushed from one lecture to another and one town to another. Between 1864 and 1890, eight states, Nevada, Colorado, North and South Dakota, Montana, Washington, Wyoming, and Idaho, were carved out of western territories prior to the frontier's official "closure." In each one of these new states, woman suffrage was debated in territorial and then state legislatures.

Amidst all these physical and political changes, women forged new careers. During the Gilded Age, women became professors, editors, journalists, artists, and traveling lecturers, pushing back barriers by perseverance and recourse to the courts. Law and medicine, unwillingly, finally opened to women as well.

The first women's medical school opened in Philadelphia in 1850. Harry Blackwell's sister, Elizabeth Blackwell, fought her way into Geneva Medical College in upstate New York, becoming, in 1849, the first woman to get a medical degree in the United States. The first women's medical school, the Female Medical College of Pennsylvania, was founded in Philadelphia the next year. In 1867, Rebecca J. Cole became the nation's second African American physician and the first African American to graduate from the institution renamed the Women's Medical College of Pennsylvania. She practiced with Emily and Elizabeth Blackwell.[4] By 1890, 560 new doctors had marched out from the doors of the Women's Medical College of Pennsylvania.[5]

More women fought their way into the classrooms of higher education. In 1869, new public universities in Kansas, Indiana, and Minnesota began admitting women, and a year later Missouri, Michigan, and California followed suit. Back East, new women's colleges joined Mount Holyoke, with Wellesley College in Boston founded in 1870, Hunter College in New York in 1870, and Smith College in Northampton, Massachusetts, a year later, in 1871. Gradually, more colleges opened their doors to women.[6]

Obstacles were continually thrown up before these pioneers. In state after state, women fought their way into law schools or taught themselves the law, then came up against judges who would refuse to admit them to the bar or allow them to practice in state or federal courts. Many were suffragists, as was Myra Colby Bradwell, one of those women who had worked with the U.S. Sanitary Commission during the war and had become a lifelong suffragist. Bradwell had formal legal training under her lawyer husband. Her application to the Illinois bar was denied on the grounds that she was married, and therefore could not enter into any legal contracts by herself. Myra Bradwell appealed, continuing her fight to the U.S. Supreme Court. The Supreme Court denied her petition, decreeing that "the natural and proper timidity and delicacy which belongs to the female sex evidently unfits it for many of the occupations of civil life."[7]

Many other well-known suffragists struggled to enter the law. Some eventually succeeded, though no woman in the South was able to breach this barrier. Women were prohibited from practicing in front of the U.S. Supreme Court then Belva Lockwood, admitted to the District of Columbia bar in 1873, lobbied successfully for legislation to overturn the U.S. Supreme Court rule. Benjamin Butler, chairman of the House Judiciary Committee, and Senator Aaron Sargent, both suffragists of some long standing, shepherded Lockwood's legislation through the House and the Senate. Although not supported by either national suffrage association, Lockwood ran for President of the United States in 1884 and 1888 on a woman suffrage plank.[8] For women who were already suffragists, their experience fighting for access to professions reinforced in their minds the absolute need for the power of the ballot to change laws.

With the great expansion of the population, the recruiting possibilities for suffrage were also magnified, yet the pool of possible women was still constrained by income, access to free time, and the ability to travel. By 1880, there were roughly fourteen million women in the United States, two-thirds of whom were farm women, working as producers in a household economy. Freedwomen in the South labored in the fields and ran households, as did poor white women, whether as tenant farmers or sharecroppers. These women had little, if any, leisure time, and travel between farms and towns was difficult. Their lives were not conducive to be able to gather on any regular basis.

The remaining third of women were urban, living in towns and cities. More than a million worked for wages as domestic servants, other single women worked in factories and shops, and women whose husbands worked in steel mills, factories, construction, mines, and other industrial jobs took in boarders, sewed at home, and brought in income to keep the household going. These women worked long hours, brought up children, and saw to their families; they, like their rural counterparts, had little, if any, leisure time.

Within the group of urban women, there were those who were the largest source of suffrage converts—the relatively prosperous white middle-class women whom historian Anne Firor Scott labeled the "unusually favored." These women, who had household servants and some leisure time, are identified by Scott as those who joined the voluntary women's associations which blossomed in these decades: mission societies, women's clubs, temperance groups, charity organizations, and suffrage associations. Predominantly white and Protestant, these women had taken on new roles during the Civil War and did not relinquish public work at its end. Antebellum reformers did not abandon reform; instead, they moved to new kinds of organizations, including the suffrage movement. The set of values that defined women as the keepers of the nation's morality and domestic order, known as the "domestic ideology," continued as the backbone of this reform spirit. These women clung—at least in their public statements—to the notion of woman as moral being, whose special public responsibility was to bring the principles of the well-run Christian home into community life.

These women were members of the middle class. Defining this nineteenth century middle class has always been difficult because historians and social scientists differ over the boundaries and characteristics of this class. For the purpose of woman suffrage, Anne Firor Scott's list of characteristics gives a good starting point: "income, values, concepts of respectability and propriety, education, behavior, self-definition, even clothing and patterns of church going, distinguish the middle class from the emerging working class on the one hand and the handful of homegrown, self-defined aristocrats on the other."[9] Add to this the fact that within this middle class existed ethnic, regional, and racial differences, and we have an operating definition for the women of the suffrage movement.

African American women, with a history of abolitionist leadership and woman's rights work, moved into both the American and the National suffrage organizations. Charles and Sarah Remond lectured on woman suffrage up and down the length of New York state during 1867. They were joined by a new generation of women like Harriet (Hattie) Purvis, Jr., who had been recording secretary and corresponding secretary for AERA. Hattie Purvis' father, abolitionist and woman's rights activist Robert Purvis, was almost alone among black men in maintaining that if his sons could vote, how could he deny the vote to his daughters. Both Hattie and Robert supported the Stanton-Anthony wing of the suffrage movement, and Hattie worked with Susan B. Anthony for the next decades.

Overall, more black women joined the American than the National. The racist rhetoric of Elizabeth Cady Stanton and Susan B. Anthony combined with their call for "educated suffrage"—a thinly disguised attack on illiterate African American men—gave black women good cause to join with the Boston-based AWSA. AWSA members included Charlotte Forten, Frances Ellen Watkins Harper, Mrs. K. Harris, Charlotte Remond Putnam, Charlotte (Lottie) Rollin, Louisa Rollin, Frances Rollin Whipper, Josephine St. Pierre Ruffin, and Sojourner Truth. This list included educated, prominent, and nationally respected women. Caroline Remond Putnam from Boston was at the founding meeting of the Massachusetts Woman Suffrage Association, which was allied with the American. She remained on the executive committee until she and her sister Sarah, despairing of equality in the United States, decamped for Italy in 1885. Josephine St. Pierre Ruffin (whose husband, suffragist George L. Ruffin was a Massachusetts state legislator) emerged into the public eye first as a journalist and woman's club leader. She joined the American, she said, because Lucy Stone, Julia Ward Howe, and the AWSA members did not make any distinction of race or sex. Black women in Boston in the 1870s were supported by six African American legislators in the Massachusetts State House who promoted woman suffrage legislation.[10]

Frances Watkins Harper had supported Frederick Douglass when he attacked the racist speech of Paulina Wright Davis at the last AERA meeting. Harper commented acidly that, "when it was a question of race she [white women] let the lesser question of sex go," and she referred to Davis's comments on black "tyrants" and brutes, who, with the vote, would threaten white womanhood.[11] Harper also joined the American instead of the National.[12] She and other black leaders saw the vote, according to historian Elsa Barkley Brown, as a community issue, a "collective possession." Black women must work toward woman suffrage, but they could not ignore the plight of black men. For black women, racial uplift and woman suffrage were intertwined.[13]

Some black women did join the National. Mary Ann Shadd Cary, wartime army recruiter, black nationalist, labor activist, and lawyer, gave testimony before the House Judiciary Committee in 1874, arguing that as a citizen, a taxpayer, a resident of the District, an African American, and a woman, she had the right to be heard and to vote.[14] Shadd Cary founded a suffrage society for African American women in 1880 in Washington, DC. She wrote to Susan B. Anthony in 1876 on behalf of ninety-four black women from Washington who wished to have their names included as signers of the Centennial Woman's Declaration of Independence. This request must have been ignored, as the women's names do not appear, a fact that historian Rosalind Terborg Penn notes as evidence of the increasingly hostile climate in the National for black women.

The South was inhospitable to woman suffrage. Yet, in South Carolina, black women in the Sea Islands, encouraged by Freedmen's Bureau agents, went to vote as the war was ending. Immediately after the war, during Radical Reconstruction, the suffrage efforts of the Rollin sisters in South Carolina shows a moment when it was possible for some woman suffrage lobbying. There were supportive black representatives in the State house, and during this short period, the Rollin sisters, children of a wealthy lumberyard owner, educated in Charleston's Catholic schools, in Boston, and in Philadelphia, became a force in politics in postwar Columbia. Frances Rollin, a writer and teacher, married state senator and later judge William J. Whipper, who was a woman suffrage ally. Frances' network of abolitionists and suffragists reached north into Philadelphia, including Sarah M. Douglass and Charlotte Forten. Frances' sister Charlotte (Lottie) Rollin was secretary of the South Carolina Woman's Rights Association, affiliated with AWSA and elected to the AWSA executive committee in 1872. Lottie Rollin addressed a meeting in Charleston saying, "we ask suffrage not as a favor, not as a privilege, but as a right based on the ground that we are human beings, and as such entitled to all human rights." A third sister, Louisa Rollin, addressed the South Carolina House of Representatives on universal suffrage in 1869.[15]

Women suffragists required male allies to get legislative action. In March 1872, in South Carolina, state senator Beverly Nash, with Frances Rollin's husband, William J. Whipper, called for a state amendment for woman suffrage. Alonzo J. Ransier, president of the South Carolina Woman's Rights Association and U.S. Congressman from South Carolina, argued for woman suffrage in the U.S. House of Representatives in 1874. All this work was destroyed with the racial violence and terror that swept black politicians out office and restored white power, a reversal consolidated by the withdrawal of federal troops after 1877. The fight for woman suffrage and racial uplift continued, but, of necessity, outside of the white political structure.

BUILDING THE NATIONAL

The 1870s were difficult years for Elizabeth Cady Stanton and Susan B. Anthony. In some ways, they both had to reinvent their lives and direction. The massive disappointment of the Fourteenth and Fifteenth Amendments, the Kansas fiasco, and the financial struggles of their newspaper, *The Revolution*, left both Anthony and Stanton floundering as they sought to restore their reputations and regain their central place in the woman's movement. Susan expressed a rare moment of despair telling Martha Coffin Wright, "I am feeling today that *life doesn't pay* the way seems so blocked up to me on all sides."[16]

Money was a problem. Both women took to the road as traveling speakers. In 1869, wanting funds to pay for her children's education, Stanton signed up with the James Redpath Lyceum Bureau and spent until 1880 on the road during the lecture season in the fall and winter. Anthony raised money to pay off the huge $10,000 debt from *The Revolution*. Stanton seems never to have considered that she should help with this debt.

Stanton got little pleasure from her appointment as president of the National. She wanted to be free to think, to write, to be unfettered, released from having to consider her words carefully in consideration of the increasing number of moderate suffragists. Organizing details and the shackles of an administrative post were not then, or ever going to be, her métier. In the balancing act that was the friendship of Stanton and Anthony, it was Anthony who provided the organizational brilliance, while, at the same time, begging Stanton over and over again, for every convention and suffrage event, to write a provocative speech, one that would thrill a suffrage audience. Stanton, although pleading to be left alone, would eventually give in. Anthony regarded annual conventions and testimony before Congress as necessary and effective strategies to lay the foundation for legislation. Stanton hated conventions and loathed giving congressional testimony. Stanton left it to Anthony to organize conventions and deal with administrative detail, which Anthony willingly did.

New women, with new ideas of where the movement should go, were an irritant to both women as they faced a new generation of suffragists who did not easily cede authority to elder women. Faced with the young Isabella Beecher Hooker, sister of the Rev. Henry Ward Beecher, Stanton reacted with irritation when Isabella wanted to make the NWSA more "respectable"—Elizabeth did not. She labeled these new women as "hunting after notoriety," expressing annoyance at the young women who showed a lack of deference and commenting dismissively that they "talked a great deal of nonsense." Anthony, responding to a reporter's comment that she had been called an "autocrat" by young women, snapped that, now that the woman's movement was a success, "everyone is ready to jump aboard the train," implying that these women needed experience and training and should remember who was present at the movement's founding.[17]

For Anthony, the 1870s were also difficult personally, as she suffered the grief of several deaths in her family: her sister Guelma died in 1873, sister Hannah in 1877, and her mother soon after in 1880. Anthony's biographer, Kathleen Barry, describes Anthony as taking less and less pleasure in the rigors of recruiting and state campaigns. For Anthony, "these were years filled with the repetitiveness of one campaign after another. It was work that had to be done whether or not it held the excitement or challenge of the earlier days."[18]

Despite the defeats of the 1860s, and the scandals of the early 1870s, Anthony and Stanton were now nationally known, indeed internationally known figures. Even with grueling travel, huge administrative tasks, and upstart youngsters, there were rewards that came with their increased national fame and reputation. Newspaper reports of the two women's travels in the 1870s and 1880s read as reports of a triumphal progress "like receptions given more often to rock stars rather than to radicals," writes historian Lori Ginzberg.[19]

Throughout the 1870s, the enmity between Susan B. Anthony and Lucy Stone deepened. Their correspondence about each other is filled with criticism, and at times snide remarks. Anthony accusing Stone of using a "cabinet of lies" while attacking NWSA. Lucy Stone rejected working with Anthony "after all the experiences we have had," whereupon Anthony replied, "Lucy, like the South, is incapable of understanding magnanimous overtures (thousands of which have been made to her)." Antoinette (Nette) Brown Blackwell described the division between Stone and Anthony as a great "civil war."[20]

LUCY STONE, HENRY BLACKWELL, AND THE AMERICAN

Meanwhile, in Boston, the American flourished. Lucy Stone hoped to lessen her work and travel, but the 1870s were as filled for her as the 1850s had been. She traveled giving lectures, organizing local suffrage societies, and attending conventions and fundraising events, all the time writing scores of letters to politicians, suffragists, and prospective donors. Her one constant concern, however, was the editing and funding of the AWSA newspaper, the *Woman's Journal*.

The first edition of the *Woman's Journal* came out on January 8, 1870. Stone and Blackwell raised capital, recruited subscribers, and persuaded Mary Livermore to join Lucy as editor. In fact, despite help from Mary Livermore until 1872, and some from Thomas Wentworth Higginson, Julia Ward Howe, Lucy's daughter Alice Stone Blackwell, and Henry Blackwell, Stone continued to carry the heaviest burden. For the rest of her life, Stone spent endless hours each week editing, raising money, and selling subscriptions. Henry and Alice went on vacation to Martha's Vineyard, but Lucy stayed at home, refusing to relinquish her post at the helm. Ceding control to others was as difficult for Lucy Stone as it was for Susan B. Anthony.

SUFFRAGE STRATEGY IN THE 1870S: TAX PROTEST AND THE NEW DEPARTURE

The hope that federal action would get women the vote was gone. Suffragists dreamed up new ways of bringing woman suffrage to the country. It had always been an irritant that women who owned property were taxed without representation. In 1852, Lucy Stone and Elizabeth Cady

Stanton had together called for propertied women to refuse to pay taxes. Said Stanton, "like the English Dissenters, and high-souled Quakers, of our own land, let us suffer our property to be seized and sold," until women have their political rights recognized. Stone freely acknowledged that this would be difficult because "it may involve the loss of friends, as it surely will that of property," but it was necessary, for suffrage will come "*when we ourselves are willing to incur the odium*, and loss of property." Lucy Stone returned her own tax bill in 1858 to the tax collector in Orange, New Jersey. Stephen and Abby Kelley Foster had their belongings auctioned by the town authorities when they refused to pay their taxes. Friends bought back their belongings. Starting in 1858 and continuing for twenty-five years, Sarah Wall refused to pay her taxes, continuing even after 1863 when the Massachusetts Supreme Court in *Wheeler v. Wall* ruled that suffragists had no legal standing to claim tax relief.[21]

The most famous tax resisters were the elderly Smith sisters, from Glastonbury, Connecticut. Julia and Abby Smith refused to pay their taxes in 1873 and sat calmly when their cows were sold at auction by the county to cover the tax cost. Undaunted, they welcomed reporters to their home to publicize their case. Wealthy, educated, and witty, the Smith sisters caught the imagination of the public. They were unwilling to be made paupers by continuing their protest, so they negotiated to pay interest on their tax debt, and fought off the tax collectors who tried to have them pay the entire debt. Only the death of Abby Smith in 1878 ended this particular tax rebellion.

The centennial of the Boston Tea Party provided a perfect opportunity to bring "no taxation without representation" in front of the public. Lucy Stone organized a gathering to observe the anniversary at Faneuil Hall for December 15, 1873. Susan B. Anthony addressed 600 people at the New York Woman's Suffrage Society celebration of the Boston Tea Party.[22] Other tea party celebrations were held that December, all reiterating the New York resolution, declaring that it was "the undoubted right of all men and women, that no taxes be imposed upon them but by their own consent."[23]

"Taxation without Representation" echoed with patriotic Americans, but, as a viable long-term strategy, refusing to pay taxes was flawed. There were relatively few women who owned taxable property, so there could never be large enough numbers to be effective as a means of getting all women the vote. By 1900, suffragists also generally avoided tax resistance because accusations of militancy appeared to align them with British militant activists, a charge they sought to avoid. A frequently substituted tactic, less economically fraught, was to attach a protest to tax payments.

THE NEW DEPARTURE

In 1869, a new theory was proposed, asserting that woman suffrage was already lawful because the Fourteenth and Fifteenth Amendments contained language implying that citizens could not be denied their "immunities and privileges," which included the right to vote. Women were citizens, and therefore could vote.

The first to argue this position, called the New Departure, were a couple from Missouri, Virginia Minor and her lawyer husband, Francis Minor. Virginia Minor spent the war years working for the Western Sanitary Commission, and at the end of the war was convinced that she must fight for "universal suffrage." She circulated a woman suffrage petition in 1867, which resulted in wide debate and a failed bill in the Missouri legislature. In response, getting ready for a long campaign, Minor and her allies organized the Woman Suffrage Association of Missouri with Virginia Minor as its president.[24]

Francis Minor wrote a letter to *The Revolution* about the new approach, while reporting on a convention in St. Louis. A resolution had passed describing a new approach to woman suffrage. "We no longer beat the air—no longer assume merely the attitude of petitioners. We claim a right, based upon citizenship." Minor laid out the argument of what would become known as the "New Departure," a phrase attributed to Elizabeth Cady Stanton. Put simply, the claim was that the Constitution via the Fourteenth and Fifteenth Amendments already gave women the right to vote and the states could not take that right away. Francis quoted his wife's speech: "I believe that the Constitution of the United States gives me every right and privilege to which every other citizen is entitled; for while the Constitution gives the States the right to regulate suffrage, it nowhere gives them power to prevent it. The power to regulate is one thing, the power to prevent is an entirely different thing. Thus, the State can say where, when, and what citizens may exercise the right of suffrage," but the state cannot refuse "rights and privileges" owed to a citizen, including the right to vote. Virginia concluded with a call to test this position through the courts.[25]

Anthony promptly published Minor's letter in *The Revolution*, and had 10,000 additional copies printed, at some expense, even as the newspaper faced huge deficits. Copies were given to every member of Congress and mailed to men and women all over the country. Everyone was invited to the National's annual convention in Washington, DC, in January where the "new departure" would be considered.[26] Women were citizens and therefore had the right to vote.[27] This "New Departure" logic was strong, but it conflicted with current political and social mores. Opposition centered as much around the implied threat to the domestic ideology, and the challenge to women's proper roles, as it did around the actual legal logic of the constitutional interpretation.

As the Minors were shaping the New Departure, passage of the Enforcement Act in 1870 (also known as the Civil Rights Act) gave the federal government power to enforce the Fifteenth Amendment, including using federal marshals and the army to prevent discrimination by state officials. The Enforcement Act allowed access to federal courts over voting problems, meaning local officials could be sued if they blocked a lawful vote. Suffragists, intending to test the New Departure logic, went to the polling places and asked to be registered. When rejected, they turned to the legal system for redress, with the first cases reaching the courts in 1871.[28]

WOMEN VOTE

Across the country, from California to Maine, women took action. Women went to the polls, arguing that they had a right to vote—because they paid taxes, because they had worked to support the Union in the war, or because they were just plain "citizens." Women persuaded local registrars to enroll them, and for one or two election cycles women placed their ballots in the ballot box. Some efforts began before the New Departure, while some were inspired by the New Departure.

In 1870, black women went to the polls in South Carolina, encouraged by federal agents.[29] In Topeka, Kansas, in 1868, between fifty and eighty women voted. In Detroit, in 1872, Nannette B. Gardner voted. In North Carolina, in July 1871, 200 black women dressed in men's clothing registered and voted. Others were turned away, as was Sojourner Truth, who in 1872 went to vote in Battle Creek, Michigan, where she paid taxes and owned a home. Hundreds of women who went to the polls and demanded to be registered, and the many who voted between 1868 and 1873, have been carefully documented by the Elizabeth Cady Stanton and Susan B. Anthony Papers Project at Rutgers University.

In 1871, attorney Belva Lockwood led an interracial group to City Hall in Washington, DC, with a petition asking to be registered as voters in the district. Supporters of these women, including Frederick Douglass and "society" people, flocked to join the petitioners.[30] Sara Spencer, Sarah Webster, and seventy others sued election officials for failing to let them register and vote under the Enforcement Act. Judge Daniel Carrter ruled against them, saying, amidst much comment on how women voting would be destructive of civilization, that enforcement legislation would be needed.[31] California suffrage leader Ellen Van Valkenburg rebuffed trying to register in Santa Cruz, then had her case rejected by the California Supreme Court. Carrie S. Burnham, a lawyer who had fought her way into the legal profession, tried to vote in Philadelphia in 1871, then took her appeal to the state Supreme Court, which ruled against her.[32]

The constitutional question raised by the Minors was debated from court to court, state to state, to end with the Supreme Court case, *Minor v. Happersett* in 1875. In 1872, the Minors began their test case, filing against the St. Louis registrar, Reese Happersett, who refused to accept Virginia Minor's registration. Francis Minor argued to the Missouri courts that the state of Missouri, by limiting the vote to men, was acting in contradiction to the U.S. Constitution, whose Fourteenth Amendment gave the vote to all "citizens." The Missouri courts promptly ruled for Reese Happersett, upholding the Missouri law allowing only men to vote, irrespective of the language of the Fourteenth Amendment. The state, in this interpretation, was the sole decision maker on who should have the right of suffrage. The Minors appealed, but much happened before the final court decision on the Minor's case was rendered. Other events connected to the suffrage cause took over the front pages.

VICTORIA WOODHULL MAKES A SPLASH

In January 1871, just as the National convention was being held in Washington, a new suffragist arrived with a splash on the national arena. Public attention to the New Departure was raised by the entrance of a glamorous and controversial woman whose rise and fall transfixed the reading public. Victoria Woodhull, a suffrage newcomer arrived in the nation's capital. In January 1871, the House Judiciary Committee welcomed into its smoky committee room a striking young woman, who, with Cornelius Vanderbilt's backing, had captured the attention of Wall Street as a stockbroker and editor and now set out to tell Congress why the Fourteenth Amendment gave women the vote.[33] Woodhull had gathered some strong political supporters, including among them war hero and abolitionist, Massachusetts Congressman Benjamin Butler, who probably helped couch her speech in the right framework for the Judiciary Committee. A composed Woodhull stunned the country when she gave the congressional committee a well thought out and delivered argument. The Fourteenth Amendment, she claimed, gave the control of suffrage to Congress and the federal government, and it was thus Congress's obligation to protect the vote of women. Voting was, she argued, a right not a privilege.[34] Whether voting is a right or privilege is debated still.

The House Judiciary Committee issued two reports after Woodhull's speech. The Minority Report supported her interpretation that the Fourteenth Amendment gave the federal government broad responsibilities for suffrage. The Majority Report argued that decisions over suffrage remained fully with the states. The central question was about the relative balance of power between the states and the federal government. Does control of who shall vote lie with the states alone or with both the federal government and the states? The question worked its way through the courts.

Elizabeth Cady Stanton was particularly impressed by Victoria Woodhull. The National was meeting in Washington at the time of Woodhull's address, and with Stanton's persuasion, they suspended proceedings to join the audience in the galleries. The National then took up Woodhull's cause. Isabella Beecher Hooker called for women to put pressure on their congressmen to support the Minority Report of the Judiciary Committee.

For many months after her congressional debut, Victoria Woodhull was the most famous defender of woman's right to vote, but then a scandal broke which consumed her and anyone who had supported her. During her public lectures, Victoria Woodhull spoke on the need for women's control over their own bodies and their own lives. On one fated occasion, peppered by questions, irritation overcame her political sense, and she finally replied to a heckler "Yes, I am a Free lover, I have an inalienable, constitutional and natural right to love whom I may . . . to change that love every day if I please."[35] Instantly, newspapermen in the audience scrambled over each other rushing to file their columns. Newspapers exploded with this evidence of such moral laxity by a suffragist. Outrage then blossomed into a full-fledged scandal. Woodhull and her sister Tennessee Claflin were accused of a history of prostitution, bigamy, and criminal charges in their past, all detailed and reported to eager readers. Elizabeth Cady Stanton, always willing to question conventional beliefs, supported Woodhull. Woodhull, wrote Stanton, "has done a work for women that none of us could have done. She has faced and dared men to call her names that make women shudder. She has risked and realized the sort of ignominy that would have paralyzed any of us who have longer been called strong-minded."[36] Stanton's support did not hold back the onslaught of bad publicity for the National. Because of Woodhull's connections to the National, suffrage supporters deserted in large numbers, leaving NWSA struggling to survive. Lucy Stone and the American tried to hold themselves above the fray, but they too were seriously tainted by the Woodhull brush.

Victoria Woodhull did not give in easily, retaliating by publishing salacious details of another scandal to show the hypocrisy of those who attacked her morals. She revealed adultery by leading Brooklyn Protestant minister, Henry Ward Beecher, with one of his parishioners, Elizabeth Tilton. Woodhull knew of this affair from Elizabeth Cady Stanton, who had confided the details to Woodhull in an ill-fated and unguarded moment. A famous preacher and president of the AWSA, Beecher was the son of one of the nation's most famous evangelists, Lyman Beecher, and brother to famous author Harriet Beecher Stowe and education reformer Catharine Beecher. He was immediately embroiled in church hearings. Because Woodhull had published her story in her newspaper, mailed to readers, she was arrested for promoting obscenity under the Comstock Act and spent time in jail, which infuriated her so much that she threatened to expose more scandals and tried to raise funds to keep her paper going by blackmailing some suffragists. Elizabeth Tilton's husband, Theodore Tilton, sued for divorce, citing Beecher as the correspondent, and also sued

Beecher for huge damages. Newspaper reports fueled the public perception of suffragists as a group rife with sexual license and radical mores.
The legal cases dragged on for years. Eventually, Beecher retained his
church, with his reputation restored. Elizabeth Tilton fled to England, as
did Victoria Woodhull who married there and spent the rest of her life
quietly in the country, never more in the public eye. Theodore Tilton's
career was ruined.[37]

Public attacks and the size of the outcry caused huge personal embarrassment to Lucy Stone, Julia Ward Howe, and other Boston-based
woman suffrage leaders. Everyone scrambled to dissociate woman suffrage associations from any of the people involved in the court cases or
with Victoria Woodhull. The setback for woman suffrage was enormous.
People cancelled their membership in suffrage organizations. The suffrage
movement was tainted for decades by its links to Woodhull. The issue of
"free love" was effectively and repeatedly used to attack woman suffrage.
The taint of immorality was feared throughout the whole woman suffrage
campaign, and it was difficult to dismiss easily. The National was more
seriously weakened, although they never publicly acknowledged it.

SUSAN B. ANTHONY'S TRIAL FOR VOTING

At this juncture Susan B. Anthony decided that she would test the New
Departure in courts. Clinging still to her old party loyalties, Anthony
intended to vote the straight Republican ballot, convinced Ulysses Grant
would win and that the Republicans would recognize the New Departure
logic once the election was over. She was more hopeful than realistic, as
it turned out.

Anthony and fifteen other women went to register and vote in Rochester on Election Day in 1872. Anthony persuaded the young men acting
as inspectors of elections that the women had consulted a respected local
lawyer, Judge Henry Selden, who agreed that the Fourteenth Amendment entitled women to vote. The young men conceded the point,
and the women placed their votes in the ballot box on November 5.
"Well, I have been & gone & done it!! Positively voted the Republican
ticket—strait—this A.M. at 7 o'clock & swore my vote in at that," wrote
Anthony to Stanton.[38] Not unexpectedly, a few weeks later Anthony was
arrested by federal marshalls accused of violating the Enforcement Act

(intended to protect voters) by falsely presenting herself as a legitimate voter. The other women voters from Rochester and the election inspectors were also charged.

The hearings and trial that followed Anthony's arrest were heavily reported in the newspapers. Anthony, knowing that she was not allowed to testify in court on her own behalf, promptly canvassed the county to educate the jury pool about the case. In response, the State Attorney General moved the trial venue and waited until newly appointed Associate Supreme Court Justice Ward Hunt was available to preside. At that time, Supreme Court judges also rode the trial circuit and oversaw cases. In June 1873, Anthony was tried in the Ontario County courthouse, an impressive building in the Greek manner. Ironically, the structure was topped with a gold dome where a twelve-foot high sculpture of Lady Justice gazed down on Canandaigua.

Anthony's lawyer, Henry Selden, took three hours giving his closing speech to the visible annoyance of Justice Hunt. Hunt had actually arrived in court with his opinion already written or written in haste during the testimony. He took only ten minutes speaking to the jury, directing the jury to return a guilty verdict, and refusing to allow the jury to debate. Susan B. Anthony was found guilty of a crime without recourse to a jury of her peers. Even if the case had gone to the jury, Anthony was quick to point out, unless there were women on the jury, there could not be any jury that was actually made up of her "peers."[39]

Hunt's ruling was that the Reconstruction amendments, although they included woman as citizens, did not give women the vote. Decisions about who could register and vote still rested with the states, not the federal government, because the right to vote was not among the "immunities and privileges" of U.S. citizens. States were prevented from barring men from voting "on account of race, color or previous condition of servitude," but states retained the right to control suffrage otherwise. A state could decide that only men with gray hair could vote, if they wished, because the Fourteenth Amendment had not, in Hunt's ruling, changed the right of the states to set qualifications for voting.

A comedy of sorts then ensued. Justice Hunt, who had quashed all efforts Anthony made to speak throughout the proceedings, asked if Anthony had anything to say before he passed sentence. Of course, Anthony did, and proceeded to speak eloquently for an hour, with Justice

Hunt interrupting in a futile effort to get her to stop. Anthony's words were forceful, with an eloquent summary of the whole trial.

Hunt promptly lost his temper and expostulated that the court could not listen to arguments that her counsel had already taken three hours to deliver. Anthony replied that she was not arguing the case again, but "simply stating the reasons why sentence cannot, in justice, be pronounced against me. Your denial of my citizen's right to vote is the denial of my right of consent as one of the governed, the denial of my right of representation as one of the taxed, the denial of my right to trial by a jury of my peers as an offender against law, denial of my sacred rights to life, liberty, property, and . . ." there Hunt interrupted again. Finally, Anthony finished and sat down, only to have Hunt make her stand immediately for sentencing. The courtroom reacted with unseemly amusement.

No-one was surprised when Anthony refused to pay her $100 fine nor did the other women who had voted or the registrars of elections. Justice Hunt would not hold Anthony in custody because to do so would have given her a route to a Supreme Court appeal. The male registrars were later pardoned by President Grant at the behest of Senator Benjamin Butler. Susan B. Anthony was now both a heroine and a criminal, and her skill in publicity had brought her plight to the entire nation's attention. Newspapers were largely in favor of Anthony, and attacked the conviction as a far-fetched use of national power. The *Rochester Evening Express* called Anthony's directed verdict and the conviction of the election inspectors "a petty but malicious act of tyranny."[40]

Significantly for Anthony's verdict, Justice Hunt was an ally of machine politician Roscoe Conkling and supporter of President Grant. Hunt may well have consulted with Conkling and Grant. Anthony's lawyer observed at the time that "there never was a trial in the country with one half the importance of Miss Anthony's. . . . If Anthony had won her case on the merit it would have revolutionized the suffrage of the country . . . There was a prearranged determination to convict her. A jury trial was dangerous and so the Constitution was deliberately and openly violated."[41]

Historian Ellen DuBois thinks that Anthony's arrest was both a sign that the Republicans felt strong enough to dispense with the question of women voting and believes that it was more than likely that her arrest "had been authorized at the highest level of government."[42] Woman suffrage, if supported by the courts and resting on the Fourteenth and Fifteenth Amendments, would have solidified the reach and power of the federal government at the expense of state power.

Congress showed increasing apathy to the question of civil rights. Hunt's decision echoed other cases that limited federal power in favor of states' rights. In 1873, the U.S. Supreme Court decision in the Slaughterhouse Cases further limited the power of the Fourteenth Amendment, making it virtually useless in enforcing civil rights or the immunities and privileges clause. Absent federal power, interest, or law to prevent conservative white southerners from doing away with Reconstruction-era civil and voting rights gains for blacks, southern states moved to disenfranchise black male voters with state legislation and state constitutional changes that imposed literacy tests, poll taxes, grandfather clauses, and other stratagems, which, reinforced by violence, by the turn of the century removed black men from voting rolls but also eliminated the vote of some poor white men.

The former Confederate states opposed a strong federal government. Northern Democrats now agreed. There was probably cold political calculus as well as cultural objections to women voting. Republican Senator Simon Cameron from Pennsylvania was willing to sacrifice woman suffrage in return for support from Southern Democrats for Republican efforts to increase tariff protection for industry. The reactions of Justice Hunt, Senator Cameron, and President Grant to Anthony's case appear as a simple effort to maintain Republican control of its congressional agenda.

The New Departure was hopelessly entangled in Republican political goals, states' rights forces, and the waning of Reconstruction—a fact that did not auger well for women getting the vote. Indeed, it sank the suffragists' hopes.[43] These hopes sank further when *United States v. Cruikshank,* heard by the U.S. Supreme Court a day after Justice Ward delivered his opinion on Anthony, handed down a ruling that the 1870 Enforcement Act was unconstitutional, repeating the argument that the Constitution alone did not grant suffrage to anyone. In *United States v. Reese,* the U.S. Supreme Court further narrowed the reach of the Fifteenth Amendment, finding that the plaintiff, although a black man, could not prove that he was denied the vote on the grounds of race, and so was not covered by constitutional protection.

MINOR V. HAPPERSETT: THE SUPREME COURT ENDS THE HOPE OF THE NEW DEPARTURE

The final glimmer of hope for woman suffrage through the New Departure logic disappeared when *Minor v. Happersett* came before the U.S. Supreme Court in February 1875. The decision handed down in favor of Happersett defined women out of the suffrage equation once more. The Supreme Court ruled that women's voting status had not been changed by the Fourteenth Amendment; women had always been citizens and women had always been denied the vote. The states might not prevent specific groups—that is black men—from voting but they had the sole right to confer suffrage.

Woman suffrage became just another one of the casualties of growing political conservatism. Historian Alex Keyssar has detailed the retreat toward "antidemocratic sentiments." Suffragists, both women and men, were unable to surmount barriers placed in their way by sweeping social, economic, and political movements outside their control. Industrialism trumped Reconstruction and universal suffrage. The leading historian of suffrage, Keyssar writes that, "leading intellectuals and politicians voiced deep reservations about universal or manhood suffrage . . . in the wake of the Civil War." As the United States became the leading manufacturing nation in the world and its population rose from thirty-five million to nearly seventy-five million by 1890, more than ten million people worked in manufacturing, mining, construction, and transportation.[44] With the changes wrought by an influx of southern, central, and eastern Europeans, including many Jews, public debate centered on the problem of extending the franchise to the poor, the uneducated, and the foreign born. The national mood did not favor expansion of the franchise.

Of additional importance is the conclusion Keyssar reaches that, "efforts to restrict the franchise commonly emanated from the middle and upper classes, from business and rural interests, as well as professionals; resistance to these efforts, as well as sentiment in favor of looser voting requirements, tended to be concentrated in the urban working class." Republicans were far more likely than Democrats, or third-party advocates, to favor restrictive reforms. We should note that suffragists came, on the whole, from the same middle and upper class, the very class that contained the male voters who favored restrictive reform, and who, like many suffragists, spoke out on their racial and nativist fears. Keyssar sums this situation up noting, "distinctive as this (woman suffrage) history may have been, it always ran alongside and frequently intersected with other currents in the chronicle of suffrage."[45]

1876: THE CENTENNIAL EXHIBITION IN PHILADELPHIA

In June 1876, still determined to draw the attention of Americans, Susan B. Anthony and Matilda Joselyn Gage planned a great publicity coup at the Fourth of July celebrations for the Centennial Exhibition in Philadelphia. They set up NWSA headquarters in Philadelphia, and, when Stanton arrived, they wrote a "Woman's Declaration of Independence" accompanied by a petition signed by as many suffrage leaders as they could muster on short notice. General Joseph Hawley, in control of the Independence Hall celebration, refused all requests from Stanton for time to present the woman suffrage message to the President. Anthony decided upon direct action.

The Fourth of July dawned hot, as usual, for Stanton described that summer in Philadelphia as "simply intolerable, only a seven times seven heated furnace could match it." Susan B. Anthony, Matilda Joslyn Gage, Lillie Devereux Blake, Phoebe Couzins, and Sara Spencer had passes so they could be seated in the audience. As Virginian Richard Lee finished reading the Declaration of Independence, Anthony and Gage rose from their seats, walked up to the platform, and presented a surprised Senator Thomas Ferry, the acting Vice President, with the Woman's Declaration of Rights on a large scroll rolled up and tied with red, white, and blue ribbons. A stunned, but not discomposed, Ferry gave Anthony a graceful bow, whereupon she turned and retreated down the main aisle. Anthony, Gage, and the other women distributed copies of the women's Declaration to an entertained audience who stood and clamored for copies.

The suffragists retreated to the steps of Independence Hall, where Anthony read out the Declaration of Rights. Women, she said, wanted to celebrate the great exhibition and the industrial achievements shown in the buildings. "Yet," she said, "we cannot forget even in this glad hour, that while all men of every race and clime and condition, have been invested with the full rights of citizenship under our hospitable flag, all women still suffer the degradation of disfranchisement."[46]

Anthony and Stanton left Philadelphia and turned to a new project, compiling a history of the woman suffrage movement, which was to occupy them for decades and would consume six volumes, with the first published in 1881.

Lucy Stone and AWSA had never believed the New Departure would work and so maintained its steady pace of work in the states. Examination of woman suffrage efforts in Wyoming, Utah, Washington, and later in the 1880s in Oregon and California sustains the claim that state suffrage movements were a successful strategy. It was the only option that had a record of success, although even in these states women got the vote, only in some cases, to have it taken away. Stone, Anthony, Stanton, other American and National leaders, and paid agents of both organizations traveled constantly from state to state, recruiting and working with state suffrage campaigns.

Lucy Stone and Susan B. Anthony had succeeded in undermining the image of them both as unsexed radicals. They both were now respected and judged respectable by friend and foe. Lucy Stone maintained her public image as a virtuous woman through the years of the scandals. Susan B. Anthony was able to turn back the waves of disapproval engendered by the taint of "free lovism." The *Toledo Blade* praised Anthony at the time of her trial, saying "Whatever may be said of Susan B. Anthony, there is no doubt but she has kept the public mind of the country agitated upon the woman's rights question as few others, male or female, could have done. She has displayed very superior judgment and has seldom been led into acts of even seeming impropriety. She has won the respect of all classes by her ability, her consistency and her spotless character."[47] By the 1880s, the woman suffrage movement was becoming respectable, or at the least was no longer seen as radical as it had been to the many people who had been horrified by the women and the cause in the antebellum era, or during the scandals of the 1870s.

The two national organizations were in constant public conflict and claimed deep differences. The National stood for federal campaigns and the New Departure, and continued fights for equal rights issues. The American focused on state suffrage campaigns. In reality, they both employed agents who worked in state campaigns, and National leaders, like their American counterparts, traveled constantly, recruiting for state and local societies.

NOTES

1. Francis Minor to *The Revolution*, October 14, 1869 in Elizabeth Cady Stanton, Susan B. Anthony, and Matilda Joslyn Gage, eds., *History of Woman Suffrage*, Vol. 1 (New York, NY: Rochester, 1881).

2. Rebecca J. Mead, *How the Vote Was Won: Woman Suffrage in the Western United States, 1868–1914* (New York: New York University Press, 2006), 37.

3. Ruth Barnes Moynihan, *Rebel for Rights: Abigail Scott Duniway* (New Haven, CT: Yale University Press, 1983).

4. Darlene Clark Hine, Elsa Barkley Brown, and Rosalyn Terborg Penn, *Black Women in American History*, Vol. 1 (Brooklyn, NY: Carlson Publishing, 1990), 261–2.

5. Nancy F. Cott, *No Small Courage: A History of Women in the United States* (New York, NY: Oxford University Press, 2000), 323.

6. Cott, *No Small Courage*, 313–5.

7. Louis Fisher, "The Rights of Women," in *Congress: Protecting Individual Rights* (Lawrence: University Press of Kansas, 2016), 70–72.

8. Jill Norgren, *Belva Lockwood: The Woman Who Would Be President* (New York: New York University Press, 2007).

9. Anne Firor Scott, *Natural Allies: Women's Associations in American History* (Urbana: University of Illinois Press, 1991), 80–83.

10. Rosalyn Terborg-Penn, "African Women and the Suffrage Movement," in Marjorie Spruill Wheeler, ed., *One Woman, One Vote: Rediscovering the Woman Suffrage Movement* (Troutdale, OR: NewSage Press, 1995), 135–54; Rosalyn Terborg-Penn, *African American Women in the Struggle for the Vote, 1850–1920* (Bloomington: Indiana University Press, 1998), 34–52.

11. C.C. O'Brien, "'The White Women all Go for Sex': Frances Harper on Suffrage, Citizenship, and the Reconstruction South," *African American Review* 43, no. 4 (2009): 605–6.

12. Alison M. Parker, *Articulating Rights: Nineteenth-Century American Women on Race, Reform, and the State* (DeKalb: Northern Illinois University Press, 2010), 122–3.

13. Elsa Barkley Brown, "'What has Happened here': The Politics of Difference in Women's History and Feminist Politics," *Feminist Studies* 18, no. 2 (Summer 1992): 295–312.

14. Jane Rhodes, *Mary Ann Shadd Cary: The Black Press and Protest in the Nineteenth Century* (Bloomington: Indiana University Press, 1998), 185–208; Martha S. Jones, *All Bound Up Together: The Woman Question in African American Public Culture, 1830–1900* (Chapel Hill: University of North Carolina Press, 2007), 90–91.

15. Hine et al., *Black Women*, 990; Darlene Clark Hine and Kathleen Thompson, A *Shining Thread of Hope: The History of Black Women in America* (New York, NY: Broadway Books, 1998), 156.

16. Kathleen Barry, *Susan B. Anthony: A Biography of a Singular* Feminist (New York, NY: Ballantine Books, 1990), 294.

17. Lisa Tetrault, *The Myth of Seneca Falls: Memory and the Women's Suffrage Movement, 1848–1898* (Chapel Hill: University of North Carolina Press, 2014), 46–47.

18. Barry, *Susan B. Anthony*, 237.

19. Lori Ginzberg, *Elizabeth Cady Stanton: An American Life* (New York, NY: Hill & Wang, 2009), 148.

20. Sally G. McMillen, *Lucy Stone: An Unapologetic Life* (New York, NY: Oxford University Press, 2015), 199.

21. J. Tutt, "'No Taxation without Representation': The American Woman Suffrage Movement," *Stanford Law Review*, 62, no. 5 (2010): 1473–512.

22. Speech by Susan B. Anthony to the Centennial of the Boston Tea Party in New York City, December 16, 1873, in Ann Gordon, ed., *Selected Papers of Elizabeth Cady Stanton and Susan B. Anthony*, Vol. 3 (New Brunswick, NJ: Rutgers. University Press, 1997), 22.

23. Stanton et al., *History of Woman Suffrage*, Vol. 3: 395–443.

24. "Virginia Minor," in Edward T. James, ed., *Notable American Women, 1607–1950: A Biographical Dictionary*, Vol. 2 (Cambridge, MA: Belknap Press of Harvard University Press, 1971), 550–51.

25. Francis Minor to *The Revolution*, October 14, 1869, in Stanton et al., *History of Woman Suffrage*, Vol. 2.

26. Martin J. Naparsteck, *The Trial of Susan B. Anthony—An Illegal Vote, A Courtroom Conviction, and a Step Forward* (Jefferson, NC: McFarland & Company, 2014), 33–34.

27. Ellen Carol DuBois, *Woman Suffrage and Women's Rights* (New York: New York University Press, 1998), 113–4.

28. DuBois, *Woman Suffrage and Women's Rights*, 117.

29. DuBois, *Woman Suffrage and Women's Rights*, 853.

30. Norgren, *Belva Lockwood*, 58.

31. DuBois, *Woman Suffrage and Women's Rights*, 857.

32. Tamara Gaskell, "A Citizen's, Not a Woman's, Right: Carrie Burnham v. the Pennsylvania Supreme Court," *Pennsylvania Legacies* 8, no. 2 (2008): 20–27.

33. Victoria Woodhull declared herself a candidate for President of the United States on April 2, 1870, for the 1872 campaign, although her effort was largely theoretical.

34. Norgren, *Belva Lockwood*, 56.

35. Ellen Carol DuBois, "Taking the Law into Our Own Hands: *Bradwell, Minor*, and Suffrage Militance in the 1870s," in Nancy A. Hewitt and Suzanne Lebsock, eds., *Visible Women: New Essays on American Activism* (Urbana: University of Illinois Press, 1993), 19–40.

36. DuBois, *Woman Suffrage and Women's Rights*, 857.

37. Although it was not widely known, Theodore Tilton may have had a brief affair with Victoria Woodhull.

38. Barry, *Susan B. Anthony*, 297.

39. Hunt's actions were outlawed soon after this trial. Judges could no longer direct a jury's verdict.

40. Naparsteck, *The Trial of Susan B. Anthony*, 143, 183.

41. DuBois, *Woman Suffrage and Women's Rights*, 129.

42. DuBois, *Woman Suffrage and Women's Rights*, 31.

43. Alexander Keyssar, *The Right to Vote: The Contested History of Democracy in the United States* (New York, NY: Basic Books, 2009).

44. Keyssar, *The Right to Vote*, 119–20.

45. Keyssar, *The Right to Vote*, 172–221.

46. Declaration of Rights of the Women of the United States, 4, 1876, *Selected Papers*, Vol. 3: 234.

47. Naparsteck, *The Trial of Susan B. Anthony*, 85.

CHAPTER 4

WOMAN SUFFRAGE BECOMES RESPECTABLE, 1870–1900

"As soon as a new railroad ran through a village of five hundred inhabitants that could boast a schoolhouse, a church, or a hotel, and one enterprising man or woman, a course of lectures was at once inaugurated as a part of the winter's entertainments."

—Elizabeth Cady Stanton[1]

THE LYCEUM CIRCUIT AND THE "BUSINESS OF FEMINISM"

Lillie Devereux Blake inherited a sizable amount of money, but at her first husband's death, she found to her horror that her inheritance was gone. She worked as a correspondent during the Civil War and later found she still needed to earn money because her second husband did "not get on in business as he ought." Giving public lectures was considered unbecoming by her conservative middle-class family; once she took to the lecture circuit only one sister remained speaking to her. Blake worked hard to learn the art of drawing in an audience, becoming a proficient writer and eloquent speaker and finding pleasure in the profession. After a lecture in Newport in 1869, she wrote to Paulina Wright Davis:

A thrill of intense excitement rushed through me as I saw how my audience was giving me their best attention. . . . A new delight and a new joy swelled in my heart, surged in my veins, I uttered my appeal with passionate earnestness and sat down at its close glowing, intoxicated and triumphant with the knowledge that I had a portion of heaven's divinest gift, eloquence![2]

Elizabeth Cady Stanton commented on the October to June lyceum season, when, "like the ferryboats in New York harbor, running hither and thither, crossing each other's racks, the whole list of lecturers were on the wing, flying to every town and city from San Francisco to New York."[3] The number of women (and men) on the speaker circuit who gave lectures on woman's rights shows that audiences were eager to hear lectures on married women's property rights, guardianship of children, and control over women's own bodies, as well as woman suffrage. Speakers moved from town to town with a traveling case full of three or four speeches and were paid well to deliver a range of talks. Suffragists realized quickly that the way to earn an income, and a good income at that, was to go on the road. The speaking circuit was a major source of income for many suffragists who worked within the two national associations. Their lectures were a significant source for spreading the word for woman suffrage and other woman's rights issues.

Abigail Scott Duniway estimated that she had given 1,750 lectures over thirteen years after her husband had an accident that prevented him from earning a living. Susan B. Anthony kept meticulous records of her earnings; in 1871, she earned $4,300, while a female teacher might earn $1,000 a year, and a factory worker scraped by on less than $500. In 1878, Mary Livermore gave 114 lectures on woman's rights, temperance, and other topics, earning perhaps $18,000.[4] Such substantial sums were rare, but they are evidence that other less well-known women, like Matilda Joslyn Gage or Lillie Devereux Blake, could earn enough to live on. In the South, rural isolation and poverty, and opposition to women's rights, did not support women speakers. Black women found it difficult to join this white-dominated profession. The exceptions were Sojourner Truth, as well as Frances Ellen Watkins Harper who when widowed during the war, supported herself and her daughter lecturing. In general, however, the lyceum circuit was dominated by white, Anglo-Saxon and Protestant lecturers and audiences.

Historian Lisa Tetrault has pointed out the central role of suffrage speakers who traveled the country to recruit women to the cause. These speakers built the suffrage movement from the grassroots and reveal the strong role the funds they generated played in supporting both national suffrage organizations. Tetrault examined the lyceum phenomenon, concluding that "business reshaped American feminism" because of the numbers of activist women who earned a good income on the speaker's platform.[5] Few women spoke publicly about the need to earn a living. The public image of the suffrage movement was as a cause in which women were volunteers only; the reality was that some suffrage women had to support themselves and their families.

SPREADING THE NEWS: THE SUFFRAGE PRESS

The lyceum brought the woman suffrage cause but so too, increasingly, did newspapers and journals, handed around from home to home, family to family. As more women received more education, they read what they could find on woman suffrage and woman's rights. On the frontier, women's newspapers and journals were effective recruiting agents, read by multiple eager readers purveying word of the cause as never before. For sixteen years Abigail Scott Duniway published *New Northwest* (1871–1887) in Portland. In Utah, Emmeline Wells published the *Woman's Exponent* for Mormon women from 1872 until 1914; and in Colorado, Caroline Churchill published her paper, *Queen Bee*, from 1879 until 1895. The length of time each paper lasted is significant evidence of the increasing support for woman suffrage, even in isolated towns.

The moderate *Woman's Journal* dominated the field. Started in 1870 after energetic fundraising by Lucy Stone and Henry Blackwell, it became the main source of news for all suffragists, edited and managed by Stone and then by her daughter Alice Stone Blackwell, until 1920. Seed money came from wealthy suffrage sympathizer Elizabeth Eddy and the New England Woman Suffrage Association. The AWSA provided support with fundraising bazaars and kept it financially solvent.

The *Woman's Journal* reflected the moderate views of its founders and reached more moderate suffragists. It covered state suffrage campaigns, printed foreign news, and had columns of general interest on "what women were doing."[6] Activities of the suffrage movement, transcripts of conventions, suffrage debates in legislatures, activities of the antisuffragists (called "Remonstrants"), and news of suffrage activities in other countries were covered. The journal managed to remain aloof during the national furor over the Beecher–Tilton scandal, which enhanced its reputation as a serious and moderate organ of the movement. Harry Blackwell had the idea of offering a column by Lucy Stone on news items about women to newspapers. Between 100 and 200 newspapers picked up the column in 1882, reaching women through mainstream national and state papers. The *Woman's Journal* annoyed Susan B. Anthony with every edition because it didn't cover National Woman Suffrage Association (NWSA) events thoroughly and made condescending references to "Miss Anthony's party." Stone believed that, despite NWSA's "flawed" strategies, their work should be reported, so coverage was included, but often not in detail. With the New Departure gone as an option, it was lyceum speakers and newspapers that were important in broadening the base of women in support of a suffrage campaigns.

As hopes for any federal amendment were dashed, the option to win woman suffrage in the territories and the states became the chief way forward. In this work, the American was more active than the National, but the first successes, in Wyoming and Utah, had little to do with the Eastern organizations.

STATE BY STATE: SUCCESS IN THE WEST

The only state campaigns that were successful before the end of the century were in the sparsely populated West. On first look, it would seem contradictory that the frontier regions, with the sparsest populations, should be the first to enfranchise women when it was the East that was the site of both national organizations. In 1869, soon after Wyoming was connected to the East by the transcontinental railroad, women won the vote in the territory. Two other territories passed woman suffrage before 1890—Utah a few months after Wyoming in 1870 and Washington in 1883. In every territory and new state, the topic of woman suffrage was debated. With small populations and small legislatures, suffragists had better opportunities to persuade legislators than did Eastern suffragists facing large, heavily party-controlled state legislatures.

Wyoming: The First Success

Woman suffrage was debated in the Wyoming territory as early as 1854, and woman's rights issues surfaced again in 1869, when two pieces of legislation succeeded—equal pay for women teachers and a married women's property rights measure. Even so, people were surprised when late in the legislative session a Democrat and a Southerner, William H. Bright, introduced woman suffrage legislation with the support of the territorial secretary, Edward M. Lee. Bright's wife was a strong suffragist with women allies who joined her to support the bill. Bright's logic, according to his wife, was a racial one; if black men could vote, then so should white women. In a letter in the *Denver Tribune*, his position was somewhat different; he wrote that, "I knew it was a new issue, and a live one and with a strong feeling that it was just, I determined to use all my influence." Race and anti-Chinese prejudice were certainly part of the equation in Wyoming, with one legislator remarking, "Damn it, if you are going to let the niggers and pigtails vote, we will ring in the women, too." Some Democrats favored the publicity for the territory that would follow woman suffrage. Antisuffrage Democrats hoped to embarrass the new Republican governor, John Campbell, by putting the woman suffrage proposal in front of him, assuming he would veto it. Campbell surprised everyone by signing woman suffrage into law.

Wyoming women supported Republicans in the next elections in 1871, helping erode the Democratic monopoly. The Democrats promptly tried to repeal woman suffrage, but they could not override the governor's veto. Even so, the press was full of comments describing women voting a success. Polling places did not erupt in riots, as some had predicted. Women were generally considered to bring their morality and ethical strengths to politics. Californian Congressman and suffragist Aaron Sargent said that woman suffrage worked so well in Wyoming that it had "rescued that Territory from a state of comparative lawlessness to one of the most orderly in the Union." Woman suffrage had delivered its promise that women in politics would bring an improved, more civilized society.[7]

When Wyoming applied for statehood, women worked successfully to elect prosuffrage delegates to the state constitutional convention. An effort to sideline woman suffrage by calling for a popular referendum was narrowly defeated with the support of these men. A popular referendum posed huge obstacles to any woman suffrage campaign as the suffragists did not have the numbers to cover every part of a state, or to persuade a majority of the men of the state. They could more successfully convince a targeted population of state congressmen and senators. Another defeat was narrowly avoided when Democrats in the U.S. Congress tried to block the woman suffrage clause in the Wyoming constitution despite the fact that this put them in the awkward position of undermining states' rights. Wyoming delegates telegrammed that they would become a state with woman suffrage or not at all. In 1890, a close congressional vote gave Wyoming statehood with woman suffrage.

Utah

Utah, with the overwhelming influence of the Mormon Church, presented a different scenario. Polygamy, along with slavery, was for Republicans evidence of "barbarism" in a civilized country. Woman suffrage in Utah would rise and fall on the question of plural marriage. There were both women and men suffragists within the Mormon Church and the territory. After two weeks of discussion, the Utah legislature voted for woman suffrage. On February 12, 1870, the territorial governor signed the law.

The *New York Times* supported woman suffrage in Utah, arguing that surely women in Utah who suffered from the degradation of a plural marriage would vote to end polygamy.[8] Non-Mormons may have thought that woman suffrage would be a means to end polygamy, but Mormon Elders thought otherwise, and banked upon Mormon women voting to support them in the continuation of polygamy. They also counted upon women to help Mormon voters outnumber non-Mormon voters.

To the amazement of outsiders, there were woman suffragists who were in plural marriages. A protest meeting was held where five thousand Utah women who supported polygamy and opposed antipolygamy legislation gathered in January of 1870, leading the New York *Herald* editors to comment "the so-called degraded ladies of Mormondom are quite equal to the women's rights women of the East."[9] In 1887, Congress passed the Edmunds–Tucker Anti-Polygamy Act, which, among other provisions, disenfranchised women in the territory. Male suffrage was restored in 1890, and woman suffrage was not restored until 1896, with the entry of Utah into the Union.[10]

Washington

Woman suffrage came within one vote of success in 1854 in the largely Republican Washington territory. In 1867, a law to disenfranchise

Confederate soldiers seemed by its language to enfranchise white women, and in 1868, prosuffrage legislator Edward Eldridge wrote a series of articles arguing the "New Departure" logic for woman suffrage. Mary Olney Brown tested the New Departure argument by going to the polls in 1869. An official at her polling place told her that she was not an American citizen, and that "the laws of congress don't extend over Washington Territory." The swelling crowd disagreed, with one man yelling, "It would be more sensible to let an intelligent white woman vote than an ignorant nigger," to general applause from others in the audience. Another official worried that if they accepted Mary Brown's vote, it might invalidate the votes of the whole precinct. She was denied the ballot. The Washington legislature reacted by passing a law in 1871 that explicitly prohibited women from voting.

Woman suffrage came up before the legislature again and again. Often the votes in the 1870s were very close; the Constitutional Convention of 1878 rejected woman suffrage by one vote. In 1883, enough Republicans supported the measure that it passed, though with the sentiment that this was not the end of the question. It was, said one legislator, "as good a time to try to experiment—if experiment it was—and if it proved a failure, it could be corrected when we become a state." There was talk of women bringing "purity, progress, and reform." Women turned out at the polls, and there were reports that women voting improved ethics, that it was "a warning to the undesirable class of the community."[11]

The "undesirable class" responded with a backlash that showed that woman suffrage was an unsettled proposition, even after successful legislation. Though some suffragists, pragmatically, but taking a low road, used the racial argument that woman suffrage (for white women) would balance the black vote and the likelihood of Chinese enfranchisement, it was not enough. Woman suffrage was linked with prohibition, and women serving on juries was particularly disputed. Strong opposition coalesced to disfranchise women. Heavy Democratic (antiprohibition) influence appears to have led to the territorial Supreme Court, ignoring the precedents of Wyoming and Utah, into ruling that a territorial legislature had no right to enfranchise women. Abigail Scott Duniway had been the loudest voice in opposition to the connection between woman suffrage and prohibition or temperance, arguing that it doomed the woman suffrage movement.

Stunned and believing, correctly, that their vote had been stolen, angry women suffragists organized, leafletted the territory, gathered signatures for petitions, brought in Matilda Hindman from Pennsylvania to traverse the state, and readied the Equal Suffrage League to fight at the state constitutional convention in July 1889. Clara Colby, in her *Woman's Tribune*, appealed for help against "machine politics and the allied forces of vice and corruption."[12] In the end, the majority of delegates believed that woman suffrage was too radical and would doom ratification of the state constitution, so they took the easy route of calling for a popular referendum on both suffrage and prohibition, which avoided any one representative showing his hand on woman suffrage. Strong Democratic Party influence, the opposition of liquor interests, and antireform political factions doomed woman suffrage in Washington. Twenty years of heavy campaigning by suffrage organizations, the Woman's Christian Temperance Union (WCTU), and a Populist coalition followed. Washington finally passed woman suffrage in 1910.

Failure in Oregon

Abigail Scott Duniway played a large role in most of the women's rights successes in Washington and Oregon in the 1870s, leading successful campaigns from her home in Portland, for legislation allowing women to own a business alone, a Married Woman's Property Act, and woman's right to vote in school elections.[13] In 1882, the Oregon legislature defeated woman suffrage by one vote. Despite the energy of Duniway and fellow suffragists, woman suffrage in Oregon proved elusive; suffrage bills passed the legislature in 1880 and 1882, but the public referendum vote failed badly. Opposition from the liquor industry remained strong, and it took until 1912 to get woman suffrage.

Colorado: The First State to Win Suffrage by Referendum

On January 19, 1870, Representative M.S. Taylor rose to address the Colorado territorial legislature on woman suffrage. Reminding his colleagues that he was a Democrat and therefore opposed "negro suffrage in any shape or form," he spoke against giving women the vote because it would enfranchise black women. In both Idaho and Colorado, there were common elements to the suffrage debates that reflected national prejudices as well as Western prejudices. Native Americans were not considered civilized enough to be suitable candidates to vote. Anti-Chinese sentiment ran strong. Southern Democrats moved to the northwest after the Civil War and were an influence in elections against woman suffrage. Racism pervaded the discussions. Opposition to African American men or women voting was led by Democrats in both Colorado and Idaho. Black women formed suffrage organizations, only to be ignored by white women. Susan B. Anthony, after a defeat in Colorado in 1877, disparaged the Mexican workers as too ignorant, too drunk, or too much under the thumb of the Roman Catholic Church to support woman suffrage. Class divisions also played a part; in the 1893 campaigns, Denver club women, who were "society" women, were unable to form coalitions with the strong Knights of Labor and other workers organizations.

Colorado was the first state to vote in woman suffrage by popular referendum. Suffrage agitation began early in Colorado as it had in Wyoming, Utah, Oregon, and Washington. The territorial governor, Edward M. Cook, was a suffragist, who in 1870 tried to convince the territorial legislature to vote for woman suffrage, asking them to match Wyoming in leading the way to universal suffrage. The territorial Council then passed woman suffrage with a one vote margin, but the legislature balked and hopes for legislation died.

Debate and suffrage organization revived in 1876 as Colorado approached statehood. The suffragists managed to get a referendum before the state's voters in 1877. Support came from William Bright, the Wyoming suffragist now in Colorado, and from the state governor, John L. Routt. Both the National and American were in action, with Lucy Stone, Henry Blackwell, and Susan B. Anthony joining the campaign. Suffragists ran a strong lecture program in as many towns and cities as they could manage. Many newspapers came out in support. Strong opposition came from Roman Catholic Bishop Joseph P. Machebeuf, joined by a leading Presbyterian, the Reverend Mr. Bliss, who lambasted suffragists as "brawling, ranting women, bristling for their rights."[14]

The suffrage campaign embraced a variety of opinions that reflected the surrounding society, with its prejudices and preferences. One of the strongest local leaders was Caroline Nichols Churchill, a leading suffragist, journalist, and lecturer, and later editor of *Queen Bee* (1879–1895).

Churchill was unusual in her pro-Chinese stand, and yet she was also fiercely anti-Mormon and anti-Catholic. She endorsed the Knights of Labor, but disliked its leader, Terence V. Powderly, because he was Catholic. Like Abigail Scott Duniway, Churchill grew away from a protemperance position, and clashed with WCTU women, who were more traditional, more conservative, and horrified by Churchill's "flamboyance."[15]

Once the votes were tallied from the 1877 referendum, it was clear that it was a severe loss for the suffragists. In Denver and other cities, the majority of voters supported woman voting, but the campaign had not reached voters in small towns, particularly the mining towns. Liquor industry funds had also been spent liberally and effectively. Much was also made in the antisuffrage newspapers about Easterners interfering with Colorado politics. Anthony, taking a nativist tack, blamed the defeat on Spanish-speaking voters. She was wrong in that large numbers of Anglo males also voted against woman suffrage. An organized suffrage movement fizzled.

Colorado lay as a fallow field for suffrage until Matilda Hindman, suffragist lecturer and organizer from Pennsylvania, and a mainstay of all the western campaigns, returned to Colorado in 1890 and managed to raise enough interest for the establishment of a renewed state suffrage organization. Colorado suffrage association leader Ellis Meredith Stansbury then appealed to the newly created united national association, the National American Woman Suffrage Association (NAWSA), for help. Newly recruited to the national scene, Carrie Lane Chapman (later Catt) came from Iowa and was the genius behind the successful organization. Her skills were so effective, and local suffragists so energetic, that in 1893 the general assembly passed a bill providing for a woman suffrage referendum vote. The 1893 referendum result was a solid victory, especially in counties where the Populist Party was strong.

Women in Colorado did not stop with their own victory, but organized to learn parliamentary process and to send workers into Utah and Idaho. Woman voting in Colorado was declared a success in 1896 by the state's governor, and women seemed to be voting in equal proportion as men.

The role of the Populists in the campaign was vital to the success. The Populist Party had adopted a national prosuffrage plank in 1893, and with that came the support of miners and working men of Colorado for the 1893 campaign. The Knights of Labor sent energetic and effective

Leonora Barry, and the WCTU committed its support. The Brewers' Association was slow to act in opposition, which helped the women's cause as there was little other organized opposition. Colorado's suffrage success was made possible by the presence of a third party and working-class voters. Populist Party representatives in the lower house provided 22 votes in favor, balancing out 21 opposing votes from Republicans, and joining with 5 supporting Republican votes. Populists in the state Senate also provided essential support.

After the 1877 loss in Colorado, Henry Blackwell reviewed the failure. He attributed it to the lack of support or opposition from state politicians, concluding that the "Lesson of Colorado" was: "Woman suffrage can never be carried by a popular vote, without a political party behind it."[16] The year 1893 proved the accuracy of Blackwell's theory. The 1893 victory came because the Populist cause was strong.

Another essential aspect of the Colorado campaign was Carrie Chapman Catt's organizational skill. Using newspapers, speeches to party organizations, public demonstrations to reach male voters with an aggressive campaign, and financial support from the East, Catt won women the vote and established her national reputation. One aspect of Catt's plan, later labeled the "Society Plan" and employed across the country, was based upon her work in Denver, where, taking the advice of Lucy Stone, she sought the support of elite women from Denver's high society and women's clubs. These were intensely respectable suffragists, radical in their suffragism, but deeply rooted in the city's growing elite. Yet, in addition to the Society Plan it was actually her organization of a mass of volunteers, largely from Populists, who worked in mining towns and small communities, and with trade union support, who went house to house canvassing voters and handing out educational tracts that won the referendum.

Progressive women claimed that with the vote they succeeded in getting a state home for delinquent children established and helped elect the progressive reform judge, Ben B. Lindsey, who created juvenile courts. Probably 40–50 percent of eligible women voted in the first years of woman suffrage. There was no "woman's bloc," says historian Rebecca Mead, but Colorado women moved into the Republican, Democratic, and Populist parties, creating women's political clubs. There were African American clubs, as well as ethnic women's political clubs. In the late 1890s, Republicans, Silver Republicans, Democrats, and Populists ran and elected women candidates. Colorado State Senator Helen Ring Robinson claimed successful progressive reforms, such as minimum wages for women, pure food legislation, juvenile courts, joint guardianship, and child labor laws. Women became school superintendents and public officials and entered politics, albeit to be employed at low levels in the party hierarchies. The aftermath of suffrage in Colorado was substantive. It was, however, significant for expectations at the national level that women did not vote for one party or create their own party.

Idaho

The last woman suffrage success in the West before 1900 was in Idaho. The proximity of Utah and Wyoming was the most important factor in that success, particularly because of the overflow of Mormon settlers from Utah into Idaho. Abigail Scott Duniway's suffragist newspaper was readily available there, and Duniway herself visited Idaho often, and eventually moved there. Duniway created the early suffrage associations, but her influence waned when she attacked Mormons because she feared increasing the Democratic Mormon vote.

Duniway warned against upsetting the liquor interests in Idaho, and her influence was strong enough that the Idaho suffrage movement was divided between pro-WCTU suffragists and antitemperance suffragists. Despite this split, a swing toward suffrage came when the national Populist Party adopted a woman suffrage plank and the Idaho Populist Party followed the national lead. Jane Ellen Foster, the President of the National League of Republican Women, toured the western states in 1894 and reported from Boise that the Republicans in Idaho would support woman suffrage, predicting that woman suffrage would soon be on the state ballot. Foster had been a member of WCTU, but she forsook it for direct political involvement, as did many women in the late nineteenth century. Though their story is separate from organized suffrage, women played a strong role within the Republican Party structure in a way that increased over the decades.[17]

In 1896, woman suffrage came up for a vote. Republicans, Populists, Democrats, and Silver Republicans all supported it. There was little organized opposition. The woman suffrage amendment was carried by a nearly 2–1 vote, but the state board of canvassers ruled that the amendment had not passed because it did not receive the majority of all votes cast in the overall general election. The question was then placed before the Idaho Supreme Court where William E. Borah and James H. Hawley led the case on behalf of the equal suffrage association. The justices ruled in their favor, and Idaho became the fourth state to award women the vote. Borah went on to become a Republican Senator, known for his isolationism, and Hawley became Idaho's governor; both men were supported by suffrage women in getting their offices.

The votes of re-enfranchised Mormon men in the counties adjacent to Utah were significant in the woman suffrage success in Idaho. Women who moved into Idaho from Utah expected to continue to vote, and their communities went strongly for woman suffrage. Historian Beverley Beeton points to Mormon communities being heavy subscribers to the *Woman's Journal*, while there were few subscribers from non-Mormon Boise.

Despite Abigail Scott Duniway's efforts to keep out what she viewed as interfering Eastern suffragists, NAWSA had significant influence in the campaign, running effective educational outreach to communities across the state. But the main key to woman suffrage success in the West was the work of local women. Many came from back East and brought with them first-hand experience of suffrage lectures, or they had been members of suffrage societies, and these were the backbone of the western successes. At times, western women felt that organizers from the national associations were more of a hindrance than a help. These were grassroots campaigns and success depended upon local conditions and local politics.

WOMAN SUFFRAGE AND TEMPERANCE: AN EFFECTIVE UNION?

While western campaigns were underway, a new force grew across the county—the Woman's Christian Temperance Union (WCTU). When the WCTU committed to supporting woman suffrage, its members transformed the national movement. In doing so, they solidified the already existing link between temperance and suffrage. Susan B. Anthony was a temperance agent, Lucy Stone worked for temperance, and many other abolitionists were temperance advocates. They did not necessarily call for complete prohibition, but for limiting alcohol consumption.

A series of spectacular street protests against the selling of alcohol, called the Woman's Crusade, started in the winter of 1873 and created a new mass movement that gave rise to the WCTU. Eliza Jane Thompson, respectable, educated, and from a family of status and substance, never expected to speak in public or put herself in the public eye, but on a cold winter Monday in December 1873, with light snow impeding her progress, Eliza led a parade of hymn-singing women into downtown Hillsboro, Ohio. Taking up the challenge of a traveling temperance lecturer, Dr. Diocletian Lewis, they intended to stop saloons, drug stores, physicians, and any other distributors from selling alcohol. None of the women had ever been in a saloon and were perhaps as astonished at their own actions as were the proprietors who greeted them when they swept in, knelt on sawdust strewn floors, and commenced praying. The marches and invasions of saloons continued, until within a few weeks, the number of businesses selling liquor in Hillsboro dropped from thirteen to four.

The Hillsboro protests marked the start of the "Woman's Crusade" spreading nationwide and ending with the establishment of the WCTU. For months, the spirit of the Crusade ran white hot. Saloon-keepers, druggists, grocers, physicians, innkeepers, all the various dispensers of alcohol, signed pledges to cease alcohol distribution. When spring came, women counted among their successes 130 towns in Ohio, 36 in Michigan, 34 in Indiana, 26 in Pennsylvania, and 17 in New Jersey where women had shut down saloons.[18] The streets were no longer denizens where only women of questionable morals loitered, or public spaces traversed by respectable women on their way from one place to another. They were now places for respectable women to hold public protest. The tradition of public protest was refined and expanded by the woman suffrage organizations in the following decades.

Historian Ruth Bordin wrote in 1981 that the WCTU had become a "cheap joke, the epitome of blue-stocking bigotry."[19] It has been dismissed as simply the efflorescence of intolerant Protestant women who had little, if any, long-term impact. A close reading of the evidence and the rise and fall of the WCTU tells a very different story. In 1892, nearly 150,000 women paid dues to the WCTU, and another 50,000 young women belonged to the Young WCTU. The World WCTU spread across the globe in the 1880s and 1890s. In comparison, at this time, the united National and American (NAWSA, founded in 1890) had perhaps 13,000 dues-paying members. WCTU members cut across class lines; there were Catholic and Protestants, immigrant women, and African American women, although its leadership was almost all from the ranks of white, well-off women. Such a mass movement, run by women alone, was more than a footnote in the history of reform movements.

Alcohol abuse and addiction was a real and persistent problem in the nineteenth century. When drinking water was often dangerously polluted and milk could carry tuberculosis, alcohol was a cheap alternative. Working men, people generally agreed, needed alcohol to warm themselves in freezing weather and to sustain them for hard physical labor. As a disinfectant and sterilizer for wounds, alcohol was the only effective drug available.

Alcohol consumption increased after the Civil War, as it had after the American Revolution. Both periods spurred temperance campaigns with towns and states banning the sale of alcohol, only to find the laws difficult to enforce or challenged in the courts.[20] Consumption of alcohol after the Civil War increased because the numbers of saloons and distribution outlets increased in the 1860s and 1870s. In Ohio, in 1873, there was one saloon for every 200 people—an astonishing figure. In Chicago, at the turn of the nineteenth century, Bordin writes that the number of saloon customers was equal to half the city's population—another staggering fact.

Drinking was a problem that caused enormous suffering for women whose breadwinners spent their wages at a saloon. Excessive drinking accompanied physical abuse of women and children, which temperance advocates believed stemmed from the liquor industry and the moral failure of the male drunkard.[21] Compounding the problem was the continuing legal subservience of wives and their inability to maintain guardianship of their children even when married to an abusive and alcoholic husband. Given this reality, it is not surprising that, once ignited, a fire for temperance swept across the country in the 1870s, with added fuel coming from the economic crisis of 1873 making every cent earned needed to feed, clothe, and shelter a family.

In 1900, one in every 116 people was employed in some aspect of the liquor industry. Americans spent $1 billion on alcoholic beverages compared to $9 million on meat and less than $200 million on public education. The liquor industry was inextricably intertwined with politics and political corruption. Political party events and recruiting were held in saloons, which were male-only institutions. Half of the Democratic precinct workers in Chicago were saloon-keepers.[22] The producers and sellers that made up the liquor industry, as well as their consumers, had a vested interest in opposing the WCTU.

With every Woman's Crusade and WCTU success, the liquor industry roused itself further in opposition, getting injunctions and restraining orders to prevent women from singing and praying in saloons and beer gardens. Women in their turn kept track of drinking after hours, or barkeepers serving liquor to minors, and went to court to shut down the saloons.

In 1874, Cleveland, Ohio, hosted the first national convention of the WCTU. Men participated as guests but were never voting members or competitors for office or national leadership in the new organization. Women held all the leadership positions and ran the business organizations connected to their mission, including their newspaper. The WCTU was a training school for effective organizers, business managers, and lobbyists. The public did not label WCTU women as radicals, rather saw them as pious Christians bent on improving society in ways that were rooted in women's domestic roles of protecting children, providing charity, and elevating moral values.

WCTU recruits came from Protestant churches, from home and foreign missionary societies, from charitable groups, and from women's clubs. The vast majority of WCTU members were white middle-class Methodists, Presbyterians, and other Protestants, but were also African American women, immigrants, native-born Americans, women from diverse ethnic groups, and Catholic women. The WCTU even succeeded in recruiting some southerners who were just beginning to form women's organizations. Cutting across class lines, the women who joined were seamstresses, physicians, lawyers, educators, and the wives of artisans, businessmen, and professional men. Historian Ruth Bordin argues convincingly that the WCTU was the "first mass movement of American women."

From the WCTU emerged new national women leaders, whose rhetoric of change was based in biblical texts, and in references to women's moral authority and religious duty to protect their homes, their families, and their children from evil and corruption. Moral suasion gave way to political action and a wide reform agenda of charitable endeavors attacking poverty.

The WCTU emerged just as the suffrage movement was facing the huge loss of membership caused by the Woodhull and Beecher scandals, providing a timely infusion of energy to a movement attacked on all sides. The major influx of women into the suffrage fight came when, in 1881, the WCTU adopted a woman suffrage plank. This shifted the outlook and actions of the entire woman's rights movement. The WCTU was a vast grassroots organization with political aims and the ability to lobby and get legislation introduced and passed.

The WCTU shift to political activity and legislative action sprang from the incredible charisma and leadership skills of their second president, Frances Willard. President from 1879 until her death in 1898, Willard was the most famous American woman of her time, known internationally as well as at home. She forged friendships with suffrage leaders, including Mary Livermore who became a lifelong friend. Livermore helped Willard begin temperance work in Chicago, which became her base for the rest of her career. Her life's work had begun.

Frances Willard spent the 1870s developing a program of work for the WCTU that was labeled "Do Everything," meaning expansion of women's work beyond moral suasion for temperance. Willard and her allies came to believe that heavy drinking was a symptom, not the cause, that both men and women turned to alcohol to alleviate the miseries of poverty. "Do Everything" meant, said Willard, "Woman's mighty realm of philanthropy encroaches each day upon the empire of sin, disease and misery that has so long existed, we thought it must endure forever."[23] Doing everything also meant "Home Protection" by way of political action. The ballot was therefore a natural extension of women's proper sphere. "We have carried ballots to men year after year, urging them to vote; but we have made up our minds that it is just as easy for us to vote ourselves."[24] The WCTU committed to campaigning for woman suffrage in 1881. "Home Protection" implied nurturing women, with womanly virtue, protecting family. This work could not be attacked as coming from woman's rights radicals. It stemmed from the religious imperative to protect the home and women's proper sphere. "Home Protection" meant using the ballot for temperance but also as a means to attack social problems that directly or indirectly affected the home. In this way, the WCTU brought their brand of social justice work to the woman suffrage movement and with it the respectability of WCTU women.

According to historian Ruth Bordin, Frances Willard was a consummate politician, a "successful manipulator," and a "canny pragmatist, always willing to compromise or equivocate." She was also charismatic, a superb platform speaker, and an effective organizer with a gracious and gentle demeanor. Women liked Willard, and, indeed, loved her. Her immense ability to attract supporters, coupled with the stability of her long leadership, contributed to the organization's vast impact.

With Chicago as the hub of both the WCTU and Progressive reform, the WCTU boosted the progressive reforms that blossomed there in the 1890s. Well versed in petitioning, lobbying, and administrative organization, the WCTU women achieved prison reforms, with matrons provided for women prisoners, special facilities for women, and homes for young offenders. They funded kindergartens where children of working mothers could be cared for, provided social rooms to replace saloons as a gathering spot, and established model facilities for dependent and neglected children. This was work that presaged the work of settlement houses and is evidence of the WCTU's major role in urban charity in the 1880s. Other WCTU-fostered legislation brought temperance education to Sunday schools and later into public schools.

Willard's skills with people contributed to her increasing fame, public stature, and international renown. She not only led the WCTU in the United States but also became a global temperance figure. In England, Willard found a woman whose close friendship and joint work dictated Willard's life and travels in the early 1890s. An heiress who became a Christian Socialist after a failed arranged marriage, Isabel Somerset (referred to as Lady Henry Somerset) turned to temperance and social reform causes. Lady Somerset became the president of the British Women's Temperance Association, and together Willard and Somerset led the swelling international movement. The two women traveled together across both Great Britain and the United States on temperance work, while also overseeing a large administrative staff housed at Lady Somerset's home in the south of England and the WCTU staff in Chicago. Internationally, the WCTU had an enormous impact. The first country where women got the vote, in 1893, was the faraway frontier nation, New Zealand. In New Zealand and Australia, temperance workers were the mainspring of woman suffrage. International temperance meetings led women into the world suffrage movement in the 1890s. The far-reaching work of the WCTU and its alliances with woman suffrage across the globe had immense consequence for woman suffrage campaigns in the United States, however, as the WCTU became inextricably intertwined in the public mind with woman suffrage.

KANSAS AS A CASE STUDY IN THE CONNECTION BETWEEN SUFFRAGE AND PROHIBITION

The fate of woman suffrage in Kansas in the Gilded Age provides an example of the impact of this linking of temperance and woman suffrage. The WCTU began in Kansas in 1878 at a one hundred thousand–strong temperance camp gathering. The Kansas WCTU threw workers into a campaign. In 1880, Kansas approved an amendment prohibiting the manufacture and sale of "intoxicating liquors," making it the first state to enact a statewide constitutional prohibition.

The Kansas Equal Suffrage Association (KESA) was formed in 1884, and its growth was intertwined from the start with the WCTU membership. It reached moderate, urban women, growing into a sizable lobby. The national WCTU had already declared for woman suffrage. Rural farm women, who could not easily travel from their homes, were largely left out of this first WCTU and KESA organizing drive, but in the late 1880s and early 1890s, the Farmer's Alliance and the Populist Party took hold of political power in Kansas, which changed this situation. Rural women were active members of both the Farmers' Alliance and the Populist Party and joined both suffrage and temperance organizations.

Membership of the WCTU and KESA overlapped to such an extent that one KESA member commented that "the familiar faces of so many 'white ribboners' [WCTU women] made us feel we were at a WCTU convention."[25] Laura Johns, president of KESA, was simultaneously state Superintendent of Legislation and Franchise in the WCTU. Fanny Rastall, a suffragist and WCTU member, said in her presidential KESA address in 1891, "I realize I am at home once more among you; that I am with women who know and trust me and whom I know and trust; women who have united their efforts with mine for years."[26]

In Kansas there were tensions created by Eastern directives from NAWSA. Laura Johns wrote later that Kansas women were better off without interference from the East. Helen Kimber, a delegate to NAWSA, wrote candidly about Susan B. Anthony in Kansas in 1894, noting that Anthony's brother, newspaperman D.R. Anthony, said to his sister, "Susan, you're a damn fool—go home."[27] Not everyone welcomed being given advice by Eastern suffragists.

From the start, KESA and the Kansas WCTU strove to appear culti-vated. It was the "best women, the best mothers, wives, and housekeep-ers, who were for woman suffrage," said John McDonald, editor of the *Western School Journal.* Suffrage women in Kansas rejected any notion of mannishness, striving to appear respectable and fashionable. Laura Johns urged women coming to a suffrage fair to bring "any article that would prove that voting in municipal elections had not unsexed them." Dress-ing fashionably required sufficient income, of course. Kansas suffragists were examples of the new generation of suffrage women, respectable and feminine, striving not to be undermined by accusations of radicalism or the lingering taint of "free lovism."

In 1890, a woman suffrage bill passed the House in the Kansas Leg-islature, but failed in the Senate. The Southern Farmer's Alliance sent workers north into Kansas, finding support among the economically hard-pressed men and women there, with the result that in 1892 the gov-ernor's office and the state Senate were taken over by the Populist Party, which had emerged from the Farmers' Alliance. Populists were suffrage allies and were now politically able to sway the vote. Kansas women kept campaigning, with near successes in 1893 and 1894. Suffragists in Kansas now saw themselves as part of a tradition of progressivist reform. Accord-ing to Laura Johns, KESA president, through the "emancipation of all men from slavery to King Alcohol," the women of Kansas have been part of the "progressive" party, and with "grand courage, strength and faith, ever with uplifted glance, borne their large part."[28]

There were three African American WCTU locals in Kansas. Letters to the press show black women supporting municipal suffrage and woman suffrage, with constant references to "race progress." For these black women, suffrage would help uplift the black race, not simply its women. In 1888, the WCTU hired a black organizer, Naomi Anderson, to work in black communities. Some white temperance women showed an egalitari-anism that was unusual, with one Kansas leader calling for white women to make black women "not mere recipients of favors, but helpers and allies in this cause."[29] Frances Watkins Harper, as she toured the country in the

1880s lecturing on temperance, drew huge desegregated crowds in Kansas, giving us some evidence of racial tolerance in this state that had voted down both black male suffrage and woman's suffrage in 1867.

As Kansas women with the WCTU connection gathered their strength, however, in reaction the antisuffrage forces increased. The liquor interests were the strongest organized opposition, but they were joined by immigrant groups who were puzzled and angry at attacks on their traditions and culture. In Kansas, of its ethnic migrant groups, Germans were the strongest in opposing woman suffrage because of the prohibition connection. Anti-WCTU Germans and some German religious groups did not want any increase in women's control over property or expansion of women's educational opportunities. In their turn, the WCTU and suffrage women looked with disdain upon men who were of such moral laxity that they insisted upon their right to drink in beer gardens, take Sunday pleasure outings, and play cards. The Kansas WCTU thought that their model of good Anglo-Saxon womanhood would bring Americanization, and they vowed to "enlighten" immigrants to prevent any attack on "free institutions," which they believed was imminent.

Liquor industry opposition to suffrage increased after 1900, and in response, the Kansas WCTU gave up all other work to devote all its forces to woman suffrage. This succeeded, and women won the vote in 1912. The suffrage and WCTU alliance in Kansas bound suffrage and temperance together with strong threads.

Historian Ruth Bordin concludes that "with its tens of thousands of members it [the WCTU] did provide the mass base from which the twentieth-century suffrage movement could take off." Bordin disputes the conclusions of suffrage historian Ellen DuBois, who argues that the suffrage movement brought the WCTU to the fight, persuading its leaders to adopt the goal of woman suffrage.[30] Bordin's position is that the WCTU came to the ballot through its own leadership and brought its own goals into the suffrage movement. The WCTU had a key role in shifting the suffrage movement to focus on progressive reform, rather than relying on claims for the vote based on individual equal rights. The slogan "votes for women" now meant more than equal access to the vote for women; suffragists could also be social and "progressive" reformers, who would erase political corruption, improve living conditions, and rectify the misery caused by industrial growth. Women needed the ballot so that they could bring to the government of the nation their particular moral virtues and piety. A new generation of suffragists rising to power in the 1890s and 1900s were drawn from the ranks of temperance women and social reformers influenced by the WCTU.

Even as the WCTU waned in power as a national social and political reform organization after Willard's death in 1898, its indelible mark on the public view of woman suffrage campaigns remained. The Anti-Saloon League, led by men, took over as the main organization of prohibition in the United States. But the two decades of global WCTU ascendancy increased the likelihood of women suffrage beyond the United States. Woman suffragists were in touch with each other across the world.

THE GROWTH OF AN INTERNATIONAL NETWORK

Elizabeth Cady Stanton and her daughter Harriot renewed Elizabeth's networks in the United Kingdom at the same time that Frances Willard was directing suffrage campaigns across the other side of the world. Transatlantic travel was easier than in 1840, and Elizabeth Cady Stanton quickly took advantage of the comfortable staterooms of the new ocean liners.

In Britain, there was no universal white male suffrage as there was in the United States. Women in Britain could not say that they were left out of the vote simply because of their gender. It would take two great reform bills, in 1832 and in 1867, before adult males who owned or rented property could vote. Only in 1918 did all men over age twenty-one gain the vote. Unlike in the United States, there was little question, but that the vote was a privilege, not a right. British suffragists needed to persuade Parliament to pass a bill for woman suffrage for the nation; there could be no "state by state" campaigns, which provided some forward movement in the United States.

John Stuart Mill, author of *The Subjection of Women*, and by the 1860s regarded by many as the hero of woman's rights in both the United States and Great Britain, began the suffrage battles in England by presenting a woman suffrage bill to Parliament in 1866, followed by an amendment to Prime Minister Benjamin Disraeli's election reform bill in 1867 which began the organized movement in Britain. In August, 1867, a Manchester Women's Suffrage Committee was formed with a Member of Parliament,

Jacob Bright, as president. In Edinburgh, Jacob's sister, Priscilla Bright McLaren, became the president of the first Scottish woman suffrage society. Her husband, Duncan McLaren, an Edinburgh MP, was also a suffragist—another example of the strong links these British women suffragists had to influential politicians.

While the differing political structures dictated different strategies, suffrage leaders in both the United States and the United Kingdom were linked by the common goal. Suffrage papers in Britain carried news of American events, and the *Woman's Journal* was read in Britain. A *Woman's Journal* piece in 1872 said, "The cause is the same on both sides of the ocean, and on each side will be carried all the sooner by every real help given the other."[31] Ernestine Rose and Julia Ward Howe lectured in England in the 1870s. American Mary E. Beedy wrote a regular piece for the *Woman's Journal* on British events called "Our Letter from London." Leader of the British campaigns, Millicent Garrett Fawcett, was introduced to American audiences through the *Woman's Journal*, and many American suffragists traveling in Britain met with Fawcett and her husband Henry, a suffragist, a Member of Parliament, and later Postmaster General.

When Elizabeth Cady Stanton traveled to Europe in the 1880s, and when her daughter Harriot married Englishman William Henry Blatch, she made her home for months at a time with Harriot in Basingstoke, outside London. Harriot's friendship with the Pankhurst family forged links with the radical, or militant, wing of the British movement, which would develop over the next decades, fueling militancy in the United States. Stanton met most of the Bright family and developed connections with both Scottish and English reformers.

As an international network flourished, at home in the United States, a new generation of suffragists were emerging as the founding generation grew to old age. Lucy Stone wrote that "we are all passing away." Paulina Wright Davis died in the fall of 1876, William Lloyd Garrison in 1879, Lucretia Mott in 1880, and Wendell Phillips in 1884. Sojourner Truth and both Thomas and Mary Ann McClintock were gone by 1890. The new generation did not understand the depth of ill-feeling engendered by the 1869 split. Lucy Stone and Susan B. Anthony came to believe that the time for unification had come.

NOTES

1. Elizabeth Cady Stanton, *Eighty Years and More: Reminiscences 1815–1897* (1898; repr., New York, NY: Schocken Books, 1971), 308.

2. Grace Farrell, *Lillie Devereux Blake: Retracing a Life Erased* (Amherst: University of Massachusetts Press, 2002), 123.

3. Stanton, *Eighty Years and More*, 308.

4. Lisa Tetrault, "The Incorporation of American Feminism: Suffragists and the Postbellum Lyceum," *Journal of American History* 96, no. 4 (2010): 1027–56.

5. Tetrault, "The Incorporation of American Feminism,"

6. Martha M. Solomon, *A Voice of Their Own: The Woman Suffrage Press, 1840–1910* (Tuscaloosa, AL: University of Alabama Press, 1991), 88.

7. Beverly Beeton, *Women Vote in the West: The Woman Suffrage Movement, 1869–1896* (New York, NY: Garland, 1986), 14.

8. Beverly Beeton, *Women Vote in the West*, 23–4.

9. Carol Cornwall Madsen, *Battle for the Ballot: Essays on Woman Suffrage in Utah, 1870–1896* (Logan: Utah State University Press, 1997); Sarah Barringer Gordon, "The Liberty of Self-Degradation: Polygamy, Woman Suffrage, and Consent in Nineteenth-Century America," *Journal of American History* 83, no. 3 (1996): 815–47.

10. Rebecca J. Mead, *How the Vote Was Won: Woman Suffrage in the Western United States, 1868–1914* (New York: New York University Press, 2006), 45.

11. Rebecca J. Mead, *How the Vote Was Won*, 47.

12. Rebecca J. Mead, *How the Vote Was Won*, 49.

13. Ruth Barnes Moynihan, *Rebel for Rights, Abigail Scott Duniway* (New Haven, CT: Yale University Press, 1983), 178–9.

14. Beeton, *Women Vote in the West*, 106–7.

15. Mead, *How the Vote Was Won*, 29–30.

16. Mead, *How the Vote Was Won*, 59 (italics in the original).

17. Susan Melanie Gustafson, *Women and the Republican Party, 1854–1924* (Urbana: University of Illinois Press, 2001).

18. Ruth Bordin, *Woman and Temperance: The Quest for Power and Liberty, 1873–1900* (Philadelphia, PA: Temple University Press, 1981), 22.

19. Bordin, *Woman and Temperance*, xxv.

20. Ian R. Tyrrell, *Woman's World, Woman's Empire: The Woman's Christian Temperance Union in International Perspective, 1880–1930* (Chapel Hill: University of North Carolina Press, 1991); Ian R. Tyrrell, *Sobering Up: From Temperance to Prohibition in Antebellum America, 1800–1860* (Westport, CT: Greenwood Press, 1979).

21. "Drunkard" was the usual derogatory term used for an alcoholic.

22. Bordin, *Woman and Temperance*, 6.

23. Bordin, *Woman and Temperance*, 95.

24. Bordin, *Woman and Temperance*, 100.

25. Fran Grace, *Carry A. Nation: Retelling the Life* (Bloomington: Indiana University Press, 2001), 111.

26. Grace, *Carry A. Nation*, 71.

27. Grace, *Carry A. Nation*, 120.

28. Michael L. Goldberg, *An Army of Women: Gender and Politics in Gilded Age Kansas* (Baltimore, MD: Johns Hopkins University Press, 1997), 60–61.

29. Goldberg, *An Army of Women*, 2.

30. Ellen DuBois, "The Radicalism of the Woman Suffrage Movement: Notes toward the Reconstruction of Nineteenth-Century Feminism." *Feminist Studies* 3, no. 1/2 (1975): 63–71.

31. Patricia Greenwood Harrison, *Connecting Links: The British and American Woman Suffrage Movements, 1900–1914* (Westport, CT: Greenwood Press, 2000), 8.

CHAPTER 5

THE *HISTORY OF WOMAN SUFFRAGE* AND UNIFICATION, 1880–1890

In 1879 Elizabeth Cady Stanton left the lyceum circuit, thoroughly tired of packing, unpacking, traveling from town to town. She longed to be at home and planning her retirement in peace. Still "combative, keen witted, self-centered, and uninhibited" at the age of sixty-five, she was "ready to become an imperial old lady," says biographer Elisabeth Griffith. Not only was Stanton giving up traveling she was not going to any more conventions; "My work in conventions is at an end, they are distasteful to me."[1] Between 1880 and her death in 1902, Stanton drew further and further away from the organized movement.

She was, however, ready to write, and for the next years, she bent over her desk, pen in hand, and wrote the grand narrative of the history of the movement. Stanton and Susan B. Anthony were determined to record the efforts women had made up until 1880. Stanton, Anthony, and Matilda Joslyn Gage, editor of the *National Citizen Ballot Box*, had tossed about the idea of creating a history of the woman's movement during the 1876 Philadelphia Centennial celebrations. Anthony, ever the organizer and strategist, responded to the defeats of the New Departure and lackluster recruitment to the National membership by writing a history of the long battle for equality as a way to secure their record in history and publicize the great work of the movement. All the material Susan and Elizabeth had amassed was bundled up and sent to Stanton's house in Tenafly. In

October 1880, Anthony joined her there, ready to begin the grand history. What they expected to take several months grew into a huge undertaking lasting years.

Long, tiring, and often cantankerous hours occupied them in Tenafly. They sent out requests asking for summaries of suffrage work and short biographies. Material flooded in so much that Stanton complained bitterly of the tendency of authors to be overly wordy. Matilda Joslyn Gage, staying at her own home in upstate New York, worked from a room piled high with books, letters, and other documents. Anthony and Stanton quickly tired of the drudgery of sifting through the masses of letters, notes, convention minutes, and documents they hoped to synthesize into a story of the past that was as "true" as they could make it. The draft quickly grew to two volumes, the first on the antebellum era and the next on the postwar decades. The first volume of the *History of Woman Suffrage* (*HWS*) came out in 1881, the second in 1883 as expenses far outweighed profits. Anthony finally found a solution in 1885 by using money from Eliza Eddy's bequest of $40,000 (to both Anthony and Stone) to buy back the rights to the first volumes and take over publication herself. The *HWS*, published between 1881 and 1922, eventually took up six volumes and 5,700 pages.[2]

Lucy Stone was furious when asked for her biography and a summary of her own contributions to the cause. "In regard to the History of the Woman's Rights Movement, I do not think it can be written by any one [sic] who is alive today. . . . Your 'wing' surely are [sic] not competent to write the history of 'our wing,' nor should we be of yours."[3] In retrospect, her decision to boycott was a mistake because the consequence was the disappearance of the AWSA and Lucy Stone from historical memory for over a century.[4] Stone feared, correctly, that a history written by one set of suffragists would glorify the roles of some and ignore the work of others. In turn, Stanton and Anthony exploded to friends that Stone's reaction was "narrow pig-headedness."[5] In the end, the work of the *HWS* went on without the cooperation of the American.

Stanton worked long and hard for weeks on end. While Elizabeth Cady Stanton normally celebrated her own robust health, which she attributed to daily long naps, she fell ill in 1881 with what may have been malaria, with its accompanying fevers. A worried Harriot quickly sailed from England to nurse her mother. Harriot and the family blamed Susan for Stanton's breakdown, complaining that she had left too much of the burden to Elizabeth.

As Stanton recovered, Harriot was put to work on the *HWS*, quickly seeing that Lucy Stone and the American had been ignored. Despite protests from Anthony, Harriot hastily wrote a chapter whose final hundred pages would be the only section on the American in the whole six volumes. Stone and Blackwell would not contribute themselves, but they responded angrily to the results. They were particularly outraged at the second *HWS* volume, which failed to mention George Train, Victoria Woodhull, or the Beecher–Tilton scandal, skipped over the split of 1869, and generally ignored any events that reflected badly upon the National or the authors. They tried to address their version of the past later with their own history, but they were never able to replace the *HWS*'s version of the past. Anthony wanted, and got, a history that was a propaganda coup for the National, both as a recruitment vehicle and a grand history of the movement. The massive *HWS*, which, in its compilation of detail and evidence, and its narrative of success, in which Anthony and Stanton alone figure as heroines of the long battle, became the shaping force of many later women's rights and suffrage histories.[6]

Whatever its faults, the *HWS* is a treasure house for historians. Filled with reports, letters, convention minutes, and a strong narrative tracing the history of the suffrage movement to Seneca Falls, the massive *HWS* and its triumphalist narrative became the main source for later writers. Re-evaluation of this narrative by scholars who had not lived through the Nineteenth Amendment fight began with Eleanor Flexner's *Century of Struggle: The Woman's Rights Movement in the United States* (1959), followed by Aileen Kraditor's *The Ideas the Woman Suffrage Movement* (1965), and continue into the present.[7]

Historian Lori Ginzberg describes Stanton as having created a "mythic story of struggle and resistance, with the 1840 London Convention, New York State, Seneca Falls, and Elizabeth Cady Stanton herself at the very center of the action." In Stanton's telling, the *HWS* told a particularly motivating story of the woman's movement and its leaders. In that story, "Stanton alone articulated the demand for woman suffrage, and Anthony led the charge; there was only one major organization (theirs); and the differences of principle that led to the division brooked no debate."[8] Historian Ellen DuBois, while noting the omissions and editorial bias, observes that it is still hard not to be fascinated with the *HWS* volumes, whose massive collection of documents, letters, biographies, and convention minutes is "linked together by a loose narrative, a lovely, long string of separate historical jewels."[9]

As historians began to write about a wide range of suffrage leaders, including Lucy Stone, Mary Livermore, Lillie Devereux Blake, black suffragists like Ida B. Wells, temperance suffragist Frances Willard, and western leaders like Abigail Scott Duniway, and as new histories of the movement delved deep into other sources, the history of woman suffrage was revealed as more complex and more layered than the story told in *HWS*. These histories analyze conflicts over philosophy and strategy, explore clashes of personalities, and raise questions of race, nativism, and xenophobia. The story of the Nineteenth Amendment becomes a richer one as a consequence, less a story of constant upward progress than one of relentless, and often unsuccessful struggle.

The most recent analysis of the impact of the *HWS* upon public memory is from historian Lisa Tetrault, who labels the volumes as inventing women's history; she traces the process whereby Stanton and Anthony's version of Seneca Falls and the history of the movement became the central narrative of woman suffrage and woman's rights.[10]

Black women's activism was marginalized in the *HWS* and their suffrage work and involvement in the woman's rights movement barely noticed, as historians Elsa Barkley Brown, Rosalind Terborg-Penn, Ann D. Gordon, Bettye Collier-Thomas, and others have carefully detailed.[11] The near disappearance of Lucy Stone meant one of the three most influential leaders of the woman suffrage movement and the leader of one of the two national organizations was also nearly absent from the narrative.[12] Those who opposed Anthony and Stanton's leadership were written out of the story. Matilda Joslyn Gage ran afoul of Anthony because she published work on atheism and the oppressive impact of Christianity. Lillie Devereux Blake, like Gage, a radical feminist who continued to promote wider rights issues as well as suffrage, was forgotten to women's history until Grace Farrell's *Lillie Devereux Blake: Retracing a Life Erased* (2002).[13]

Anthony ensured that the history was distributed freely. The *HWS* was published just as the nation was producing collective memories of the Civil War; the North produced articles, memoirs, official histories, and biographies of war heroes, while Southerners did likewise and constructed the "Lost Cause" of the Confederacy. The strength of the *HWS* is that it inserted women's rights, women's war efforts, and woman suffrage into that national discussion. Congressmen and Members of Parliament in the United Kingdom were all given copies, as were libraries around the world. Anthony and Stanton handed out copies wherever they and their lieutenants traveled. The *HWS* was able to draw attention to the National and away from the work of the American in the 1880s.

THE WORK OF THE NATIONAL IN THE 1880S: THE FATE OF THE FEDERAL AMENDMENT

Anthony re-entered the fight even as the writing went on. The federal amendment was, to Anthony, the only way to the final prize of universal woman suffrage.[14] Anthony did not want to be working on state campaigns and her irritation often voiced itself. To her, it was a waste of energy to work for electoral college representatives through woman suffrage in each state. Despite having to expend resources on state work because others in the National wanted to do so, Anthony was determined to push forward a federal amendment, with the small force of women at her disposal and with few funds.

In the middle of the acrimonious 1869 schism, two men in Congress proposed woman suffrage resolutions; in December 1868, Republican Senator Samuel Pomeroy from Kansas proposed a Sixteenth Amendment for woman suffrage, then the following March another Republican, Congressman George Julian, asked for a joint resolution calling for universal suffrage without "any distinction or discrimination whatever founded on sex."[15] Neither was taken up. Congress, the Supreme Court, and the nation turned from universal suffrage toward limiting who voted.

Ten years after Pomeroy's proposal, Californian Senator Aaron Sargent introduced the Sixteenth Amendment in the form that would eventually be passed as the Nineteenth Amendment in 1920. It was written by Elizabeth Cady Stanton but later called the Susan B. Anthony Amendment by Alice Paul.[16] Despite the hostile political climate in Congress, Sargent was able to get a hearing in 1878 from the Senate Committee on Privileges and Elections where Elizabeth Cady Stanton gave a speech before an inattentive and irritated audience. She persisted as several men walked in and out of the chamber and conversed loudly over her. Congressional sympathy increased somewhat from that low. In 1882, both the U.S.

House and Senate appointed a Select Committee on Woman Suffrage after maneuvering by long-time suffragist Republican, George Hoar, of Massachusetts. Suffragists hoped this admittedly glacial advance was the start on the path toward serious consideration of the amendment.

Year after year, while Congress was in session, delegations of suffragists went to Washington, DC. Painfully slowly, some favorable reports emerged. The Senate Judiciary Committee produced four reports in the 1880s in which the majority voted for woman suffrage. Each one of these reports required strenuous effort by Anthony as she coordinated with congressmen and senators and arranged for effective speakers.

Then, at last, the full Senate took up the amendment. In December 1886 and January 1887, the proposed Sixteenth Amendment was debated for the first time on the Senate floor. The Woman's Christian Temperance Union (WCTU) produced two hundred thousand signatures on petitions and women filled the galleries in support of the suffrage men on the floor. Senator Henry Blair of New Hampshire spoke in favor, pointing to woman suffrage successes in Wyoming, Utah, and Washington. Ten women, from across the country, were allowed to speak. The opposition quickly attacked. Senator George Vest of Missouri laid out the consequence of woman voting—she would be taken down from the "pedestal where she is today, influencing, as a mother, the minds of her offspring, influencing by her gentle and kindly caress the action of her husband toward good and true." Vest gathered up all the usual images of the domestic sphere in one speech and laid out the ultimate threat—women would become as corrupted by politics as were men.[17] The final vote of sixteen ayes and thirty-four nays was a weighty defeat.

This vote marked the end of anything but token efforts by suffragists for a federal amendment until 1913. As she had done so often before, Anthony looked for another way ahead, turning this time to an idea that had surfaced while she was in Europe in 1883. She began to plan for a great international gathering in 1888 to celebrate the fortieth anniversary of the Seneca Falls Convention.

THE AMERICAN AND STATE CAMPAIGNS

Lucy Stone, hampered by increasingly debilitating rheumatoid arthritis and bronchitis, continued on the state-by-state path. Stone's pace, despite

ill health, was bruising. With Henry Blackwell and Alice Stone Blackwell, the American fostered new state and local associations, sent organizers out into the field, and, to the frustration of Anthony and Stanton,
made the *Woman's Journal* the main voice of the suffrage movement.

National and American organizers actually crossed paths in the field
working on the same state campaigns. Despite Anthony's dislike of the
state efforts, she and her NWSA organizers participated. Opposing leaders even worked together when necessary; Stone, Blackwell, and Anthony
spoke at the same legislative hearings in Rhode Island in 1884. State campaigns were undertaken, each involving hundreds of suffragists who lobbied legislators, gathered signatures for petitions, wrote articles, and made
sure that male suffragists turned out at the polls. Years of campaigning
gave women activists well-honed political skills and lobbying expertise
but brought few results.

SEEKING POLITICAL ALLIES

Anthony did not want to work with any one political party, thinking
that to do so risked alienating potential supporters in other parties. Others disagreed Lillie Devereux Blake, lecturer, fiction writer, and suffragist, in the 1880s tried to move the suffrage movement into more active
work with both main political parties. Women needed political power,
she believed, and to get it they must develop political skills and build
relationships. In 1879, Blake and Matilda Joslyn Gage founded the New
York State Woman Suffrage Association, with Blake serving as its president from 1879 to 1890. Using the organization as a base, Blake set about
opposing the re-election of Governor Lucius Robinson, who had vetoed a
bill to allow women to sit on school boards. Robinson was defeated, and
Blake and her cohorts honed their campaign skills. Male politicians took
note—the newly elected governor signed the bill. President Chester A.
Arthur received her "with marked cordiality," and Grover Cleveland took
her into his office ahead of a roomful of waiting men.[18] Blake's conclusion
was to propose to the National convention in 1880 that the organization put less focus on petitioning (the main strategy for the movement
since the 1860s) and turn toward organizing women to campaign for the
presidential candidate who best committed to woman suffrage. Significantly, Anthony was not enthused, which Blake interpreted as the result

of Anthony so long regarding suffrage as a moral reform that she could not see that it could be made into a "living political issue."[19] It would be an ongoing debate.

INTERNATIONAL NETWORKS: THE 1888 INTERNATIONAL GATHERING OF WOMEN

In 1887, Anthony and Stanton drew up plans for an international gathering sponsored by the National. An international gathering was another example of Anthony's consistent effective political intellect when faced with defeats. The final plans for 1888 were for an international celebration, not just for suffrage women but for organized women from around the world. An international gathering of women from all women's organizations, not just suffrage groups, would attract more women and be a fitting celebration of the forty years since Seneca Falls. It also brought together respectable, upright, not radical women to bolster Anthony's conviction that the days of the movement as a radical vanguard of society were gone.

In late March, three thousand men and women gathered in Washington, DC, where eighty speakers addressed representatives of fifty-two women's organizations from across America and eight foreign countries. This International Council of Women gathering marked the solidification of an international women's movement—women's clubs, temperance women, and suffragists. The 1888 gathering resulted in the formation of an International Council of Women, with Frances Willard elected president. The International Council of Women met again in 1894 in Berlin, in London in 1899, and again in Berlin in 1904, where an international suffrage organization, the International Woman Suffrage Alliance, was born.

THE PROCESS OF UNIFICATION

As with many others, growing older for Lucy Stone brought a tendency to think a new generation lacked one's own spirit, grit, and initiative. Despite reservations about the younger generation, she was looking for those who might take over the lead, and unification was a step in that direction. When Stone learned of Anthony's plan for the 1888 celebration, she proposed that the two associations sponsor the event as "United Societies." This was intended as a first step toward cooperation, if not unification. Susan B. Anthony had no intention of sharing the limelight with the American and quickly rejected Stone's offer.

Stone continued to work toward unification. A resolution passed at the annual convention of the American in November 1887 which authorized Stone to discuss a merger with Anthony. Just before Christmas, in the Boston office of the *Woman's Journal*, Stone and Anthony met, with Alice Stone Blackwell and Rachel Foster in attendance. Anthony was caught off guard and put in the public position of blocking the unification, which she had been publicly supporting for the last two decades. On top of this, she knew that many young suffragists comprehended little of the 1869 split. Anthony had to tread carefully. Profoundly unenthusiastic, she put forward a number of propositions that would disadvantage the American. The battle lines were drawn, and both sides readied to attack.

Lucy asked first whether men would be accepted on equal footing. Strangely, Anthony dismissed the notion that men were ever excluded from office in the National. It is unclear whether it was true; most people believed that men were banned from office in the National. After unification, no men were officers of the joint movement with the exception of Henry Blackwell, who continued to be a central figure.

The subject of the name for the unified organization was consequential. Anthony's preference for a name was agreed to—the National American Woman Suffrage Association (NAWSA). The National was symbolically first and would remain first in terms of the leadership of the new organization. Stone next proposed "all kinds of suffrage work," rather than just the passage of the Sixteenth Amendment. Anthony demurred. Lucy Stone stood for a wide-ranging organization that would be a bigger tent, allowing a range of women's rights work as well as local and state work. This is significant in light of the usual characterization by Stanton and Anthony of the American as the staider, more conservative, and less radical wing of the suffrage movement.

The question of leadership of the unified association was the most explosive. Stone proposed that none of the old leaders, Anthony, Stanton, or herself, should be considered for the post of president so that suffragists would not see the new association as partisan toward either the National or the American. Rachel Foster and Anthony reacted negatively, rejecting Stone's suggested alternatives. Anthony and Foster saw Stone's suggestion as forcing Anthony and Stanton out of the leadership, even as Stone tried to suggest that the three women could be on an executive committee.

Negotiations broke down. Lucy Stone was furious, convinced that Susan B. Anthony "so much wishes to be president herself! To bring her to the top at last would be such a vindication she cannot bear to forgo it."[20] As negotiations ended, it was clear that there would be a "takeover" from the National. Lucy Stone was never a force in the new association, and her public life as a suffrage leader was almost over. Determined to save her mother and father from too heavy a load, Alice Stone Blackwell pushed through the unification process to its successful conclusion. Stone feared that the AWSA would be swallowed and its history obliterated, which was largely what happened.

Lillie Devereux Blake had been an early believer in the union of the two associations. She often attended both the National and the American conventions. When the negotiations for unification grew serious, Anthony used Blake's powerful reputation to push unification; Blake delivered the unification motion and managed the often contentious debate. Blake retold the long fight in her autobiography, noting that she "threw all my influence in favor of Union."[21] She carried the day. Sadly, it was the last of Blake's work with Anthony. Once her usefulness during the unification negotiations was done, Anthony pushed her aside as being another woman who had become too radical for the suffrage organization.

There was opposition from both National and American rank and file. Eventually, a consensus emerged, and a joint letter, issued on February 8, 1889, as an "Open Letter to the Women of America," began the formal process. Although both sides continued to trade barbs about past conflicts, a joint meeting was organized for Washington, DC, for February 1890, under the new name, the NAWSA. Stanton was present at the first convention of NAWSA, with her two daughters, and was duly elected president, but departed the day after her opening speech, leaving New York once again for England. As Lucy Stone had feared, Susan B. Anthony took over the running of the new organization. Stone's ill health prevented her from being in Washington for the NAWSA meeting, and there was little she could do to stop the new direction of the joint organization.

Lucy Stone made a few more public appearances after unification. She and Elizabeth Cady Stanton testified before the House Committee on the

Judiciary. Stone's final trip was in 1892 to the great World's Columbian Exposition in Chicago (known as the Chicago World's Fair), where a sculptured bust in her honor was unveiled, and where she was much feted. Stone returned to Boston where in October 1893 she died from stomach cancer. Henry Blackwell remained on the road, working on state and federal campaigns.

AFTER UNIFICATION: A WHITE SOUTHERN ALLIANCE

Soon after unification, NAWSA turned its attention southward. Anthony, Henry Blackwell, and others thought the white suffragists of the South might provide a substantial membership boost and provide a number of state successes. This policy shift was predicated on trading the support and work of black suffragists for the support of a segregated South, which maintained white rule by intimidation and violence. The alliance with white Southern women proved barren of results and evidence of an expediency repellent to present-day taste.

White women were at the core of building the "Lost Cause" myth glorifying the Old South. The "Lost Cause" developed to a fever pitch with the erection of memorials to the Confederacy in the 1890s.[22] White women developed a mythical vision of the beneficent slave South and created a "fruitful history of the War Between the States," keeping alive the memory of the "noblest knights of the race," as said one prominent society woman in North Carolina.[23]

Woman suffrage in the South was a descendant of the Memorial Associations, which paved the way for white women to women's clubs and then a small number to the suffrage movement. This Southern path lagged the North and West by one or two decades. Linking themselves with the Old South, the Confederacy, chivalry, and domesticity, women groups and then suffragists ameliorated fears of women's public activism, which were still very strong.

The growth of organized womanhood in the South was hindered by the overwhelmingly rural economy, where black and white families wrenched a bare living from the land. As expanding urbanization, the growth of small towns, and increasing ease of travel by railroad drove the development of women's organizations in the North and West, so did southern woman's associations grew as factories appeared on the Piedmont and commercial centers were established. Women's groups and woman suffrage never had anything but a toehold anywhere in the rural South of tenant farmers, subsistence farms, and widespread poverty, but they gained ground in the towns and cities of a "New South."

The WCTU enrolled members from across the South and was officially committed to woman suffrage, but temperance work in the South generally avoided this explosive issue, allied still in the minds of southerners with abolition. Frances Willard toured the South in 1883 ignoring suffrage in her speeches. Suffrage leaders in the South emerged who had studied and traveled in the North and West, returning to their homes inspired by the work of women they had encountered. In North Carolina, Suzanne Bynum organized a local league after a winter in New York. Annette Finnigan graduated from Wellesley College, joined a suffrage club in New York, and returned to start suffrage work in her native Texas.[24]

The suffrage cause showed some strength in the 1890s. The growing movement campaigned on the platform that white woman suffrage was a way to overwhelm the black male vote. Moreover, white women's votes would have even more impact if combined with "educated suffrage," eliminating almost all black men and women (and poor white men and women). A coalition of white southern women and NAWSA emerged.

Southern leaders were almost all members of elites, both wealthy and educated. They had grown up in political families, which made them familiar with the process of petitioning legislators and commanding a hearing for their cause. Madeline McDowell, great-granddaughter of Henry Clay, was married into the equally powerful Breckinridge family of Kentucky. Nellie Nugent Somerville's heritage included a chief justice of Mississippi as well as a state senator. Her father, William Louis Nugent, a former Confederate officer, was a leader in restoring "home rule" to Mississippi. Her daughter recalled that she could do no wrong in Greenville, suffragist notwithstanding, because of her father's standing. Another important driver of the southern strategy of NAWSA was Laura Clay. Kentucky suffrage leader and member of the NAWSA board, she was the daughter of antislavery lecturer Cassius Marcellus Clay, owner of over two thousand acres of plantation, a hero of the Mexican War, and foreign minister to Russia. All the Clay women became suffragists after their parents' divorce left them with few resources. Laura Clay believed in racial superiority and supported the argument that woman suffrage could "neutralize all the alarming elements of the race question."[25]

Clay told NAWSA leaders, "you have worked for forty years and you will work for forty years more and do nothing unless you bring in the South." In 1892, she pleaded with NAWSA to expand its work in the South and to provide funds to the suffrage groups there. At the instigation of NAWSA leadership, Clay formed a Southern Committee, quickly enlisting representatives from Arkansas, Tennessee, Louisiana, Georgia, Missouri, Texas, and South Carolina.[26] Clay became a national figure, joining the NAWSA board as auditor in 1896. A bequest directly to Clay for stocks and real estate valued at $5,000 gave her the funds to solidify her control of the Southern suffrage movement. Until the race-based southern strategy failed, Anthony and NAWSA followed Clay's advice.

A sign of the turn to the South for support was a segregated convention in New Orleans in 1903, which was almost certainly the lowest point of NAWSA's record on racism. Even holding the annual convention in the South was a concession to the Southern white suffragists. Belle Kearney from Mississippi delivered a deeply racist and nativist speech arguing that (white) woman suffrage would ensure white supremacy in the South. It would also provide a bulwark against the degradation of northern society caused by immigration. Kearney insisted that:

> The enfranchisement of women would secure immediate and durable white supremacy, honestly attained, for upon unquestioned authority it is stated that in every southern State but one there are more educated women then all the illiterate voters, white and black, native and foreign combined. . . . The civilization of the North is threatened by the influx of foreigners with their imported customs; by the greed of monopolistic wealth and the unrest among the working classes; by the strength of the liquor traffic and encroachments upon religious belief. Someday the north will be compelled to look to the South for redemption from those evils on account of the purity of its Anglo-Saxon blood, the simplicity of it social and economic structure, the great advance in prohibitory law in the maintenance of the sanctity of its faith which is being kept inviolate.[27]

This was the southern white suffrage theory encapsulated in two paragraphs. Nowhere was there space for African Americans, in the South or anywhere in the country. Kearney's speech resonated among northerners who were anxious about universal suffrage, those who wanted "educated suffrage," and those who wanted to disenfranchise black male voters.[28]

When a *New Orleans Times-Democrat* editorial questioned the NAWSA position on "the race question," Carrie Chapman Catt retorted quickly with the rationalization that decisions over admission to suffrage organizations belonged to the state associations.

> The association as such has no view on the subject. Like every other national association, it is made up of persons of all shades of opinion on the race question and on all other questions except those relating to its particular object. The northern and western members hold of the views on the race question that are customary in their sections: the southern members hold the views that are customary in the South. The doctrine of State's rights is recognized in the national body and each auxiliary State association arranges its own affairs in accordance with its own ideas and in harmony with the customs of its own section. . . . The National American Woman Suffrage Association is seeking to do away with the requirements of a sex qualification for suffrage. What other qualifications shall be asked it leaves to each state.[29]

Catt, in this way, publicly condoned racism as an expedient position. The women's rights movement's roots in abolition and equality were a long way in the past.[30] This was, writes historian Marjorie Spruill Wheeler, the height of racist rhetoric delivered under the umbrella of the national suffrage association.[31]

In 1891, Arkansas debated white woman suffrage, South Carolina discussed woman suffrage in 1895, and Louisiana considered woman suffrage in 1898, as did Alabama in 1901. All these states eventually chose to limit black male suffrage directly. Democratic politicians were not persuaded that woman suffrage would ensure black disenfranchisement. Southern Democrats were reinforced by the U.S. Supreme Court, which declined to enforce civil rights for black men or women, retreating far from the Fifteenth Amendment's intended commitment to black male suffrage. Democratic Party men did not see the need to risk the unforeseen changes that woman's suffrage might bring.

After Susan B. Anthony's retirement in 1900, NAWSA policy shifted. In 1904, President Carrie Chapman Catt withdrew all southern aid that came from central headquarters, thinking that it was money that could be better spent out west. In 1907, Kate Gordon of New Orleans, on the board of NAWSA, put forward a new scheme for "whites only" woman suffrage in Mississippi. Laura Clay supported the plan, but Anna Howard Shaw, now NAWSA president, refused to send funds, and Alice Stone Blackwell opposed it. There were, Blackwell revealed, limits to the NAWSA support of southern white suffragists. Blackwell told Laura Clay and Kate Gordon that they had gone too far with their plea for woman suffrage as a race solution. Alice Blackwell wrote to both women asking them to stop this "whites only" campaign. If only a few people still stood by universal suffrage, to enforce whites-only voting was going too far and was "regarded everywhere outside the South as an unmitigated iniquity."[32] By 1910, male Democrats in the South had solved the "race question" by disenfranchisement of blacks by constitutional devices and various electoral means, and even violence—all without woman suffrage. The national suffrage movement put its efforts elsewhere, even as southern suffragists fought on. The NAWSA southern suffrage strategy failed.

AFTER UNIFICATION: BLACK WOMEN'S SUFFRAGE AND RACIAL UPLIFT

With NAWSA's turn to the white South, black women were ignored and shut out. In the South, white women were almost wholly oblivious to the parallel work of black women working on racial uplift and suffrage. Antilynching crusader and black suffragist Ida Wells-Barnett met with Susan B. Anthony in 1894 asking why "expediency" led Anthony to reject black suffragists' support. Anthony related to Wells how she had asked Frederick Douglass not to attend the suffrage convention in Atlanta, and also refused to meet with a group of black women, "on the ground of that same expediency."[33] Anthony did not want to have race issues upset the carefully cultivated white southern suffrage movement. Anthony was not a strict segregationist, but she did maneuver to remove discussion of race from NAWSA. In the 1890s, with the rise of white southern suffrage associations, the balancing act failed, and Anthony and NAWSA consolidated itself as a whites-only organization.

Black suffragists in the forty years of the "nadir" of race relations, from President Rutherford B. Hayes to Woodrow Wilson, built regional and national women's organizations and suffrage organizations, even as they were shut out of NAWSA. National federations of black women's clubs were formed during the 1880s and 1890s, then a joint national group, the National Association of Colored Women (NACW) led by Mary Church Terrell, was formed in 1896. Committed to woman suffrage with the motto of "Lifting As We Climb," the association fought segregation and raised funds to provide welfare and education in communities lacking hospitals, welfare institutions, and schools. The Woman's Convention of the National Baptist Convention, founded in 1900, became the largest black women's organization in the country and served as a major source of suffrage work.

Black suffragist leaders in the 1890s came from the ranks of the nation's black elite, women with access to higher education, generally middle class and social leaders. Many were professional women. Josephine St. Pierre Ruffin, Mary Church Terrell, Adella Hunt Logan, and Gertrude Mussell, from a prominent Philadelphia family, all began long public careers as journalists. Black women suffrage leaders in the South were restricted to educational institutions like Tuskegee, but outside the South, black suffragists organized out West and across the North and were particularly strong in the nation's capital. In 1895, four chapters of Woman's Loyal Union suffrage societies in Pennsylvania collected over 10,000 signatures for a petition delivered to Senator Henry Blair of New Hampshire. That same year, Josephine St. Pierre Ruffin, Margaret Murray Washington, and Victoria Earle Matthews were invited to attend the Republican Party convention in Detroit, a first for black women. Black women's suffrage work continued alone into the next century, despite constant outreach efforts by black suffragists to NAWSA.

IMPERIALISM AS AN INTERNATIONAL SUFFRAGE MOVEMENT

The increasingly racist climate of the age was reinforced by a major shift in science and philosophy known as "evolutionary science," which we now describe as the pseudoscience of racial hierarchy. In 1859, Charles Darwin had published *On the Origin of the Species* describing his revolutionary theory of the evolution of species. Darwin's theories gradually dominated the world in which suffrage leaders moved. Nearly as important was the reinterpretation of Darwin's work by Herbert Spencer, who coined the term "Social Darwinism," which theorized that Anglo-Saxons and north-ern Europeans were at the top of a human evolutionary pyramid. Those from southern and eastern Europe sat securely below, and at the bottom of this pyramid were native American Indians, Africans, Chinese, and other Asians. The idea of racial hierarchy and the racial superiority of the "race" of "Anglo-Saxon" and "Nordic" peoples drove social, polit-ical, and foreign policy. Seeing itself as a rising world power and striving to build a navy to control the Western Hemisphere and project its power into the Pacific, the United States turned to imperialist endeavors, taking democracy and Christianity to those nations viewed as needing uplift and civilization.

The Spanish American War in 1898 brought the question of citizen-ship and suffrage to the forefront. After the ten-week "splendid little war," the United States claimed Puerto Rico, Guam, and the Philippines as U.S. territories. The United States also acquired American Samoa through diplomacy and annexed Hawaii. Cuba was held temporarily. Questions regarding the status and future of the new acquisitions arose. Should these new acquisitions progress from territory to state, as had acquired land on the North American continent? Should the peoples of these lands be citi-zens? Should women in the conquered lands get the vote? The question of territorial status for the Philippines was complicated by the Filipinos themselves when they rejected American control, and their rebellion was brutally repressed by American troops. The Philippines would remain in American hands until after World War II, but never with the prospect of statehood. Future statehood was debated for Puerto Rico and Guam. Whether the Constitution followed the flag became a question the Supreme Court settled by saying no, so that pressure to extend American rights to the "darker peoples" of the new acquisitions was answered for the time in the negative. Still, both organized suffragists and the WCTU were concerned about this question of woman's rights in the colonial acquisi-tions, as well as across the globe, in general.

The WCTU added woman suffrage to its crusades in new American acquisitions, and was hard at work in Hawaii, annexed in 1898. Democ-racy, republicanism, and Christianity were the gifts that Frances Willard and her followers believed they brought to the world.[34] Whether this uplift included absorption into the United States remained up in the air.[35] Most suffragists subscribed to the idea that the "lesser peoples" of the overseas territories could be educated into democratic habits and, therefore, to the proper use of the vote.

The practical result for woman suffrage was that the worldwide reach of the WCTU in the late 1880s and 1890s affected the international suffrage movement. Frances Willard went to England in 1892 and was greeted in London by an audience of notables—from Members of Parliament, leaders of Protestant denominations, labor leaders, and temperance leaders, to the Salvation Army. Newspapers lauded her. There Willard found a close friend and an ally in building the women's world temperance movement. Lady Henry Somerset, president of the British Women's Temperance Association (BWTA) became Willard's inseparable companion, traveling with her back and forth to the United States over the next four years. They created an international movement that spread woman suffrage as much as it spread temperance ideas. Together Willard and Somerset sent women out across the world who believed deeply that they were bringing Christianity, civilization, and uplift. These intrepid WCTU missionaries also traveled with the conviction that women should vote.

In what turned out to be a momentous decision, in the mid-1880s Willard had sent WCTU organizer Mary Clement Leavitt to Honolulu to explore WCTU expansion there. Leavitt was a former schoolteacher and a divorced mother of three who began what became a globe-circling tour that lasted until 1891. Leavitt's excellent organizational skills bolstered temperance and, at the same time, provided key organizational and political skills that led to successful suffrage wins—particularly in the countries of the British colonies. Under Leavitt's tutelage, women around the world learned political skills and lobbying expertise. If they had been in Britain or the United States, many of these women may have directly entered the suffrage movement, but in the southern hemisphere, where there was no such opportunity, the WCTU provided the outlet for activist women that led to woman suffrage successes. The first nation to vote in woman suffrage came from these WCTU roots.

Late in 1893 came news of a vote making New Zealand, a self-governing colony of Great Britain, the first country to send women to the polls. Recalling when Parliament voted in woman suffrage, historian and former Minister of Labor, William Pember Reeves claimed that women woke up one morning and had the vote. Both political parties claimed to be responsible. Victory in the South Pacific was attributed to the fact that

New Zealand was a sparsely populated frontier, and that men had actually led the suffrage fight.[36] In fact, New Zealand suffragists, who had benefited from WCTU training, had worked for over fourteen years, producing petitions and lobbying the two houses of the legislature. In 1888, leading New Zealand suffragist Kate Sheppard wrote a pamphlet, *Ten Reasons Why the Women of New Zealand Should Vote,* using the argument of John Stuart Mill, the British theorist and suffrage leader, that simple justice demanded it, but at the same time arguing the need for women's vote to secure moral and social reform. This combination of justice and "expediency" arguments was used throughout Australasia and South Africa. Coming on the heels of the New Zealand victory, Australian women won the vote at different times in the several independent colonial provinces, beginning in 1894. With the creation of one united Commonwealth of Australia, the national women's vote was secured in 1911. After the New Zealand and then Australian victories, Kate Sheppard went to England in 1907 to work with suffragists there, reinforcing the international nature of the woman suffrage movement by the first decade of the twentieth century. Suffrage campaigning was linked across the globe. Women learned from each other's successes and failures.

A RETREAT FROM TEMPERANCE

Meanwhile, when Frances Willard returned to the United States in 1896, her star began to fade. The crash of 1893, coming right at the time when the WCTU had huge debts from a new headquarters in Chicago, added to her problems. Willard's critics charged that the Chicago building was financial misfeasance. At this point, Willard's health began to fail and she was diagnosed with pernicious anemia. Practically speaking, Willard's death in 1898 signaled the end of the suffrage/temperance strong alliance. Willard's successor as president abruptly narrowed the focus of WCTU work, relegating suffrage to something honored on paper but paid little attention in practice.[37]

The WCTU also lost some of its energy and cachet. After 1900, young women no longer joined the WCTU, which became an institution with an aging population who restricted themselves to temperance and prohibition. The national Prohibition Party and the Anti-Saloon League, both with male leadership, began to dominate the political battle for a national amendment. At the same time, doubt as to the usefulness of official temperance support grew within NAWSA. In 1896, even Susan B. Anthony, who was a lifelong temperance supporter, took a step back, convinced that a suffrage vote in San Francisco would be at risk if the WCTU held its convention there. She persuaded Frances Willard to change venues.

The suffrage movement in the early 1900s had slipped into the "doldrums." The alliance with white women in the South produced no state wins. Connections with temperance organizations increased the opposition to suffrage from the liquor industry. Unification created a new organization, but a new generation of leadership was still in the future. The conflict over unification still rankled among many. Women were dispirited; the years between 1896 and 1910 were labeled the "doldrums" because no wind moved the ship of suffrage for those wanting a federal amendment. A generation had passed, and it took the next generation some time to adjust to the political and cultural changes that affected the fate of woman suffrage campaigns. The doldrums evolved into a period of renewal for NAWSA with attendant tensions and outright conflict. Then, suddenly in 1913, a new force for woman suffrage splashed all over the newspapers. Alice Paul and Lucy Burns organized a great parade in Washington, DC, on the eve of Woodrow Wilson's inauguration as President of the United States.

NOTES

1. Elisabeth Griffith, *In Her Own Right: The Life of Elizabeth Cady Stanton* (New York, NY: Oxford University Press, 1984), 170–71.

2. Mrs. Eliza Eddy was the daughter of Francis Jackson, whose funds had supported woman's rights in the 1850s. Eddy left money to be divided between Stone and Anthony. Her will was disputed, with $40,000 finally being divided between Stone and Anthony in 1885.

3. Sally G. McMillen, *Lucy Stone: An Unapologetic Life* (New York, NY: Oxford University Press, 2015), 223.

4. See Andrew Moore Kerr, *Lucy Stone: Speaking Out for Equality* (New Brunswick, NJ: Rutgers University Press, 1992); Joelle Million, *Woman's Voice, Woman's Place: Lucy Stone and the Birth of the Woman's Rights Movement* (Westport, CT: Praeger, 2003).

5. McMillen, *Lucy Stone*, 223.

6. The first three volumes, which cover the history of the movement from its beginnings to 1885, were written and edited by Stanton, Anthony, and Matilda Joselyn Gage. Volume 1 (1848–1861) appeared in 1881, Volume 2 (1861–1876) in 1882, and Volume 3 (1876–1885) in 1886. Some early chapters first appeared in Gage's newspaper, *The National Citizen and Ballot Box*. Volume 4 (1883–1900) was published in 1902, edited by Anthony with the help of Ida Husted Harper, although the heaviest load was carried by Harper. Volumes 5 and 6 were published in 1922 long after the death of Anthony, Stanton, and Stone.

7. See Aileen S. Kraditor, *The Ideas of the Woman Suffrage Movement: 1890–1920* (New York, NY: W. W. Norton, 1981); and Eleanor Flexner, *Century of Struggle: The Woman's Rights Movement in the United States* (1959; repr., Cambridge, MA: Belknap Press of Harvard University Press), 996.

8. Lori D. Ginzberg, *Elizabeth Cady Stanton: An American Life* (New York, NY: Hill and Wang, 2009), 154–7.

9. Ellen Carol DuBois, *Woman Suffrage and Women's Rights* (New York: New York University Press, 1998), 213.

10. Lisa Tetrault, *The Myth of Seneca Falls: Memory and the Women's Suffrage Movement, 1848–1898* (Chapel Hill: University of North Carolina Press, 2014), 9–10, 113–4.

11. See Joan Marie Johnson, *Southern Ladies, New Women: Race, Region, and Clubwomen in South Carolina, 1890–1930* (Gainesville: University Press of Florida, 2005); Elsa Barkley Brown, "'What Has Happened Here': The Politics of Difference in Women's History and Feminist Politics," *Feminist Studies* 18, no. 2 (Summer 1992): 295–312; Glenda Elizabeth Gilmore, *Gender and Jim Crow: Women and the Politics of White Supremacy in North Carolina, 1896–1920* (Chapel Hill: University of North Carolina Press, 2006); Ann D. Gordon and Bettye Collier-Thomas, eds., *African American Women and the Vote, 1837–1965* (Amherst: University of Massachusetts Press, 1997); Evelyn Brooks Higginbotham, *Righteous Discontent: The Women's Movement in the Black Baptist Church, 1880–1920* (Cambridge, MA: Harvard University Press, 1994); Dorothy Sterling, *We are Your Sisters: Black Women in the Nineteenth Century* (New York, NY: W. W. Norton, 1984); Rosalyn Terborg-Penn, *African American Women in the Struggle for the Vote, 1850–1920* (Bloomington: Indiana University Press, 1998); and Deborah Gray White, *Too Heavy a Load: Black Women in Defense of Themselves, 1894–1994* (New York, NY: W. W. Norton, 1999).

12. Sally G. McMillen, *Seneca Falls and the Origins of the Women's Rights Movement* (New York, NY: Oxford University Press, 2008), 222.

13. Grace Farrell, *Lillie Devereux Blake: Retracing a Life Erased* (Amherst: University of Massachusetts Press, 2002).

14. Susan B. Anthony to Frances Willard, December 31, 1888, in Ann D. Gordon, ed., *Their Place Inside the Body-Politic, 1887 to 1895*, Vol. V of *The Selected Papers of Elizabeth Cady Stanton and Susan B. Anthony* (New Brunswick, NJ: Rutgers University Press, 2009), 163.

15. McMillen, *Seneca Falls*, 174.

16. The wording of the Sixteenth Amendment as passed in 1920 is as follows: "The right of citizens of the United States to vote shall not be denied or abridged by the United States or by any State on account of sex. Congress shall have the power to enforce this article by appropriate legislation."

17. McMillen, *Seneca Falls*, 207.

18. Farrell, *Lillie Devereux Blake*, 153.

19. Farrell, *Lillie Devereux Blake*, 154.

20. Elizabeth Frost-Knappman and Kathryn Cullen-DuPont, *Women's Suffrage in America*, Updated ed. (New York, NY: Facts On File, 2004), 259.

21. Farrell, *Lillie Devereux Blake*, 163.

22. See Joan Marie Johnson, *Southern Ladies*; Elna C. Green, *Southern Strategies: Southern Women and the Woman Suffrage Question* (Chapel Hill: University of North Carolina Press, 1997); and Anne Firor Scott, *The Southern Lady: From Pedestal to Politics, 1830–1930* (Charlottesville: University Press of Virginia, 1970).

23. Marion W. Roydhouse, "The Universal Sisterhood of Women: Women and Labor Reform in North Carolina, 1900–1932" (Ph.D. diss., Duke University, 1980), 198. See also, Gilmore, *Gender and Jim Crow*.

24. Green, *Southern Strategies*, 9.

25. Paul E. Fuller, *Laura Clay and the Woman's Rights Movement* (Lexington: University Press of Kentucky, 1975), 54.

26. Fuller, *Laura Clay*, 58.

27. Paul Buhle and Mari Jo Buhle, eds., *The Concise History of Woman Suffrage: Selections from the Classic Work of Stanton, Anthony, Gage, and Harper* (Urbana: University of Illinois Press, 1978), 348–9.

28. Majorie Spruill Wheeler, *New Women of the New South: The Leaders of the Woman Suffrage Movement in the Southern States* (New York, NY: Oxford University Press, 1993), 118–9.

29. Knappman and Cullen-DuPont, *Women's Suffrage in America*, 287.

30. Green, *Southern Strategies*, 10.

31. Jean H. Baker, *Votes for Women: The Struggle for Suffrage Revisited* (New York, NY: Oxford University Press, 2002), 108.

32. Baker, *Votes for Women*, 110.

33. Terborg-Penn, *African American Women*, 111.

34. Ian R. Tyrrell, *Woman's World, Woman's Empire: The Woman's Christian Temperance Union in International Perspective, 1880–1930* (Chapel Hill: University of North Carolina Press, 1991), 106–15. Jad Adams, *Women and the Vote: A World History* (Oxford: Oxford University Press, 2016). The initial impetus to export American democracy by incorporating new acquisitions as future states was eroded by Social Darwinism. There was a widespread conviction that the native peoples of the Philippines and Puerto Rico were in a lesser state of development, the same way the people of Santo Domingo had been viewed in 1870 when the Senate refused to vote for annexation, as negotiated by President Ulysses Grant.

35. Allison L. Sneider, *Suffragists in an Imperial Age: U.S. Expansion and the Woman Question, 1870–1929* (New York, NY: Oxford University Press, 2008).

36. Tyrrell, *Woman's World, Woman's Empire*, 228; Adams, *Women and the Vote*, 437–41.

37. Ruth Bordin, *Frances Willard: A Biography* (Chapel Hill: University of North Carolina Press, 1986), 239.

CHAPTER 6

OUT OF THE DOLDRUMS, 1905–1915

A REVIVED SUFFRAGE MOVEMENT: THE 1913 PARADE

At 3.45 pm on March 3, 1913, President-elect Woodrow Wilson stepped off his private train at Union Station, in Washington, DC. The next day was Wilson's inauguration. President William Howard Taft had sent a White House "touring car" with two motor-cycle policemen, a chauffeur, and a footman to ferry the Wilson entourage to the Shoreham Hotel. The crowd outside the train station was enthusiastic but was oddly small. A group of Princeton students gave a boisterous cheer for their university's former president, covering up with their enthusiasm what the *New York Times* described as a "strange greeting" when it should have been a "wildly enthusiastic" event.[1] Wilson looked around as he stepped to the waiting car, asking where the people were, only to be told that they were all over on Pennsylvania Avenue, watching the woman suffrage parade. Woodrow Wilson had been upstaged. The cars with the Wilson entourage took back streets through a practically deserted city. It would not be the last time Wilson was confounded by these women. Suffragists bedeviled Wilson's presidency, endlessly campaigning for the ballot and refusing to cease their public and private campaigns to get his support as he tried vainly to focus on his own reform agenda and then the conflagration of World War I.

Alice Paul and Lucy Burns pulled off a public relations and organizational miracle that clear and bright day in March of 1913. Arriving in Washington in January with permission from the National American

Woman Suffrage Association (NAWSA) headquarters to revive the moribund suffrage lobby, the NAWSA Congressional Committee, the two young women promptly used every connection they had and pulled every string possible to raise funds and to recruit marchers. With a handful of other women recruited to work with them, they raised money frantically, managed a myriad of organizational details, gathered suffragists from across the country and even countries that already had woman suffrage—New Zealand, Australia, Finland, and Norway—and brought it all together in a huge, colorful parade up Pennsylvania Avenue. While Woodrow Wilson was being greeted by notables at Union Station, the suffrage parade had begun with the sounding of horns blown up and down the parade route as women on horseback led the way for floats, cars, and phalanxes of women dressed in yellow, white, and purple. Somewhere between five thousand and eight thousand women and men marched on that fresh spring day.

As the parade got underway and turned onto Pennsylvania Avenue, all the careful planning was destroyed. The parade was halted by spectators moving off the sidewalks in hostile bunches, yelling, pushing, grabbing at, and tripping up the marchers, making it impossible to move ahead. A troop of Boy Scouts struggled to protect the women while an inadequate police force stood by and watched, some joining in the taunting. The women kept going, but only step by step, struggling to fight through the crowds. Inez Milholland, lawyer and activist, known as the most beautiful of suffragists, sat resplendent in suffrage white—a dress, a long cape, and a crown—astride her white horse, "Grey Dawn." Milholland, seeing the mêlée, bravely drove her horse into the crowd to push them back. Grand Marshall Jane Burleson, also on horseback, looked around for the promised police escort, only to see a "horrible, howling mob."[2] Hemmed in and beleaguered, the marchers made slow headway, fighting their way up to Fourteenth Street.

A hasty phone call to the Taft White House via sympathetic connections brought relief when a troop of cavalry arrived and rode into the hostile crowds, pushing back hooting men with little delicacy, but quickly restoring order. The great suffrage parade did not go as planned, but the publicity that followed the chaos was much greater than Alice Paul could have hoped. Even the antisuffrage *New York Times* was sympathetic, writing that the event was an "insult to American womanhood and a disgrace to the Capitol City of the Nation."[3]

Alice Paul, Lucy Burns, and Inez Milholland had learned their street theater tactics firsthand in England. They were joined by others who wanted more radical action than NAWSA was undertaking. This splinter group, first named the Congressional Union (CU), later the National Woman's Party (NWP), aroused the ire of the staider NAWSA members, splitting the suffrage movement once again.

The 1913 parade signaled to Woodrow Wilson that his presidency was going to be taken up with the "woman question," although this fact was probably only brought home to him a few days later when the White House reception rooms were filled with suffragists waiting for an audience. In ten states women already voted for the Electoral College. President Wilson found it harder and harder to ignore this fact as his presidency progressed. The president, politicians, and newspaper readers alike concluded that the woman suffrage movement had changed radically, from a lethargic, or perhaps just weary, groups gathering at conventions in the 1890s and early 1900s. At least a few wondered how this change had come about.

In 1913, suffrage was fashionable as well as respectable; wealthy "society" women gave money to be used for publicity, paid staff, and enhanced state and federal work. Clever use of mass newspapers, as suffragists wrote hundreds of news releases, combined with other inventive publicity efforts like the sale of consumer items—buttons, clothing, badge, and teacups painted with "Votes for Women"—reached new audiences. Door-to-door canvassing and precinct-by-precinct organization had begun to forge a sophisticated lobbying machine at work in the halls of state legislatures and in the U.S. Congress. In 1913, the suffrage cause was also an international one, with shared methods, regular communication, and extensive personal networks.

Getting to 1913 and the spectacular show of the March parade involved overcoming the lethargy of the national movement in the last years of Anthony's presidency. It took a long period for the new leadership to rebuild NAWSA. After 1910, a stiff breeze began to blow away the doldrums; victory in Washington state in 1910 was followed by California in 1911. Change did not happen without conflict. Between 1900 and 1913, NAWSA's work was hampered by internal dissent. Susan B. Anthony's choice as her successor, Carrie Chapman Catt, only stayed in office until 1904. Anna Howard Shaw took over in 1905 and faced strong opposition from the long-seated officers of the NAWSA Board. The internal conflict came to a head between 1909 and 1911 when a new NAWSA Board was dominated by Progressives. NAWSA in 1913 reflected wider changes taking place in the nation becoming more reform oriented, supported now by social justice reformers and "municipal housekeepers."

A MORIBUND ORGANIZATION REVIVES: NAWSA AFTER 1900

In 1900, Susan B. Anthony, turning eighty, presided at her last NAWSA convention. Anthony's admiring biographer, Alma Lutz, described the event:

> there was thunderous applause from an audience tense with emotion with the thought of losing the leader who had guided them for so many years. The tall gray-haired woman in black satin, with soft rich lace at her throat and the proverbial red shawl about her shoulders, had become the symbol of their cause. Now as she looked down upon them with a friendly smile and motherly tenderness, tears came to their eyes, and they wanted to remember always just how she looked at that moment.[4]

Anthony was a symbol of the suffrage movement and, to this audience, its saint. A great gala was also held in Anthony's honor. With numerous toasts declared, poems read, and music played, the culmination of the accolades came with the procession of eighty children across the stage in single file, each one placing a red rose on Anthony's lap. When Anna Howard Shaw rose to speak of Susan's career, the audience was reduced to tears.

This kind of pageantry—banks of flowers, music, poetry, speeches, presentations—was a hallmark of nineteenth-century suffrage celebrations, each event helping to create the legends of suffrage history and establishing suffrage traditions. Susan B. Anthony dominated the public's vision of the movement; Elizabeth Cady Stanton remained as its intellectual, and its critic, but now outside of NAWSA.

Despite the glitter of the Washington events of 1900, the outlook for the movement was gloomy. Between 1896 and 1910, no states enfranchised women. These years were described by suffragists themselves and later by historians as "the doldrums," where the winds of suffrage did not blow. Eleanor Flexner and those historians who followed laid much of the blame at Anna Howard Shaw's feet, commenting on her failure as an administrator and her inability to unite her Board.[5] Then, in 1996, historian Sara Hunter Graham produced a revised interpretation, calling these the years not the doldrums, but a "suffrage renaissance." It was, Graham argued, a period of rebuilding, not of stasis but one of growth, accompanied by healthy internal debates about strategy. Trisha Franzen's biography of Anna Howard Shaw strengthens Graham's argument. The extent to which the suffrage movement was in the doldrums or in a rebuilding phase before 1910 continues to be debated.[6]

There is much to support the rebuilding argument. After 1900, membership slowly increased, taking off after 1909. By 1910, a new headquarters of NAWSA in New York City was staffed with paid, professional women and funds for the movement were increasing its ability to campaign. As the number of women who had higher education increased, as women entered professional occupations, as women sought control over their own lives as independent individuals, they turned to suffrage for the power they believed the vote would bring. The vote would clear away further hurdles to women's full participation in public forums. Woman suffrage attracted progressive reformers, labor activists, and a small number of socialists. Settlement house workers, professional women, educators, wage earners, civic or "municipal" reformers, club women, college-educated women, wealthy "society" women: all became suffragists. The rebuilding relied heavily upon the energy and innovation of NAWSA's presidents—Carrie Chapman Catt and Anna Howard Shaw. Catt's term as president lasted four years. In 1904, Anna Howard Shaw took over and remained until 1914.

In 1900, the lethargy of the movement was easy enough to see. Harriot Stanton Blatch came back from England to New York in 1902, full of lessons learned in the more active British movement and immediately scornful of the state of the suffrage movement in New York, describing it as "completely in a rut." Moreover, she continued, "it bored its adherents and repelled its opponents. Most of the ammunition was being wasted on its supporters in private drawing rooms and in public halls where friends, drummed up and harried by the ardent, listlessly heard the same old arguments."[7] Carrie Chapman Catt laid the same failures at the foot of the "hopeless, lifeless, faithless members of our own organization . . . 'It cannot be done' is their favorite motto." No funds were set aside for congressional lobbying, making any effective federal amendment campaign impossible. The total number of dues-paying members of NAWSA was a little less than nine thousand.[8] No membership dues came in from the Deep South, and most states sent little more than $10.00 a year to headquarters in New York from paid dues. Campaigns were run on gifts, an unreliable source.

This lack of energy can be attributed, in part, to the general climate of political conservatism in the 1880s and 1890s. Neither the Republican Party nor the Democratic Party could see any advantage to woman suffrage. The Populist moment waned. Many native-born white Americans questioned the whole idea of universal democracy. These men and women saw a threat to their established values in the overcrowding of cities with immigrant populations whose religious and cultural differences were reflected in the clothing they wore, the food they ate, and the places in which they worshiped. Adding women to the suffrage rolls would add illiterate women immigrants and black women.

It was in this political and cultural climate that Susan B. Anthony handed over the presidency of NAWSA. Her resignation in 1900 signaled the end of fifty years of woman's rights and suffrage work. The struggle had consumed all her energies to the detriment of her physical health, yet her indomitable will still overwhelmed the failures of her aging body. Knowing that she must train a new generation, Anthony recruited prospective leaders in the 1880s and 1890s. She gathered around her a group whom she referred to as her "honorary nieces."

Rachel Foster was initially the most likely candidate to succeed Anthony. But Foster did two things that ruined her prospects. Foster adopted a baby in 1887, and in 1888, she married Philadelphian Cyrus Miller Avery. Anthony was as angry as she had been at the defection of earlier colleagues to marriage and childbearing. Anthony believed strongly that no-one could lead the suffrage fight and simultaneously cope with marriage and children. She wanted a successor whose life could be totally absorbed in the movement.

Anthony's hopes were next pinned on the Reverend Anna Howard Shaw. Meeting Shaw first in 1887, Anthony was immediately impressed and offered her a position with NAWSA, where Shaw soon became Anthony's most trusted confidant and administrative aide. Anthony became a mother figure and mentor to whom Anna Shaw was completely devoted. Anthony then urged Shaw to hire her niece, Lucy Anthony, who became Shaw's secretary, close companion, and main emotional support for the rest of Anna's life. In 1892, when Elizabeth Cady Stanton resigned as president, Shaw became vice-president of NAWSA. Shaw's informal extended family—Lucy Anthony and some of Shaw's nieces—lived outside Philadelphia at "Alnwick," her much-loved retreat and official home.

Anna Howard Shaw wanted to carry on Anthony's legacy, but she would need a salary to do so. Money and funding were not discussed openly in NAWSA, however.[9] Shaw was Anthony's emotional choice to lead, but practicalities prevented her from being Anthony's anointed successor in 1900. First, she needed an income, and none of the NAWSA Board had even been paid for their work. Shaw could not afford to leave the lecture circuit unless funds came from the NAWSA coffers. She was bitterly disappointed.

Shaw was always an outsider among the solidly middle-class and upper-class leaders of NAWSA, in part, because of her lack of family or personal wealth. An immigrant, born in England, she grew up on a rugged frontier farm on the Michigan peninsula, 100 miles from the nearest train stop. As the family struggled to earn a meager subsistence, Anna took up teaching at a local school, living at home where she continued to dig tree stumps, work the land, and do housework. Anna left her family behind to get more education, nearly starving for lack of money while at theological school in Boston. Eventually, Shaw was ordained deacon by the Methodist Protestant Church, the first woman minister in the denomination. In Tarrytown, New York, working with a small congregation, Shaw quickly concluded that life as a small-town pastor was too confining. Shaw left and put herself through medical school and got some medical experience, but still, she had not found her métier.

In the 1880s, Shaw's life shifted irrevocably. She believed that God's will intended that she take a new path, one that would lead to the eradication of the underlying causes of women's inequality. New friends, Mary Livermore and Frances Willard, urged her take. up suffrage and temperance work. First employed by both Lucy Stone and the Massachusetts Woman Suffrage Association and Frances Willard and the WCTU, Shaw began to earn substantial fees on top of her wages as an agent; her skill at lecturing increased and her reputation as a stirring speaker spread. As a result, in 1888, she vowed never, from then on, to "give one ounce of my strength of body or purse, or mind, or heart to any cause which opposes the best interest of women."[10]

CARRIE CHAPMAN CATT TAKES OVER

Susan B. Anthony turned to another extremely well-regarded field administrator. Carrie Chapman Catt was never one of Anthony's inner circle, although she was a superbly skilled campaigner and fundraiser and regarded as a key administrator for NAWSA. In 1900, Catt presented a clear contrast to Shaw in background and in her more controlled personality. Catt was also a wealthy and economically independent woman. After a comfortable childhood, Carrie Lane graduated from Iowa State, began teaching, then quickly became the first female School Superintendent for Mason City, Iowa. In 1885, she married newspaper editor Leo Chapman, who soon died of typhoid fever. Catt joined the Iowa State Suffrage Association and began her suffrage career. In 1890, she married a wealthy engineer, George Catt, who agreed, at the time of their marriage, to Carrie spending a substantial part of each year on suffrage work. Catt, as one of a new generation not rooted in abolition or the WCTU, was not linked to the early leadership. She worked first with Lucy Stone in Colorado and was never one of Anthony's close personal friends. Biographer Robert Fowler describes her as "known as the new general, a woman in a hurry, who felt she knew the way."[11]

Catt's abilities as a leader came to the forefront at the NAWSA convention in 1895, where she minced no words in urging NAWSA to stronger fundraising and better coordination of state and national work. She proposed a new Organization Committee, which would hire trained organizers to direct state campaigns. NAWSA responded; within a few years, the new committee formed new state branches and put organizers in the field while raising and spending $5,500 to pay expenses. Catt came to the presidential election in 1900 with a strong reputation for administrative ability and Anthony's support. But she was not widely known by the general membership.

The first sign of impending internal conflict in NAWSA came as Anthony was planning for the 1900 convention. Lillie Devereux Blake ran for president against Catt. Blake received significant support, but not enough, and she withdrew before the formal election process. Most members were still loyal to Anthony and any successor she supported. However, it was a sign of how far apart Anthony and Stanton had become personally that Stanton supported Blake. Stanton commiserated with Blake after her defeat, inviting her to come and have dinner so that they could "have an exhaustive talk on the situation & the many dissatisfied women with the present rulers. I will make a list of all I know who have retired from the movement because of snubs by Rachel Foster Avery & et al" whom she referred to as "Susan's little cabinet of 'girls.'"[12] Ida Husted Harper immediately wrote to Elizabeth, admonishing her for the hurt she had caused Susan. This factionalism continued until 1915, in one form or another.

Elizabeth Cady Stanton was, in 1900, de facto exiled from NAWSA after the publication of her *Woman's Bible* in 1895. She was bedridden, nearly blind, and in ill health, but her intellectual ability remained strong and her desire to change the world around her undimmed. Matilda Joslyn Gage had worked with Stanton on the volume, as did a group of twenty-five others. Less radical suffragists feared that the *Woman's Bible* would harm the movement because of its attack on organized religion. Rachel Foster Avery led an attack on the *Woman's Bible* at the annual convention in 1896, and, despite opposition from Anthony, secured the passage of a resolution disassociating NAWSA from the book. Significantly, the incoming leadership, both Carrie Chapman Catt and Anna Howard Shaw, supported the resolution. NAWSA was now a one-issue organization, working only for woman suffrage. Its focus had narrowed a long way from the goals enumerated at Seneca Falls in 1848. Elizabeth Cady Stanton, the mighty intellectual of the woman's movement, died in 1902. Her death shook Susan B. Anthony deeply. Stanton and Anthony had drifted far apart, but they remained loyal friends and their fifty-year partnership could not be erased, even by their philosophical differences.[13]

Susan B. Anthony continued to influence NAWSA after she relinquished the presidency. She told the 1900 convention that she was retiring with "joy and relief" but reassured the audience that she had no intention of giving up all work, for "I am Yankee enough to feel that I must watch every potato that goes into the dinner pot and supervise every detail of the work."[14] Carrie Chapman Catt found herself having to cope with Susan's heavy hand. The executive committee of the Board immediately dissolved Catt's field organization committee; some feared that Catt would amass too much power as the committee's chair while simultaneously serving as president. Catt objected strongly and was horrified when Anthony did not back her. Carrie Catt was also taken aback by Anthony's opposition to an International Woman Suffrage Alliance, which Catt saw as essential to the future of women around the world.

Within NAWSA's executive committee, whose members had been long installed in power, some were first irritated, and then angry, with Catt's requests to increase national fundraising and hire more field agents. Women on the Board felt empowered to oppose Catt when Anthony failed to show complete support. Even so, Catt went on to wade in turbulent waters. She was particularly resisted by southerners Kate Gordon and Laura Clay, who promoted states' rights over any federal amendment.[15]

Catt never confronted either Gordon or Clay on the race question. The consequences were evident in New Orleans in 1903. Feeling ill with a cold, with only a few days' rest, and with little to show for the last two years' work, Catt went south to New Orleans in March 1903 for the annual convention. Personally, Catt believed that a race could elevate itself by education. Yet, if Mary Peck is to be believed, Catt wished that "there were no Negroes in the country," and did not want to be bothered with the race question.[16] Biographer Robert Fowler concludes that Catt was "no exception" to the deep racism of NAWSA. But when she deemed it politically necessary, Catt supported black suffrage.[17] The 1903 convention simply revealed the continuing rejection of black women suffragists as full NAWSA members and the failure to understand the ways in which race and suffrage could not, for black women, be separated. Elizabeth Cady Stanton had criticized Anthony's ruling out of order discussion of the "race question," writing "the magnitude and far-reaching consequences involved in the emancipation and enfranchisement of this Africo-American race lifts this above all ordinary questions."[18]

Black suffragists were faced with the option of persisting in battering at the doors of NAWSA and local suffrage societies or creating their own parallel movement. They did both. During this lowest point in race relations, when segregation hardened across the country, new black women leaders worked through their church organizations or their own suffrage associations, even as they retained some connections with NAWSA, particularly with its leadership. In 1905, suffragist Adella Hunt Logan from

Tuskegee Institute summed up the general black suffragist opinion, which was that black women needed the vote more than white women; "if white American women, with all their natural and acquired advantages, need the ballot . . . how much more do Black Americans, male and female need the strong defense of a vote to help secure their right to liberty and the pursuit of happiness?"[19]

Most white suffragists were still deeply rooted in their time and place. Specific racial and ethnic prejudices differed in relative importance in different regions; race was still the most important factor in the South; xenophobia, particularly with regard to Chinese voters, was most prevalent on the West Coast; and class divisions based in nativism had their greatest impact in the industrial swath from Chicago across to the Northeast and Mid-Atlantic. All these prejudices were in play when it came to the policies and membership of NAWSA at the turn of the century and into the first decade.

The racism of white suffragists affected the suffrage movement at different levels and in a variety of ways. Some suffragists were fully dedicated to white supremacy, others wanted to ignore any racial issues, with the justification that for practical reasons they must focus only on suffrage. Civil rights needed to be held separate, according to this view. For black women, burdened with the oppression of race and lacking the vote to influence change, these delicacies of focus were irrelevant.

Roslyn Terborg-Penn, noted historian of black woman suffrage, has the most salient point on the debate on racism within NAWSA, arguing that historians' debate on whether white suffragists were racist or not is beside the point because black suffragists thought they were racist and acted accordingly. Terborg-Penn tells us also that, although we don't yet know how many black suffragists passed as white and attended NAWSA conventions, it is clear that some did and kept abreast of NAWSA efforts.[20] These determined women carried on working for "racial uplift" and suffrage together, pushing constantly against the limits posed by racial violence and hatred. NAWSA invited a handful of black leaders to address conventions, but never fully embraced black suffragists.

By 1906, the southern strategy was not producing results and was in its last throes. Kate Gordon proposed a new southern campaign that would overtly promote white woman suffrage as a solution to the race problem. This was the line beyond which northern women would now not go. Anna Howard Shaw gave Gordon a strong no, saying that "it would be impossible for us to be allied with any movement which advocated exclusions of any race or class from the right of suffrage."[21] There were, it seemed, limits to NAWSA's tolerance of its southern members. To support whites-only suffrage would contradict the organization's "justice" argument. Bowing to southern habits was one thing, supporting the vote for white men and women only was another after 1906. By 1910, almost all signs of any health in the southern suffrage movement were gone. In practical terms, little had come of the recruiting efforts in the South where no suffrage interest was able to get a foothold in state legislatures. Anna Howard Shaw endorsed black suffrage in 1911 but still prevented a black delegate in St. Louis from proposing an antidiscrimination resolution. The single focus on suffrage was solidly in place.[22] Stanton, Anthony, Shaw, and Catt had a mixed legacy when it came to black women and equality.

NEW LEADERSHIP AND THE DEATH OF A GREAT LEADER

Carrie Catt presided over her last convention in 1904. She refused to stand for re-election, pleading exhaustion. Her husband was severely ill and needed more of her time. Catt also had a growing interest in the international suffrage movement. Initially, she told Anthony she would take a short leave, but it quickly became clear that Catt would not return to the presidency in 1905. Shaw had taken over from Catt for the interim, but the question of her long-term presidency still had to be solved by finding a salary to support Shaw and her family.

In 1905, Anna Howard Shaw, like Catt, was worn out from traveling and organizing and was no longer as eager to take over NAWSA. But Anthony, now eighty-four and in ill health, was convinced that Shaw was the only person who could carry her legacy forward.[23] Shaw reluctantly acquiesced and stood for president in 1904, telling Anthony, "Aunt Susan, love for you is all that would make me do this. You have borne so much and been to me more than a mother."[24] Shaw's agreement was that she would take over while Catt was recovering. When it was apparent that Catt would not return to NAWSA, Anthony spent the next year looking for permanent funds to pay Shaw's salary.

The international network of suffrage women was growing stronger; Shaw, Anthony, and Catt all kept up voluminous correspondence with overseas suffragists. In 1904, women had the vote in New Zealand (1893) and in the Commonwealth of Australia (1902), as well as in the Pitcairn Islands (inhabited by the mutineers from the *HMS Bounty*), in the Cook Islands in the Pacific Ocean, and on the tiny Isle of Man in the Irish Sea. As other nations passed woman suffrage, their victories were held up by American suffragists as evidence of the failure of the United States. By failing to give women the vote, it had also failed to lead the world as a model of democracy. In 1906, Finland, newly independent from Russian control, voted for full woman suffrage. In 1913, Norway followed suit. The next swath of woman suffrage nations came during World War I: Denmark and Iceland (1915), Russia (1917), Austria, Canada, Germany, Hungary, Latvia, Lithuania, Poland, and Great Britain (1918).[25] In 1919, in the aftermath of the war, five more countries followed, reinforcing to American suffragists their failure. It was galling to be lagging when their own fight had been underway much longer than in almost all these countries.

Anna Howard Shaw took up the work of NAWSA but kept lecturing to pay her own salary. Knowing the only way ahead was to create a permanent source of income for Shaw, Anthony set out to raise money. She found the difficulty of doing so intensely frustrating. Paying an officer of NAWSA was, however, controversial. Women's organizations in general did not have salaried staff; they were all volunteer institutions. Little was said publicly about the fact that some suffragists earned their own living, but anyone who did so was not on the NAWSA Board. Class prejudice and tradition combined into a belief that those who had to be paid were liable to be corrupted. Shaw's biographer notes that her financial situation was the basis for the "nastiest attacks against her."[26]

Anthony at last found support for Shaw. President M. Carey Thomas of Bryn Mawr College and her partner, Mary Garrett, heiress to the substantial Baltimore and Ohio Railroad fortune, agreed to raise a fund to pay Shaw a salary. Both women were appalled by the unprofessional and outdated methods of fundraising that NAWSA clung to. Thomas and Garrett guaranteed Shaw's salary and that of several headquarters staff by raising $12,000 a year for five years. Both women also stepped quickly into central roles in the suffrage movement, starting a new stage for the suffrage movement. Wealthy women philanthropists gave money and raised even more. In doing so, they influenced policies and promoted their own strategies. Existing NAWSA Board members, not all of them graciously, accepted Anthony's *fait accompli* at the 1905 convention and Anna Howard Shaw was elected president.

Shaw's strongest support lay in the general membership of NAWSA. She had been traveling constantly for more than a decade and had created a network of suffragists who admired and supported her. Now in her fifties and showing her age with streaks of white hair, Shaw was a nationally known figure, admired for her tremendous speaking ability. People also appreciated her public persona as a plain-spoken working woman who chopped wood, gardened, and did her own home repairs at her much-loved home outside Philadelphia. Shaw's difference lay in her ordinariness. She also stood for universal woman suffrage and was opposed to the idea of the limits intended by educated suffrage advocates. Her status as an outsider both helped and hindered her as president of NAWSA.

Baltimore, in 1906, was Susan B. Anthony's last convention. Mary Garrett paid for around-the-clock nurses during the convention. So ill that she was barely able to get to the podium to speak, Anthony uttered the phrase that would become the suffrage motto—"failure is impossible." She struggled to get home to Rochester, where she lingered for a few days on the edge of death. With Shaw at her side, Anthony died on March 13, 1906. Rochester and the nation mourned as condolences poured in from around the world. Susan B. Anthony was, at her death, a saint of the movement, a revered figure who had become the one central figure of its history, eclipsing Stanton and, of course, Stone, in public memory.

WEALTHY WOMEN AND "COERCIVE PHILANTHROPY" IN THE SUFFRAGE MOVEMENT

Conflict over leadership in NAWSA broke into the open with Anthony gone. Between 1906 and 1911, Anna Howard Shaw fended off efforts to unseat her, then was able, with M. Carey Thomas's backing, to elect a new kind of woman, Progressives, to the NAWSA Board. Increasingly, Anna Howard Shaw turned to Thomas, asking her support for moving the NAWSA headquarters away from the isolation of Harriet Upton's house in the small town of Warren, Ohio. The money for a new headquarters eventually came not from Thomas, but from a new convert whom Shaw had cultivated assiduously.

In 1909, Alva Smith Vanderbilt Belmont, newly widowed, the possessor of a huge fortune, a woman of drive and administrative skill, with strong opinions and the desire to control any project she took up, quickly became a huge presence in the suffrage movement. Alva Belmont's friend, another wealthy woman, Katherine (Kitty) Duer Mackay, the wife of Clarence Mackay, the founder of International Telephone and Telegraph, was already a suffragist and had recruited Belmont.

Alva Belmont met Carrie Chapman Catt, Harriot Stanton Batch, Fanny Garrison Villard, and Ida Husted Harper at a suffrage lecture at the exclusive new women's club, the Colony Club, in New York. Anna Howard Shaw was then invited to the Belmont mansion and talked suffrage long into the night. Catt and Shaw in turn invited Alva Belmont to attend the International Suffrage Alliance in London in April 1909. The militant Women's Social and Political Union (WPSU), founded by Emmeline Pankhurst in Manchester in 1903, was now thriving and in strong opposition to the more conventional National Union of Women's Suffrage Societies (NUWSS) under Millicent Garrett Fawcett. It was the Pankhurst women who most attracted Belmont. By 1909, their militancy was in full flight. Emmeline, Christabel, and Sylvia Pankhurst regularly interrupted speeches of members of Parliament, and WPSU women began to break windows in government offices and were promptly jailed, whereupon they went on hunger strikes. Impressed by a suffrage parade and a rally at Albert Hall, Belmont returned to New York ready to join the fight and to stir NAWSA into copying British tactics.[27]

In August 1909, at the height of the Newport society season, Alva Belmont opened her extravagant summer home, Marble House, to raise funds for NAWSA. Already skilled at manipulating the press from her years in New York society, Alva Belmont organized an event that resonated across the country. Alice Stone Blackwell admitted that she was delighted not to have to beg people to take tickets; rather, tickets were sought after, despite being expensive. Alva Belmont became a suffrage celebrity. Interviews with her were published and her suffrage exploits intensely documented in the newspapers.

Belmont supported the founding of eleven suffrage clubs in Manhattan, the Bronx, Brooklyn, and Long Island. These were intended to bring in a more diverse group to suffrage by holding suffrage meetings and hosting public speaking classes and music and reading clubs. With a lunchroom run by suffragists, these clubs were a combination of settlement house and suffrage organization. Belmont was also ready to take on New York politicians and began to pigeon-hole opposition politicians in Albany. Between 1909 and 1913, before she transferred her loyalties to Alice Paul, Alva Belmont influenced NAWSA's actions with her funds, usually given with strings attached. She agreed to fund new NAWSA headquarters for two years, not in Washington. DC, as Shaw preferred, but in New York, where it would house the New York Woman Suffrage Association and NAWSA, as well as Belmont's own newly created Political Equality League. Alva Belmont and her friend Katherine Mackay were but two of the "Gilded Suffragists" who entered the New York suffrage scene. Their influence was profound.

Anna Howard Shaw began reviving the movement with funds from Mary Garrett and M. Carey Thomas until Garrett's death, but she also received other monies that were under her sole control. After 1910 Pauline Agassiz Shaw, a Boston philanthropist, gave money anonymously that was Anna Howard Shaw's private fund. Pauline Shaw sent $30,000 in 1913, a sum nearly 75 percent of NAWSA's annual budget, that was used for the western campaigns in Arizona, Kansas, Oregon, Wisconsin, Michigan, North Dakota, Montana, Ohio, and Nevada, and was spent at Anna Shaw's direction.[28] Legacies from wealthy women were a vital part of the post-1900 suffrage movement. Shaw also had a legacy from Mary Anthony after her death in 1907 that Shaw personally controlled.

These wealthy women expected to have a say in how their money was spent. Alva Belmont dictated not just where the headquarters would be, but later specified that unless Ida Husted Harper remained as press officer, and Anna Howard Shaw in the presidency, she would withdraw her funding support. Historian Joan Marie Johnson labels this money with strings attached as "coercive philanthropy," and likens it to the "scientific philanthropy" of Progressives intent on changing society. Without these funds, the massive campaigns of the post-1910 years, with paid traveling organizers, large press and publicity budgets, expensive parades, and other suffrage stunts, as well as sizable lobbying campaigns, could not have happened. Monied women understood that money gave them clout. These (all white) women resented their lack of power and independence in the world so that almost all wanted the vote as a means of gaining equality, rather than using maternalist arguments. Johnson concludes that their donations "shaped the trajectory, priorities, strategies, and ultimately the success of the movement. These women gave thousands and thousands of dollars because they cared deeply about women's rights."[29] But their money raised resentments. The underlying strains and tensions caused by wealthy women directing policy contributed to the crises over Anna Howard Shaw's leadership that engulfed the Board between 1909 and 1911.

CRISIS OF LEADERSHIP: ANNA HOWARD SHAW AND INTERNAL OPPOSITION, 1909–1911

In 1909, Anna Howard Shaw traveled west to NAWSA's annual convention in Seattle. On the journey, Shaw met two women whom she quickly recruited for staff positions. Rather too quickly, as it turned out. Professor Frances Squire Potter, from the University of Minnesota, who was active in Minnesota suffrage as well as in the College Equal Suffrage League, agreed to be the principal administrator in New York as corresponding secretary. Potter's close friend Mary Gray Peck gave up her faculty position to join Potter as the headquarters' secretary. A hint of problems to come emerged almost immediately when Potter alienated M. Carey Thomas. Frances Potter particularly resented Alva Belmont, fearing that her money could buy her way into office and that it would cause NAWSA to "lose its own and other people's respect." Laura Clay agreed, thinking Belmont's exploits would make people take the movement less seriously. "The chief impression we are making on the uniformed public is that we are a protégée of Mrs. Belmont," who would toy with the movement for as long as it amused her.[30]

Once the September 1909 celebrations of the grand new headquarters at 505 Fifth Avenue were over, hints of conflict between Potter and Lucy Anthony—Shaw's voice at headquarters while Shaw was on the road—soon filtered out. Harriet Upton had been unhappy about the move to New York and took Potter's side in the power struggle. Relations between other members of the Board were not smooth either; Kate Gordon thought Rachel Avery incompetent, and Harriet Upton a weak fundraiser. None of this augured well. Nor did Shaw directly address the tensions; she just ploughed on, rather than facing the conflicts, which was the source of later comments on her administrative failures and her inability to smooth ruffled feelings in her staff and on the Board.

Florence Kelley and M. Carey Thomas tried and failed to mediate.[31] Kelley believed that NAWSA should pay more attention to labor and equality issues and defended the more radical Potter. Conflict reached the boiling point; the mass of the membership, Carey Thomas, and Alva Belmont stood with Shaw. Florence Kelley quietly resigned from the Board before the 1910 convention in Washington, DC. Shaw devoutly hoped that Potter and Peck would do the same, and she thought she had come through the worst when they did actually resign. Suddenly, in a closed session at the end of the annual convention, Rachel Foster Avery, Florence Kelley, Ella S. Stewart, Harriet Upton, and Laura Clay wrote a resolution bemoaning the resignations, a move that amounted to a public attack on Shaw's leadership. In the ensuing fracas, Upton and Avery resigned. Shaw had lost five people in a widely publicized fight.

Why two women so new to the leadership caused such turmoil so quickly is unclear. Long-standing tensions between women on the Board obviously contributed. Laura Clay's biographer describes the conflict as one where the eastern wing of NAWSA came into conflict with both the southern and western delegates. Certainly, there was animosity between eastern and western suffragists. Catherine McCulloch, Chicago lawyer and long-term legal advisor for NAWSA, who served as first vice president in 1910, set up the Mississippi Valley Suffrage Conference in 1912, which held annual meetings of midwestern suffragists as a way of rebalancing the movement.

Shaw, with Carey Thomas's help, forged a new leadership team, though southerners Laura Clay and Kate Gordon remained on the Board for a few more years. Jessie Ashley, a socialist and young radical from Greenwich Village, became treasurer and was joined on the Board by Mary Ware Dennett as corresponding secretary. Dennett was a pacifist and a Progressive, who later became known for her work in birth control and sex education. The make-up of the Board shifted slightly toward younger and more progressive reform-oriented women.

The last ripples of dissent only calmed down a year later, in 1911, when Kate Gordon tried and failed to introduce new term limits for the president. Alva Belmont declared that she would not continue to fund the headquarters unless Shaw was president. This time Carey Thomas appears to have taken steps to eliminate Shaw's internal opposition completely. At the annual convention, to the surprise of many, Jane Addams was elected first vice president with support from eastern delegates. Sophonisba Breckenridge, from the prominent Kentucky Breckenridge family, was a strong Progressive and friend of Jane Addams and became second vice president. None of the long-term leaders except Shaw and Alice Stone Blackwell remained in office. NAWSA now had a nationally known group of women who were strong reformers. Even Carrie Chapman Catt, who had doubted Shaw's ability to negotiate leadership, was impressed. "I am glad the National is quarreling it betokens life and alertness. A few years ago, nothing could rouse the convention from dead calm. . . . I am beginning to think AHS is more executive and a better politician than I thought her!"[32]

NAWSA emerged from the conflict with a rejuvenated Board whose members were solidly progressive, many of whom would support Theodore Roosevelt's Progressive Party in 1912. The new NAWSA Board was better suited to the current winds of change. They were ready to build a re-energized movement with new strategies. Anna Howard Shaw presided over the growing number of state campaigns until her retirement in 1915. The suffrage movement was now more fully reflective of the Progressive reform movement well ensconced in the nation, but particularly in the states that won woman suffrage victories.

To understand those victories, we need first to understand the nature of the massive changes that had taken place in the United States since the birth of NAWSA in 1890. As the Progressive Era shunted aside the Gilded Age, the suffrage crusade became more diverse, more active, and more successful. A new kind of suffragist now populated NAWSA's leadership. These were women with roots in the Progressive movement, women for whom social justice and reform were essential to the future of American society. Suffragists now worked within a changed political arena, where Republicans and Democrats faced demands for change.

THE PROGRESSIVE ERA AND WOMAN SUFFRAGE AS A PROGRESSIVE REFORM

Progressivism, as a political and social movement, emerged out of the wreckage of Populism in the 1890s. Progressivism came into its own at the turn of the new century. A "modern" age emerged. As one California suffragist wrote in her autobiography of the time of President William McKinley's assassination in 1901, "with the advent of Roosevelt the old order changed somehow and another was born."[33] When Carrie Chapman Catt was elected President of NAWSA in 1900, the country had experienced drastic changes, with great divisions carved out between rich and poor, accompanied by monopolistic control over the economy by captains of industry working alongside corrupt political machines. When Republican Theodore Roosevelt took over the "bully pulpit" from the assassinated McKinley, he addressed a swelling audience who believed that change was needed to cope with the impact of the epochal transformations.

President "Teddy" Roosevelt's boundless energy and his conviction that the United States was still a place of opportunity echoed with expanding numbers of Americans. The most determined of these became political activists, crusaders convinced that the nation's problems could be overcome with the right people leading a great social justice crusade. Careful reform would produce the looked-for "modern age," with new technologies, new inventions, and new opportunities. If a vigorous reform spirit introduced rational limits to business and industry, if the bitter human consequences of overcrowded cities and dangerous working conditions could be attacked and ameliorated, if not eradicated, then the problems created by great growth and great wealth could be controlled for the good of the nation. Here was reason to be hopeful. Activist women were right in the center of the transformation conceived by small and large "P" progressives. Politically, they were insurgent progressive Republicans or members of Roosevelt's Progressive Party. In some states, progressive Democrats backed reform.

The conservatism of the Gilded Age receded as the number of men and women who called themselves Progressives swelled and as Progressive reforms were introduced to make food, drugs, and other products safe, reduce tariffs, limit the size and power of trusts and monopolies, clean up cities, make housing and working places safe, and limit the hours women and children could work. Women were at the lead in many of these reforms; the most well-known was Jane Addams, founder of Chicago's pioneering Hull House settlement, social reformer, urban researcher, Nobel prize-winning peace activist, writer, and lecturer. The growing settlement house movement, whose public face was represented by Jane Addams and

Ellen Gates Starr in Chicago, and Lillian Wald and Mary Simkovitch in New York, provided a place where politically minded women could find a home, and where unmarried suffragists could find like-minded women.

A look at the speakers at NAWSA annual conventions shows interest in "municipal housekeeping" and other progressive reforms increasing after 1900. In 1900, there was a discussion of "Industrial Problems Affecting Women and Children," and a committee was formed to investigate them. At the Baltimore Convention in 1905, Philadelphia Progressive, and later mayor, Rudolph Blankenburg, spoke on "Municipal Government," and Florence Kelley spoke on child labor. These Progressives' version of "separate spheres" was that women's sphere needed to expand to include the streets, factories, and corrupt political machines in their communities.

Progressive suffragists often put forward arguments that were rooted in women's differences. Most avoided any outright connection with "politics," which to them meant the corrupt and masculine enclave of party politics. Still, their reform impetus led them into the political arena, adopting previously male political tactics as they worked in state legislatures and in the U.S. Congress. This was the early twentieth-century version of the expediency argument. Suffragists did not abandon the argument that women deserved the vote as taxpayers or as citizens who were denied their constitutional rights or simply as humans who deserved equality with men. Rather they layered onto this "justice" appeal the argument that women were the bearers of stronger moral values and were the moral guardians of society. Women would bring these values to bear with the power of the vote. Progressives saw woman suffrage as an essential reform.

Despite the changed nature of the NAWSA Board, the actual suffrage advances continued to take place out on the Pacific Coast and in the West. Once more, the state campaigns provided the real movement of the country toward woman suffrage as NAWSA struggled to create a strong national organization. While NAWSA struggled, the work of women in Washington state, California, and Illinois built more diverse and more grassroots suffrage organizations, working within the demands of state politics. They created coalitions with labor and third parties and secured the support of a range of women's organizations, from the WCTU to women's clubs. Wealthy women had an increasing role to play in all these states, funding campaigns that were now huge in reach and in expense.

Washington state won suffrage in 1910, California in 1911, Illinois in 1913, and, as Anna Howard Shaw finished her years as president in 1914, two more states won suffrage—Nevada and Montana. In both states, NAWSA workers were joined by the new and more militant Congressional Union. In Montana, NAWSA organizer Jeannette Rankin led the fight, becoming a national leader, seated in 1917 as the first woman in the U.S. House of Representatives.[34] That same year, women voted in thirteen states. Presidential hopefuls and those running for U.S. Congress in suffrage states now began to consider women's votes in their political calculus. At the same time, antisuffrage organizations continued to grow, and the opposition of brewers, liquor dealers, industries that employed women and children, and political machines heightened their level of surveillance of woman suffrage campaigns.

NOTES

1. *New York Times*, March 4, 1913, ProQuest Historical Newspapers.

2. Rebecca Boggs Roberts, *Suffragists in Washington, D.C.: The 1913 Parade and the Fight for the Vote* (Charleston, SC: History Press, 2017), 18.

3. Roberts, *Suffragists in Washington, D.C.*, 52.

4. Alma Lutz, *Susan B. Anthony: Rebel, Crusader, Humanitarian* (Boston, MA: Beacon Press, 1960), 430.

5. Eleanor Flexner commented "Dr Shaw's devotion was complete and her gifts were many, but administrative ability was not among them," in Eleanor Flexner, *Century of Struggle: The Woman's Rights Movement in the United States* (New York, NY: Atheneum, 1972), 241; Aileen Kraditor echoed Flexner, writing "Miss Shaw after becoming NAWSA's president devoted her truly great oratorical powers to the suffrage cause, but by then speech-making was no longer the most important activity for a suffrage leader to engage in. The movement was stagnating, and Miss Shaw's administrative deficiencies made the organization's problems worse. By 1911 its internal splits and dissensions had become public knowledge," in Aileen Kraditor, *The Ideas of the Woman Suffrage Movement: 1890–1920* (New York, NY: W. W. Norton, 1981), 13.

6. Sara Hunter Graham, *Woman Suffrage and the New Democracy* (New Haven, CT: Yale University Press, 1996); see also, Trisha Franzen, *Anna Howard Shaw: The Work of Woman Suffrage* (Urbana: University of Illinois Press, 2014).

7. Flexner, *Century of Struggle*, 242.

8. Graham, *Woman Suffrage and the New Democracy*, 8–10.

9. See Lisa Tetrault, "The Incorporation of American Feminism: Suffragists and the Postbellum Lyceum," *Journal of American History* 96, no. 4 (2010): 1027–56; *The Myth of Seneca Falls: Memory and the Women's Suffrage Movement, 1848–1898* (Chapel Hill: University of North Carolina Press, 2014); Joan Marie Johnson, "Following the Money: Wealthy Women, Feminism, and the American Suffrage Movement," *Journal of Women's History* 27, no. 4 (Winter 2005): 62–87; *Funding Feminism: Monied Women, Philanthropy, and the Women's Movement, 1870–1967* (Chapel Hill: University of North Carolina Press, 2017).

10. Franzen, *Anna Howard Shaw*, 65.

11. Robert Booth Fowler, *Carrie Chapman Catt: Feminist Politician* (Boston, MA: Northeastern University Press, 1986), 18.

12. Ann D. Gordon, ed., *An Awful Hush, 1895–1906*, Vol. VI of *The Selected Papers of Elizabeth Cady Stanton and Susan B. Anthony* (New Brunswick, NJ: Rutgers University Press, 2012), 335. The younger women whom Anthony gathered to work closely with her in daily administration were disliked by those outside this circle, hence, Stanton referred to them as "girls." Rachel Foster was the first of these women to be given the honorary title of "niece" by Susan B. Anthony, and others followed.

13. Kathi Kern, *Mrs. Stanton's Bible* (Ithaca, NY: Cornell University Press, 2001).

14. Report in *Woman's Journal*, March 3, 1900, in Gordon, *Selected Papers*, Vol. VI: 320.

15. See Paul E. Fuller, *Laura Clay and the Woman's Rights Movement* (Lexington: University Press of Kentucky, 1975).

16. Fowler, *Carrie Chapman Catt*, 88.

17. Rosalyn Terborg-Penn, *African American Women in the Struggle for the Vote, 1850–1920* (Bloomington: Indiana University Press, 1998), 126. The NAACP was founded in 1909—suffragists among the founders were Ida B. Wells-Barnett, Mary Church Terrell, W.E.B. Du Bois, Florence Kelley, and Oswald Garrison Villard.

18. Elizabeth Cady Stanton, article in *Boston Investigator*, July 22, 1899, in Gordon, *Selected Letters*, vol. V: 305.

19. Terborg-Penn, *Struggle for the Vote*, 60–61. See also, Evelyn Brooks Higginbotham, *Righteous Discontent: The Women's Movement in the Black Baptist Church, 1880–1920* (Cambridge, MA: Harvard University Press, 1994).

20. Terborg-Penn, *Struggle for the Vote*, 65.

21. Franzen, *Anna Howard Shaw*, 109; and Kenneth R. Johnson, "Kate Gordon and the Woman Suffrage Movement in the South," *Journal of Southern History* 38, no. 3 (August 1972): 365–92.

22. Rosalyn Terborg-Penn, "Southern Suffragists and 'the Negro Problem,'" in Marjorie Spruill Wheeler, ed., *New Women of the New South* (New York, NY: Oxford University Press, 1993), 126.

23. Carrie Chapman Catt turned to international suffrage work and nursed her husband until his death in 1905. His death brought her a physical breakdown and it took her years to recover. In 1911, Catt's response to being told by doctors to rest was to first attend an International Suffrage meeting in Europe, then take off on a world cruise seeking out suffragists and reformers in South Africa, Lebanon, the Middle East, Egypt, India, China, and then home via Hawaii. With her newly acquired international network, she returned to New York in November 1912.

24. Franzen, *Anna Howard Shaw*, 94.

25. In the Pitcairn Islands, part of the British Empire and settled by the survivors of the mutiny on the *HMS Bounty*, women voted in local government (which was all they had at the time) from 1838 onward. In the Cook Islands in the Pacific, where women held positions of leadership, the British resident instituted universal suffrage in 1893, and women voted on Rarotonga Island a few days before the New Zealanders. In 1880, while the extension of the suffrage was being debated in the tiny Isle of Man, the Manchester women's suffrage organization arranged for debates on woman suffrage on the island, with the result that, in November 1880, unmarried women and widows who owned property became voters. See Jad Adams, *Women and the Vote: A World History* (Oxford: Oxford University Press, 2016).

26. Franzen, *Anna Howard Shaw*, 102.

27. Alva Smith Vanderbilt Belmont was a larger-than-life figure whose first marriage to William Kissam Vanderbilt allowed her a place in New York society. Seeking further social standing, Alva forced her daughter Consuelo into marriage with the Duke of Marlborough in 1895, an ill-fated alliance that ended with Consuelo taking up suffrage, settlement, and charity work in Britain. After twenty years of marriage, Vanderbilt's failure to keep private his adulterous liaisons provoked Alva to divorce him, thus making herself *persona non grata* in New York society. Alva soon married banker Oliver Hazard Perry Belmont, who died in 1909. See Sylvia D. Hoffert, *Alva Vanderbilt Belmont: Unlikely Champion of Women's Rights* (Bloomington: Indiana University Press, 2012). See also Johanna Neuman, *Gilded Suffragists: The New York Socialites Who Fought for Women's Right to Vote* (New York: New York University Press, 2017).

28. Johnson, "Following the Money," 67.

29. Johnson, *Funding Feminism*, 19.

30. Johnson, *Funding Feminism*, 60.

31. Florence Kelley, socialist and founder and general secretary of the National Consumers' League, became second vice-president of NAWSA in 1906, addressing the convention in Baltimore on child labor. Kelley was also the translator of Friedrich Engels's *The Condition of the Working Class in England* (which her friend Rachel Foster Avery helped get published in the United States in 1887), a pioneer of investigating industrial conditions, an organizer of the National Association for the Advancement of Colored People (NAACP), and a towering figure in protective labor legislation. On Kelley, see the entry in Edward T. James, Janet James, and Paul S. Boyer, eds., *Notable American Women*, Vol. II (Cambridge, MA: Belknap Press of Harvard University Press, 1971), 316–7.

32. Franzen, *Anna Howard Shaw*, 136.

33. Melanie S. Gustafson, *Women and the Republican Party, 1854–1924* (Urbana: University of Illinois Press, 2001), 93.

34. Barbara Sicherman and Carol Hurd Green, eds., *Notable American Women: The Modern Period* (Cambridge, MA: Belknap Press of Harvard University Press, 1980), 566.

Suffragists as Model Mothers

Elizabeth Cady Stanton, here with her daughter, Harriot, was proud of her skills as a parent and happy to share her advice on child-rearing. This daguerreotype is an example of the way in which suffragists, attacked as unsexed horrors, were careful to show that they were models of domesticity. (Library of Congress)

Lucy Stone, shown here with her only child, Alice Stone Blackwell, was known for her diminutive stature and her lively round face, which mitigated the radical nature of her message. She ran a large household always full of visitors and relatives and maintained orchards and a kitchen garden to make her homes self-sufficient. (Library of Congress)

Antisuffrage Cartoons

A common theme of antisuffrage cartoons and antisuffrage writing was the horrible consequences of women voting—notably a complete change of roles in the household. In this caricature of a household published in 1909 the wife is leaving to vote, leaving behind her anxious husband in charge of two crying children. Note the picture frame with "Votes for Women" and a ballot paper for the "Hen Party." (Library of Congress)

FEMALE SUFFRAGE.

Wouldn't it put just a little too much power into the hands of Brigham Young, and his tribe?

Votes for women in Utah posed a problem for suffragists and antisuffragists alike. Here the assumption is that Brigham Young would direct Mormon women to support polygamy and they would follow his directives. Religious intolerance mixed with antisuffrage in this cartoon. (Library of Congress)

Campaigning

Women driving the relatively new automobile were a novelty for crowds. Here, in a New York parade, Harriot Stanton Blatch sits in the front, behind her Maggie Murphy, and in the back seat Emma Bagby, and Susan Fitzgerald closest to the camera. (Library of Congress)

In Pennsylvania a suffrage replica of the Liberty Bell was funded by a wealthy suffragist, Katharine Wentworth Ruschenberger. The bell, called the "Justice Bell" had its clapper silenced until women won the vote. During the 1915 campaign it toured sixty-seven counties drumming up votes and was also used in other campaigns. (Library of Congress)

The Rise of Militant Campaigning after 1913

This group of young women marching in 1917 with the purple, white, and gold banners of the Congressional Union/National Woman's Party are striding out with the energy and determination of this last generation of suffrage fighters. (Library of Congress)

The brave women who picketed the White House, starting in early 1917, came out in the depth of winter, in rain and snow and cold. Here, a group of onlookers under the safety of their umbrellas, watch the women marching at the East Gate. (Library of Congress)

Mary Winsor was a suffragist from a Quaker family in Haverford, Pennsylvania. She was arrested and imprisoned a number of times including at Occoquan Workhouse where conditions were harsh and unsanitary. Her banner reads "To Ask Freedom for Women Is Not a Crime. Suffrage Prisoners Should Not Be Treated as Criminals," referring to the request that arrested suffragists be considered political prisoners. (Library of Congress)

The Faces of Generations of Suffragists

Sojourner Truth
Taken 1864

Abolitionist and suffragist, Truth is one of the most widely known black women in American memory, alongside Harriet Tubman. (Library of Congress)

Mary Church Terrell
Taken between 1880–1890

Suffragist leader, founder and first president of the National Association of Colored Women, Terrell believed in racial uplift, fighting discrimination all her life. (Library of Congress)

Crystal Eastman
Taken 1923

Feminist, suffragist, and radical, she represented the "new woman" of the twentieth century. (Library of Congress)

Max Eastman
n.d. probably circa 1909

Appointed secretary of the New York Men's League for Woman Suffrage, Eastman lectured and recruited for woman suffrage across the state, recruiting thousands of men to the cause. (Library of Congress)

Alice Paul
Taken 1919

The driving force behind the new wing of the suffrage movement emerging after 1912, Paul devoted her life to suffrage and women's equality. (Library of Congress)

Jeannette Rankin
Taken 1916

Suffrage organizer and pacifist, Rankin was the first woman elected to the House of Representatives in 1916. She ran as a progressive Republican from Montana. On April 5, 1917, she voted against American entry into World War I. (Library of Congress)

CHAPTER 7

NEW COALITIONS, NEW SUFFRAGISTS, AND NEW TACTICS, 1910–1915

"We shall never get the federal amendment until we get one of these big eastern states . . . New York is our only chance."

Carrie Chapman Catt[1]

"No state was ever carried for suffrage until it was sown ankle deep in leaflets."

Florence Luscomb[2]

The women who led the successful state suffrage campaigns after 1910 were an increasingly diverse set. The contrast between them and the staid middle-class suffragists gathered at a National American Woman Suffrage Association (NAWSA) convention in 1900 is marked. The first generation of suffragists broke barriers to get an education and to enter professions. The twentieth-century suffragists did the same; they flouted convention, questioned old dogma, and fought to be independent. These new suffragists climbed mountains, joined the Socialist Party, and entered partisan politics. Some were wealthy, while others were poor to the point of living on starvation wages. Some were Woman's Christian Temperance Union (WCTU) members, club women, and solid, genteel citizens. Some were Jews, some were black, and some were men. Some broke the barrier of nonpartisanship mandated by NAWSA. The story of this increasing diversity can best be uncovered by examining some of the state-by-state campaigns.

The campaigns for woman suffrage after 1910 also show the increasingly varied nature of publicity and lobbying tactics used, moving from the nineteenth-century sedate gatherings to parades where women on horseback led thousands of marching women, dressed in white with yellow sashes, followed by suffrage men, then with still more suffragists in automobiles or standing on grand floats. When Alice Paul and Lucy Burns organized their parade in 1913, they had models to draw upon. Some historians have focused on Alice Paul's mastery of publicity drawing events and concluded that Paul brought British methods to American campaigns.[3] The evidence of the state campaigns undermines this judgment. Newspapers carried the news of suffrage tactics across the country, especially from California and New York, so that suffragists were able to read about their compatriots and adopt and adapt their strategies and tactics as suited to their own needs. Among the most wealthy women travel to Europe was common. These women learned new suffrage tactics first hand, as did Alice Paul and Lucy Burns.

1910: THE BREEZE BEGINS TO BLOW

Once more, the successes were in the West and not in the East. Significantly, western suffragists now employed both justice and maternalism or expediency arguments. Their wins were also notable for political coalitions and for increased diversity in who was a suffragist. Working-class women, organized labor, socialists, farm groups, and insurgent Progressives joined with suffragists to vote for woman suffrage in triumphant campaigns. Particularly important for these suffrage victories was the surge of reform spirit nationally after 1900 combined with the success of Progressive parties in the West. Progressive reformers were elected to state legislatures, and Progressive parties declared for woman suffrage. Progressive support was a key building block in the alliances that won woman suffrage in Washington in 1910, in California in 1911, and in Illinois in 1913.

WASHINGTON WINS SUFFRAGE AGAIN

Women in Washington state had won and lost suffrage more than once in the 1880s. Impetus gathered again with the new century. In 1910, suffragists mounted a strong campaign and won. This time woman suffrage stuck. The campaign in Washington won even though the suffragists were substantially divided, which is an oddity in the history of state campaigns. The western group relied partly upon the older method, which tried not to stir up opposition from the liquor interests and antisuffragists. The veteran northwestern campaigner Abigail Scott Duniway argued strongly that any connection between temperance and suffrage meant defeat, so to be successful meant avoiding public campaigning and all discussion of prohibition. Persuading legislators one by one (the "still hunt") was the only effective method, in Duniway's opinion. It was also helpful in Washington that little sound came from antisuffragists, and, as luck would have it, the Brewer's Association focused its political work on the Anti-Saloon League and "local option" efforts underway in the same legislative session.[4]

The still-hunt was not the only approach. *Collier's* magazine described the campaign as "a new style of approach." Emma DeVoe, president of the Washington Equal Suffrage League, in an interview predicted that when they won, it would be "a triumph for strictly feminine methods."[5] Dr. Cora Smith Eaton summed up by saying that "despite the masculine use of publicity, it was essentially a womanly campaign." This comment was clear evidence of the ability of suffragists to persuade themselves and those around them that whatever they undertook as suffrage work was "womanly," as Eaton had climbed Mt. Washington and planted a suffrage flag securely at the summit. In the eastern part of the state, women took more direct action, intending to be more militant. May Arkwright Hutton, with money from mine-owning, was an outspoken advocate for taking the battle to the streets and built a strong base in Spokane.[6] Young women joined the new college suffrage leagues which thrived, particularly in Spokane.

Publicity was important but political coalitions were key. Populism had been replaced by Progressivism in Washington state, with the Progressive legislature under Governor Marion Hay passing several major progressive reforms, including direct legislation enabled by initiative and referendum. Woman suffrage and protective labor legislation were viewed as simply more of these progressive reforms. Significant support came from organized labor and farm groups—the Grange and the Farmer's Alliance—because organized labor wanted women's support for an eight-hour workday law.

The labor connection was strongest in eastern Washington. Labor women campaigned for suffrage, using the language of labor, pointing out that women voters could raise wages and support labor's goals.

On election day, suffrage campaigners were delighted with a significant victory of over 52,000 votes for suffrage, and 30,000 against. "Wet" areas of the state provided majorities, and positive urban votes reflected labor strength. The next major suffrage victory, southwards in California, took up the playbook written by Washington and added to it.

THE WESTERN ZEPHYR—CALIFORNIA

National attention was next drawn to California, where there was stronger business and political opposition than had been the case in Washington. California also had a more diverse population to reach, including immigrants from Ireland, Germany, Italy, and other European countries, as well as Chinese, Mexicans, "Californios" descended from the 1848 acquisition of California, and a relatively small African American population. Two cities dominated its politics, San Francisco and Los Angeles, but the rural vote was also be key. Organized labor was also a significant force. A dismal defeat for woman suffrage in 1896 didn't leave an encouraging outlook for any revival.

Woman suffrage faced a deep-pocketed opposition, particularly the Southern Pacific Railroad (which Progressives called the "Octopus"). The railroad paid huge bribes to the Republican Party and controlled its votes, while it also funded city machines.[7] Entrenched Republican Party stalwarts and Democrats were solidly opposed to woman suffrage. In addition, the powerful newspaper publisher, Harrison Gray Otis of the Los Angeles *Times*, a strong antiunion man and supporter of conservative Republicans, maintained continuous strongly worded editorial opposition to woman suffrage. The liquor industry also had a strong grip on the state legislature where men who were "dry" themselves voted "wet." When organized labor supported woman suffrage, it intensified business and industry opposition.

Those suffragists who wanted to remain active after the 1896 defeat turned to the women's club movement and municipal reform. As club women equated politics with corruption and partisanship with masculine party politics, to hold themselves above this kind of politics they labeled their city reform efforts as "civic activism."[8] No matter how much these club women denied it, as municipal reformers, they were embroiled in politics. When they were convinced that they needed more clout, increasing numbers of them became suffragists, thus revitalizing the California suffrage movement.

Politically savvy Lillian Coffin, long-term suffragist and Republican, led the effort to get woman suffrage going again. Urging her fellow suffragists to find support wherever they could, and to ignore party lines, she told them, "work the reform men," wherever they could be found.[9] "The men are doing fairly well in politics, but are not accomplishing as much as we believe is possible even at this day. We want clean government," said Coffin.[10] Suffragists sought and got endorsements from both Republican and Democratic parties, as well as the Socialist Party, Union Labor Party, Prohibition Party, and William Randolph Hearst's Independent League. Endorsements were short of a party plank, but it was a step in the right direction.

In 1908, women, dressed in white, marching two by two, demonstrated at both the Republican and Democratic conventions. The reform Democrats then endorsed woman suffrage. Two hundred women "handsomely gowned and bonneted" wearing white and trailing yellow ribbons marched into the Republican convention but were met with hostility because they were allied with Progressives, and the Republicans were in power. Alliances came with complications.

In 1909, Progressive men made headway with the direct primary law which allowed them to sweep the 1910 elections. Now the Republicans greeted the women effusively as they needed their support and their votes would make a difference to the fate of the party. The Progressive–suffrage alliance had at last become profitable.

In 1896, suffragists had had support from Populists and the Socialist Labor Party. In 1910, suffragists wanted the support of organized labor and working-class women.[11] This trade union–suffragist alliance took time to build and faced substantial hurdles. To start with, women's municipal corruption campaigns were regarded with antagonism by the working-class of both San Francisco and Los Angeles.

Working men and women depended for their jobs and their saloons on the party machine. In San Francisco, the Union Labor Party, with Mayor Eugene Schmitz and city lawyer and boss Abraham "Abe" Ruef, kept themselves in power by seeing to the needs of Irish, German, and Italian communities. Elite suffragists of the California Club in San Francisco had not only supported corruption trials against Ruef and Schmitz, but they had also championed the raising of saloon license fees. The places where men gathered for politics and sociability were their saloons. In a city where there may have been one saloon for every fifty people, any temperance reform pitted working men against reformers. Suffragists who wanted working men's votes had already attacked their working-class social and cultural life. These contradictions were only realized by a few suffragists.[12]

Two circumstances mitigated this class blindness. First, there were suffragists who were socialists with ties to labor. Some elite women who had joined the suffrage movement while in college became socialists. Heiress Maud Younger moved on from life in San Francisco's high society and now was renowned as the socialist "millionaire waitress." Younger, on the way to Europe for her yearly summer vacation, stopped in New York at a settlement house and left six years later as a determined activist. Women like Younger proved useful in building a (rather shaky) bridge to working-class women.

Second, California had a greater number of women in the workforce than other states, and many of these women were trade unionists. Working women were recruited to the Knights of Labor in the 1880s, and in the twentieth century, the San Francisco Labor Council recruited women working in restaurants, laundries, and factories. In 1910, over 7 percent of the city's wage-earning women belonged to trade unions, while the national average was a tiny 1.5 percent. Organized labor understood that women needed the vote to improve working hours, conditions, and wages.

As a result, a short-lived cross-class suffrage alliance emerged in San Francisco. Lillian Coffin founded the San Francisco Equal Suffrage League in 1906 for both working-class men and women. Two members, long-term suffragist Mary McHenry Keith and socialist Maud Younger, together wrestled an endorsement in 1906 from the Union Labor Party and the Californian Federation of Labor using their working-class connections. Sadly, but perhaps not expectedly, class conflict soon blew up the alliance.

When class tensions arose over union-busting, suffragists sided with the bosses. In May of 1907, five hundred women telephone operators and fifteen hundred streetcar operators went on strike and the embryonic suffrage alliance cracked. Middle-class suffragists crossed the picket lines even knowing that hired thugs had fought with picketers and that two people had died during violent confrontations. Not surprisingly, working-class women could not understand or forgive this lack of solidarity. Nor could middle-class and elite women understand why this was so. Working-class women in San Francisco formed their own suffrage group, the Wage Earners Suffrage League (WESL) in September 1908. The WESL grew into several chapters in the Bay area and one chapter in Los Angeles by 1911. Some contact with the middle- and upper-class suffrage organizations continued because Louise LaRue of the waitresses' union, while believing that her union could not rely on middle-class and elite women, still worked with them.

Even so, in 1911, many prominent trade unionists stood with the suffrage movement, including the head of the Coast Seaman's Union, the president of the Labor Council, and the state Labor Commissioner. In addition, the editor of the labor newspaper the *Labor Clarion*, whose wife was also a strong suffragist, provided vital press support.

Lillian Coffin was ready for more direct action. Coffin was the model of the elite suffragist—described by the Los Angeles *Herald* as "vivacious, keen of wit, and a brilliant speaker . . . who doesn't scorn beautiful and becoming raiment."[13] Yet, Coffin collected a broad swath of California suffragists who were ready to take to the streets, parks, and any public space to talk about suffrage. Respectable women who would once have rejected the idea of attending a public lecture now rode on a float in a spectacular suffrage parade, or drove in a newfangled automobile across the state, stopping to give speeches while standing on the seat to be seen by the gathering crowds. Because automobiles were still the purview of the well-off, women driving attracted attention.

Others were more hesitant. Elizabeth Gerberding of San Francisco broke with Coffin and formed her own suffrage league, committed to more ladylike methods of traditional suffrage campaigns. Public spaces were usual forums for men. The public man was associated with civic virtue, observes historian Linda Lumsden, and women in public spaces were associated with sexual license and with prostitution.[14] Yet, with each state campaign, fewer and fewer suffragists feared opprobrium from campaigning in public.

The state legislature passed bills to allow for a state referendum on October 10, 1911. In 1911, suffragists went to factory gates, to the waterfront, and to wherever people worked and gathered, and spoke from their perch on boxes distributing campaign literature in working-class areas. Los Angeles had restraints on public campaigning which were intended to limit labor organizing. When they could not make speeches, they sang. When one policeman tried to stop one suffragist from speaking, she read the pamphlet to him, very slowly. He finally gave up, sat down, and just pleaded with the woman to get a permit next time. Two women ascended in a balloon and threw out yellow suffrage literature which landed like "golden snow" on the baseball stadium nearby. Women canvassed in their own neighborhoods going door to door; they put up posters and paid for billboards, electric signs, and other signs in every corner of the cities—store windows, office windows, ballparks, the ferry dock. Suffragists got merchandizers to advertise suffrage, and they sold their own souvenirs and small items. Using the new technologies available, artists created striking posters in bright suffrage colors. They made slides for the "stereopticon" and made suffrage movies. As with all post-1910 suffrage campaigns, they used the press and flooded newspapers with articles and press releases.

Victory depended upon reaching every corner of the state and every group of voters. Suffragists reached out to urban working-class voters, black voters, immigrant and ethnic voters, to Catholics and Protestants, to Mexicans and "Californios" whose families had been in California when it was ceded by Mexico in 1848. Over fifty thousand leaflets were printed in Spanish. African American women had created their own suffrage associations, particularly where their numbers were more substantial in Oakland and Los Angeles. College women translated suffrage material into Greek, Portuguese, French, German, Swedish, Chinese, and other languages. Chinese voters who were for women voting were generally supporters of Sun Yat-sen in China whose revolutionary forces supported women suffrage. Women also successfully courted the vote of Chinese American businessmen. In this campaign, white, native-born suffragists muted their animosity toward Chinese labor in favor of winning the campaign. Suffragists sought support from religious leaders and churches and won significant support; Rabbi Myers of Los Angeles was a strong advocate, as was Catholic Archbishop Riordan who set his priests free to make individual decisions on woman suffrage, which was a major achievement.

The suffrage campaign came to an end with a great splash in San Francisco with speeches in Union Square by Rabbi Meyers, Berkeley's socialist mayor, and visiting suffragist leaders. Nearly ten thousand people flocked into Union Square, stopping traffic for blocks around while world-famous opera singer, soprano Lillian Nordica, standing in a flower-strewn automobile, brought the event to a close singing the "Star Spangled Banner."

The first returns came in from urban areas; as a result, the newspapers reported a defeat early next morning only to have to reverse their headlines as the day dragged on and rural and small town results trickled in. Victory came with a slim margin of 3,587 votes. The final triumph came from the rural vote, from farmers, miners, socialists, and from the progressive/organized labor coalition. California women could now vote and did so, affecting city and state elections. Los Angeles women helped elect a reform mayor in 1911 proving correct those who thought that a Progressive alliance would be productive of reform. The California election was a turning point as it was the first state to win suffrage that contained a relatively large and diversified population.

SUFFRAGE SWEEPS THE FAR WEST AND STARTS ITS EASTERN MOVEMENT

In 1912, three states passed woman suffrage hard on the heels of the California success. Arizona and Oregon used the new initiative and referendum legislation so that they did not have to win party support to get a referendum but could bypass the state legislature. Women suffrage was debated during Arizona's state constitution convention in 1910, but Governor Alexander Brodie, who had vetoed suffrage in 1903, again opposed woman suffrage. Using the power of initiative and referendum legislation, women themselves introduced legislation, and Arizona voted for woman suffrage in November 1912.

In Oregon, suffrage victory was also brought about by the passage of initiative and referendum. Woman suffrage forces used the initiative every two years from 1902 until they finally succeeded. In 1912, the women mounted a campaign appealing to state pride pointing out to voters that Oregon was now surrounded by suffrage states. Coalition building was again central to the win. Men's suffrage leagues, a Chinese American suffrage league, and an African American league were among the mix. With the successful 1912 vote, not all women were enfranchised; first-generation Asian Americans were prevented from becoming naturalized citizens, while Native American women, except those married to white men, were also ineligible.

In 1913, the Alaska Territory voted in woman suffrage using, as other territories had done, the fact that the numbers of legislators who needed to be persuaded were small in number. Again, as with Arizona, not all women could vote; the 1913 legislation prevented indigenous women from voting. In 1915, the Alaska Territorial Legislature gave indigenous women the right to vote if they gave up tribal customs—in the tradition of the Dawes Act of 1887 and other assimilation efforts.

ILLINOIS

Of more national significance was the Illinois victory in 1913. Catherine Waugh McCulloch, a lawyer and suffragist, knowing that amendment legislation would not pass the state legislature, came up with the innovative solution of "presidential suffrage" that eventually would be employed in many states where referenda had failed. McCulloch proposed a bill in 1893 that provided for women voting in presidential and state elections that were not constitutionally limited to male voters. For twenty years in a row, this legislation was doggedly introduced and failed at each session.

Then, at last, in 1913, the "Illinois idea" succeeded. Several leading suffragists had grown up in political families and knew how to work in the state legislature. The great Republican politician Mark Hanna's daughter, Ruth Hanna McCormick, with her young baby in tow, moved to Springfield to take charge of lobbying. Both Progressives and Democrats were lobbied by those who knew them well and knew how to approach them. In Springfield, the suffrage lobby was put to the test when the Speaker of the House, a young Democrat named William McKinley, told state suffrage president Grace Wilbur Trout that he would not introduce the suffrage bill unless he was convinced it would succeed. Trout set her network in action. McKinley spent the weekend in Chicago where every fifteen minutes his phone rang, day and night, at home and in his office, with both men and women suffragists at the end of the line. When he returned to Springfield, his office was filled with telegrams and messages of support. McKinley gave in.

On June 11, Grace Trout stood at the door of the Illinois House Chambers, counted heads, and sent supporters to round up absent prosuffrage men. All the first-term Progressives and three Socialist members voted for the bill, which passed handily with an 85 to 58 vote. The legislation then survived attacks on its constitutionality, winning in the state Supreme Court. The "Presidential and Municipal Voting Act" made Illinois the first state east of the Mississippi to pass woman suffrage, and its twenty-nine electoral votes were brought into the woman suffrage camp.[15] Chicago was the most populous midwestern city that had woman suffrage. The balance of electoral votes had swung toward suffrage.

In 1914, two more states won suffrage—Nevada and Montana. In Montana, NAWSA organizer Jeannette Rankin led the fight, becoming a national leader who was seated in 1917 as the first woman in the U.S. House of Representatives. Women now voted in fourteen states. Presidential hopefuls and those running for U.S. Congress in suffrage states began to consider women's votes in their political calculus. The South remained as obdurate as ever, fearing that changing anything about suffrage might allow black women to vote. The best option in the minds of NAWSA leaders was now to work for suffrage in the largely populated northeastern and Mid-Atlantic states.

NEW YORK—THE PIVOTAL STATE?

Carrie Chapman Catt believed that New York was pivotal. Harriot Stanton Blatch was also certain that New York was the state that would turn the national tide. The streets of New York City, the halls of the Capitol building in Albany, and the rural roads of upstate New York had been the haunts of suffragists from the start of the organized movement. As in other states, despite this heritage, suffrage work had diminished to a tiny state suffrage association. In the 1890s, there was some stirring of suffrage action after a long period of quiescence. In 1894 women showed their political muscle through a reform organization called the Municipal League. The Lexow Committee report, commissioned by the New York City Police Department, exposed Tammany Hall's deep ties to police corruption. The Municipal League worked with a coalition of male Progressives who envisioned a city government run by educated professionals, as well as Republicans who were shut out of city government, and anti-Tammany Hall Democrats. This reform coalition defeated Tammany Hall candidates for mayor in 1894 and fought elections after that, winning some and losing others. Women in New York city had effectively exercised political muscle.

Tammany Hall was a strong enemy. Though it did run a corrupt machine, it was also popular with those who were protected by, or benefited from, its regime; extensive patronage meant jobs as one of every eight voters in the city was a city employee, and immigrants were given jobs on public works projects. An informal welfare system gave some support to those in distress. Tammany Hall was also adept at outflanking reformers by embracing some of them into the Tammany fold and then running them against Progressives.

Municipal League women did not see themselves as politicians, but their actions were intensely political by any definition of politics. These women redefined the boundaries of what constituted "politics" in their mind, by creating a line between "political maneuvering for power" and nonpartisan reform coalitions. Their actions belied this philosophical hairsplitting, as they stumped for particular candidates, educated voters on the streets and in rented halls, and published election material, all with the intention of having an impact on the elections.

After the 1901 election a variety of suffrage groups, with Municipal League women as members, grew in New York City. After Anthony's death Harriot Blatch felt she could return to the suffrage cause and be no longer in danger of taking up tactics which Anthony did not endorse. Disdaining NAWSA organizations, she gathered a group of forty women in a "dingy little room" off the Bowery in January of 1907 and plotted. "We all believed that suffrage propaganda must be made dramatic, that suffrage workers must be politically minded. We saw the need of drawing industrial women into the suffrage campaign and recognized that these women needed to be brought into contact, not with women of leisure, but with business and professional women who were also out in the world earning their living."[16] The Equality League of Self-Supporting Women (Equality League) sprang into action. Two hundred women attended the first meeting, including doctors, lawyers, and garment workers. The Equality League was open to anyone who earned their own living, women from trade unions as well as professional women. But working-class women, as it turned out, were more difficult to recruit than professional women, somewhat to Blatch's surprise.

Two capable and influential union women did join. Leonora O'Reilly and Rose Schneiderman were initially hopeful for the new organization as a bridge between working-class women and traditional middle-class suffragists. Leonora O'Reilly was a founder of the National Consumers' League and an experienced trade unionist in the garment industry. Rose Schneiderman, from the Cap and Hat Makers Union, was red-haired, tiny in stature at four feet and nine inches, a fiery socialist, and a compelling labor speaker. Both women played central roles in recruiting working-class women. Harriot Blatch took up an offer to lecture by English suffragette Anne Cobden-Sanderson in December 1907 at the Cooper Union. Cobden-Sanderson was the daughter of famous radical politician Richard Cobden and was a member of the Women's Social and Political Union who had gone to prison for the cause. The Equality League worked hard to bring in working women, and the Cooper Union was thronged with trade unionists and suffragists. The success of the meeting meant that the Equality League was by 1908 a major influence on New York suffragism. Blatch planned to employ the tactics of outdoor campaigning she learned in England.

OPEN-AIR CAMPAIGNING

Harriot Stanton Blatch claimed to invent open-air campaigning in New York in 1908, tracing her efforts to the campaign tactics she learned in Britain. But the roots of widespread use of open-air suffrage work were more tangled. One of the first New Yorkers to take to the streets was Maud Malone, the daughter of an Irish home-rule supporter, a doctor in Brooklyn, who as a radical headed an antipoverty league and took his children to political rallies at Cooper Union. Like so many other suffragists, Maud Malone absorbed the knowledge of politics and her taste for social justice at home.[17] In 1904, as she walked every day to work, on the way she passed Salvation Army speakers, socialists, and trade unionists holding forth on street corners. Here, she thought, was a cheap way to get recruits.

Malone already had her own network of women and her own suffrage club, the Harlem Equal Rights League, but when she pleaded for women to join her on street corners, there was little enthusiasm. Eventually, a few plucky members agreed to join her on Madison Square. Late in 1907, Malone put a notice in the *New York Times*, giving notice of the planned outdoor meeting. Almost at the same time, Bettina Boorman Wells, an English suffragist, created an organization "American

Suffragettes," making clear with the name her intention that this organization would be inspired by British methods.[18] The two women began
to work together. Outdoor meetings in Madison Square Park began in
December, initially with only Malone, Bettina Boorman Wells, and
an unidentified man as speakers, but even this small band managed to
gather hundreds of signatures and the notice of reporters. Malone was
excited to see more women join her on the stump, and, as she recalled,
others started "little street meetings all around the rim of the crowd.
Sometimes I've left half a dozen orators all talking woman suffrage, for or
against. That's six meetings a night without a hall rent."[19] Malone was
particularly good as a speaker, cheerfully engaging the crowd who yelled
questions and earning the approval of reporters on the scene. Suffragists in New York were becoming more adventuresome, ready to abandon
propriety for new tactics. Harriot Blatch added her force to the work of
Malone and Wells.

Carrie Chapman Catt returned to New York in 1908, intent on bringing together the numerous city suffrage organizations. A meeting of the
Interurban Woman Suffrage Council was called, and a plan hatched for
a new, more tightly organized group. On October 29, 1909, at Carnegie
Hall, 804 delegates gathered and approved setting up new headquarters
and the publication of a new journal, the Woman Voter, with Mary Beard
as editor. The New York City Woman Suffrage Party, usually known just
as the Woman Suffrage Party (WSP), implemented Catt's goal to create a
politically savvy, hierarchical political machine that functioned as well as
Tammany Hall.

The WSP relied upon settlement houses like Henry Street and Greenwich House to reach immigrant neighborhoods. The WSP held rallies
where literature was distributed in Yiddish and Italian. Women canvassed
across the city, not always successfully; in Hell's Kitchen, three women
were chased by "thugs" throwing garbage. The police just stood by and
watched. One phone call to the police commissioner from influential
and very wealthy suffragist James Lees Laidlaw was sufficient to provide
police protection for suffrage women. This suffrage work began just as
upper-class and working-class women came together in a new cross-class
coalition, the Women's Trade Union League, modeled on similar British
efforts. The New York Women's Trade Union League (NYWTUL) was
founded in 1903, about the same time as the national organization.[20] The

WTUL grew into a national organization with substantial influence and connections to the labor movement.

WTUL's first goal was to recruit working women to trade unionism. Its second goal was to recruit working women to suffrage. Wealthy, college-educated reformers called "allies" intended to work *alongside* working-class women rather than the usual oversight model of previous efforts at coalitions. Middle- and upper-class reformers came to the WTUL from settlement houses, charity organizations, the Consumers' League, the Municipal League, and the YWCA.[21] Harriot Stanton Blatch was an early ally who was on the executive council from 1906 to 1909. Despite class tensions, over time, the WTUL provided a home for trade union women when they became disillusioned with the male-dominated labor movement's failure to organize women.

THE UPRISING OF THE TWENTY THOUSAND

The Lower East Side of New York was filled with young women who needed to work to survive. Jewish and Italian immigrant women were heavily recruited for the garment trades where conditions were harsh and wages were minimal. Pauline Newman came from Lithuania as a child in 1901 and was sent to work in the Triangle Shirtwaist factory clipping hanging threads from finished blouses. She worked from 7.30 am until 9.00 pm in the busy season for a paltry wage. With wages that were barely enough to let a family survive, tensions rose between owners, contractors, and workers. These tensions broke into outright warfare in 1909.

In late July, one of the shirtwaist factories cut piece rates and tried to negotiate even lower contracts. Two hundred workers walked out on strike at the Rosen Brothers factory starting the chain of strikes that was called the "Uprising of the Twenty Thousand"—the largest strike of women ever. Strikers endured weeks on the picket lines, and in November, a general strike was called in support. Thousands of workers went on strike. Eighty percent of the women were Jewish, but there were also Italian and native-born Americans. For eleven hard weeks, the strike dragged on.

Women on the picket lines were beaten, arrested, and jailed. One worker, Clara Lemlich, was so badly beaten that she was hospitalized. Judges who presided over arrests of strikers were almost universally in sympathy with the owners. Because picketing was legal, women were arrested on charges of vagrancy, solicitation, disorderly conduct, and assault. The WTUL launched investigations of police abuse and the hiring of strike-breakers and brought the force of its "allies" to the fight. These women were suffragists.

On November 4, Mary Dreier, president of the New York WTUL, asked that allies walk the picket lines. Suffragists who were not WTUL members joined these allies, turning out in large numbers. In doing so, they caused the tide of public opinion to turn when they were arrested on the picket lines with young women workers. The presence of middle- and upper-class women joining the strikers "was curiously disconcerting to the manufacturers," wrote Helen Marot.[22] When WTUL president Mary Dreier herself was arrested and taken to Mercer Street Station, the police hastily released her the moment they realized who she was. Too late, it turned out, as the press was already on the story. The publicity surrounding Dreier's arrest spurred even more support. The WTUL raised over $50,000 for legal aid, bail, and fines for the strikers and organized marches and rallies. WTUL publicity urged "let us stop talking about sisterhood and MAKE SISTERHOOD A FACT!"[23] Suffragists raised money, walked the picket line, sat in night court, bailed out strikers, and paid fines.

The longer the strike went, the more workers joined the WTUL, and believed they needed the power of the vote. Strikers began to wear suffrage buttons on the picket line. The woman's suffrage movement had dallied with labor issues and working-class women's concerns in the nineteenth century, but not until the WTUL entered the picture was there "any sustained interaction between working-class activists and the suffrage movement," writes historian Robin Miller Jacoby. The central role the WTUL played in the garment workers strikes in New York forged a strong link between the suffrage movement and working women.[24] Middle- and upper-class suffragists who became involved learned much about women's exploitation in the garment trades.

Some of the women on the picket line and in the courthouses were "new women," believers in radical political causes and strong feminists from Greenwich Village who represented a younger generation of suffragists. Two lawyers, Crystal Eastman and Inez Milholland, both from Greenwich Village, attended night court and wrote reports on the harsh penalties meted out. Night court was deliberately chosen as a venue because it was normally the place where prostitutes were arraigned. WTUL leader and lawyer Ida Rauh led women in a deputation to the mayor to protest police brutality. Rauh also gave legal assistance to arrested pickets. Heiress Carola Woerishoffer organized a WTUL news bureau to spread information on strikers' grievances and goals. When one judge set bail high enough to prevent the strikers from leaving jail, she put up property valued at $75,000 to secure the women's freedom. Woerishoffer also gave $10,000 for a permanent WTUL strike council.[25] These women represented a new kind of suffragist.

Various efforts were made to raise funds from club women and wealthy suffragists. Anne Morgan, daughter of J.P. Morgan, and Alva Belmont sponsored a fundraising dinner at the Colony Club which raised $1,300 to add to the $1,400 raised at a dinner in Belmont's own house. Feeling a little like animals in a zoo, strikers met with wealthy women in their homes and clubs. Alva Belmont loaned her car to the WTUL to use to publicize the strike. With her lawyer, she went into night court to provide bail for picketers who were being arraigned.[26] Outside Jefferson Market Courthouse, Belmont gave a speech calling for woman suffrage as a means of influencing police, judges, and juries. Belmont also hired the huge Hippodrome for a mass rally for December 5 and paid for another at Cooper Union. It was not just young radicals who made a difference but also wealthy women.

Gradually, some shops made agreements, and the women's strikes ended, bit by bit. Then early in 1911, the garment workers were again in the news, this time with a disaster that drew the attention of the nation. Frances Perkins, secretary of the Consumer's League, was having tea with a friend on the balmy Saturday afternoon of March 25. Both women heard a commotion and went outside. They followed gathering crowds to nearby Washington Square and saw, with dismay, smoke billowing out of the Asch Building whose upper floors were occupied by the Triangle Shirtwaist factory.[27] Word spread quickly through the East Side and shocked crowds gathered, watching in horror as workers leaped to their deaths from windows on the eighth, ninth, and tenth floors. The fire killed 123 women and twenty-three men; it was the worst industrial disaster in the nation's history. The Triangle Factory was already notorious as one of the most obdurate of the employers in earlier strikes.

The Triangle fire served as further notice, if any was needed, that working-class women must organize and need the vote. Protective legislation and an investigation of the garment industry followed the fire, but for the suffrage movement, the "Uprising of the Twenty Thousand" and the Triangle Shirtwaist fire marked the movement of industrial workers into the suffrage movement. The strikes also created the moment when wealthier women from across a great class divide began to understand the plight of working women, and a moment when both sides overcame their assumptions about each other.

THE SUFFRAGE CAMPAIGNS OF THE NEW COALITIONS OF SUFFRAGISTS

At the height of the strikes in 1909, Harriot Blatch was forced to choose between wealthy women and the WTUL. She was censored for having nonunion women employed in the offices of the Equality League, as well as for supporting an antisocialist mediator. The alliance between the Equality League and the WTUL ended. In reaction, the WTUL, with Rose Schneiderman and Leonora O'Reilly, created a separate working class suffrage organization, under the auspices of the WTUL—the Wage Earners' Suffrage League, in 1912.

Blatch now sought and got support from wealthy women to fund her shifting interests away from workers to political action in Albany. The rejection of a working-class alliance was made formal with a change of name. In November 1910, the League became the Women's Political Union (WPU). Nora Blatch—Harriot's daughter and Elizabeth Cady Stanton's granddaughter—explained the change of name this way: "We wanted to be absolutely democratic, so we decided not to discriminate against the leisure classes."[28] In 1910, Blatch established the WPU presence in Albany with money from Katherine Mackay that funded a staffed office that would remain for the whole of the legislative session. She also hired a professional lobbyist, Hattie Graham, who created a file on each legislator.

Blatch managed to get an Assembly vote—for the first time in fifteen years. Blatch also exerted her political strength on recalcitrant legislators. Artemus Ward, an antisuffrage member of the Judiciary Committee, felt the full force of the WPU's efforts to unseat him. Torchlight parades, open-air meetings, instructions on how to split a ticket, all combined to erode Ward's support. His margin of victory was reduced to only a few hundred votes. Ward was outraged, and Albany took note. But even so, the suffrage amendment went down in both chambers in 1910. Still, Blatch had shown her growing political skills.

When Carrie Catt returned to New York in late 1912, the WSP, led by Mary Beard and Harriet Laidlaw, had grown stronger and developed its publicity gathering tactics. Catt promptly installed her own choice of chairman for the city, Mary Garret Hay, and turned herself to organizing the state. In November 1913, the WSP of New York City, the College Equal Suffrage League, Katherine Mackay's Equal Franchise Society, the New York State Suffrage Association, and a newer element, the Men's League for Woman Suffrage, all joined under an umbrella lobbying group, the Empire State Campaign Committee (ESCC). The New York State Suffrage Association had 450 branches, showing significant strength. New York's NAWSA suffrage organizations were divided into twelve state districts, with assembly districts and election districts under these districts. In New York state, Catt experimented with the kind of organization that she would later implement successfully nationwide.

The year 1912 was pivotal politically for the country as Republican machines were confronted with Democratic wins. The Progressive Party in New York state endorsed woman suffrage. There probably was a connection between this and the willingness of both Republicans and Democrats in Albany to agree to a referendum, thus avoiding any one legislator having to make their suffrage stance public. Tammany boss Charles Murphy agreed to support suffrage, which was an important shift in position, driven perhaps by the need to outflank Progressives. With a new Democratic governor and both Republicans and Democrats backing the referendum, enabling legislation passed. Senate Democratic leader, Robert Wagner, announced that he was "just as much opposed to woman suffrage as he ever had been," but he introduced the Wagner–Goldberg woman suffrage bill because the party had made a pledge. Elon R. Brown, Republican Senatorial leader conceded that he was "not willing to live the rest of my life in antagonism to women, I'd rather have suffrage than war."[29] On January 23, 1913, the Senate passed the amendment 40–2 and the Assembly 128–5. In early 1915, the suffrage bill passed again, and a referendum was set up for the end of the year.

The suffrage coalitions owed much to the nature of New York society between 1910 and World War I. New York was, at the turn of the century, awash in cultural upheaval, as artists, architects, writers, and musicians rejected the values and interests of the nineteenth century. Socialists and communists gathered in New York, and trade unionists found the concentration of workers in lower Manhattan factories ripe for organization. Native-born men and women searching for a community of free thinkers converged on New York and encountered European immigrants with alternative philosophies for the first time. New York was a magnet for nonconformists and free spirits. The general atmosphere in these circles was one of hope for a utopian world and enthusiasm for deep change. From this heady cultural, economic, and political atmosphere came a new mix of suffragists

GREENWICH VILLAGE

Many writers have used the word "feminist" to describe suffragists and activist women in the nineteenth century, but as historian Nancy Cott has shown, the word was not in use in the nineteenth century, and the general use of the label feminist did not happen until 1913 in the United States.[30] Once it was in common use, to describe a young woman as a feminist or a "new woman" was to describe someone who rejected tradition, who gloried in new art and new ideas, and who intended to live an independent life. The symbol of this unconventional woman was Heterodoxy Club, founded by suffragist Mary Jenney Howe in 1912. The club, limited to forty members, had as its only stipulation for membership that a woman must "not be orthodox in her opinions."[31] Fauvism, Cubism, the work of Picasso and Matisse were all grist for the mill for the lively lectures and discussions at the Heterodoxy Club. So too were free love, trial marriage, birth control, socialism, and women's struggle for independence to develop their own paths in life, unhampered by the constraints that nineteenth-century women had placed upon them. Heterodoxy members pushed at the boundaries of existing mores and gender roles as they discussed ideas that would have shocked suffragist club women. These "new women" of the modern age expanded the diversity of the New York suffrage movement and were in stark contrast to the more conservative women of the movement upstate.

THE MEN'S LEAGUE FOR WOMAN SUFFRAGE

New York produced an innovation in the suffrage movement. Men had been necessary allies for women from the first campaigns in Wyoming.

But in New York grew a new and politically and economically influential set of suffragists who established a men's suffrage organization in New
York City in 1909. The influence of abolitionist and suffragist William
Lloyd Garrison was felt through two generations to his grandson, Oswald
Garrison Villard, whose idea began the Men's League for Woman Suffrage. Oswald Garrison Villard, with substantial family wealth and as a
publisher of two newspapers, the *New York Evening Post* and the *Nation*,
was in a prime position to influence opinion in New York.[32] Villard told
Shaw that it was time to start a men's suffrage league along the lines of
those emerging in Europe. Anna Shaw had wanted this for some years
and was delighted to agree when it became clear that what Villard envisioned would not conflict with women's control in existing organizations.
Villard's friend, the influential Rabbi Stephen Wise, agreed that he was
"prepared to share the ignominy" of belonging to a Men's League.[33] Villard and Wise believed that men needed the cover of numbers to endure
the inevitable scorn and mocking that would come with being a public
supporter of woman suffrage.

The Men's League for Woman Suffrage quickly became reality with the
hiring of Max Eastman. Eastman had a fellowship at Columbia University working with suffragist and philosopher John Dewey but needed to
make more money. A dashing and good-looking twenty-seven-year-old,
Max Eastman lived with his feminist sister Crystal in Greenwich Village. Like so many other men in the suffrage movement, Eastman's family were reformers and suffragists. Max Eastman proved invaluable to the
Men's League. He disarmed opponents with his carefully learned ability to
give well-honed speeches. When Eastman spoke on suffrage in Troy, the
reporters expected a "long haired individual" but were confronted with a
"tall, broad-shouldered, wholesome youth with a keen mind, a winning
personality, and the gift of speech."[34] Max Eastman, in the same way that
female suffragists shook off the toxic stereotypes with immaculate and
fashionable clothing, presented himself as an ordinary young man from a
good family.

The first official meeting of The Men's League for Woman Suffrage of
the State of New York was held at the prestigious men's City Club late
in the afternoon of November 29, 1909. The newspapers made much of
the thousands of dollars pledged to the League and of the political influence of those gathered that afternoon. True to Villard and Wise's goals,

these men represented influential, wealthy men of substance and reputation. In November 1909, the Men's League took on state legislators.
The Men's League assisted in mass meetings in all twenty-six districts represented by men on the Joint Judiciary Committee. In December 1909,
George Peabody met with Governor Charles Evans Hughes (already Peabody's friend) along with the state woman suffrage president, Ella Crossett,
and leaders of the state Grange and the WCTU. They wanted Hughes to
move the suffrage legislation out of the committee.

Between 1910 and 1912, the League sent men to over forty meetings
and helped establish eighteen other leagues in other states. James Lees
Laidlaw went with Harriot Blatch on two speaking tours across the country. Some were surprised that a man of Laidlaw's standing was involved
with the Men's League. Laidlaw was a financier, on the board of directors of what would become Standard and Poors, with a family name that
brought high social standing. It was exactly these men of his influence
who opened doors and raised money. By 1915, there were Men's Leagues
across the country, which were particularly influential with chambers of
commerce and fraternal organizations in the corridors of power in state
legislatures and in Washington.

The biggest test of men's devotion to the cause came when the Men's
League marched in 1911 and suffered yells and insults all the length of the
parade. Peabody, Herbert Parsons of J.P. Morgan, and the painter William
Glackens had defrayed the huge costs of designing and producing banners.
On May 7, men marched with women forty blocks down Fifth Avenue
from 57th to 17th Street to Union Square. Banker James Lees Laidlaw,
Frederick Nathan, and John Dewey led the men's section. Once the
crowd saw the over one hundred men, they erupted with hoots, jeers, and
what Rabbi Wise later described as "what now sounds like rather amusing
jabs that questioned our masculinity." Charles Strong later recalled his
admiration for James Lees Laidlaw who maintained his dignity with "calm
indifference" marching with his eyes front as members of his own clubs
looked on with disdain at the spectacle. Oswald Villard remembered the
"scoffing friends" looking out the windows of the University Club at 54th
Street where the men got into formation for the march. He never forgot
the "boos, hisses and ridicule" that kept up the whole length of the march
"without a moment's cessation."[35] The whistles, derisive taunts, and yells
continued for the men during the entire parade. Their stoicism was hailed

by the grateful women who gathered in Union Square to celebrate at the end of the march.

1915 REFERENDUM CAMPAIGN

The suffrage movement in New York state was in 1915 the most diverse of all the state movements. At one level, this diversity is not surprising given that New York City housed so many diverse immigrant populations, but the woman suffrage movement managed to recruit women across class, race, ethnicity, religious divides more than other industrial cities like Chicago or Philadelphia. The New York suffrage movement at the point of the 1915 referendum reflected the way that the national movement was becoming a genuinely mass movement.

The ESCC under Carrie Catt united all the disparate groups of suffragists: the Men's League, the WSP, the state association, Belmont's Political Equality League, Jewish women from uptown and the Lower East Side, working women connected with the WTUL, African American women, socialists, radical feminists, progressive reformers, settlement house inhabitants and workers from their suffrage clubs, wealthy society women labeled the "mink brigade," Catholic women, Protestant women, Italian, Irish, and Eastern European immigrants, WCTU women, long-term suffragists, and a new younger generation of radical suffragists. Harriot Blatch's WPU refused to unite under the ESCC umbrella but carried out its own campaign with mostly wealthy and professional women or businesswomen.

The Lower East Side campaign was particularly active, revealing substantial immigrant and working-class support. Jewish residents were canvassed and were particularly supportive of the movement. The *American Hebrew* newspaper concluded that this was expected, "when one bears in mind the fierce longing for democracy which dwells in the hearts of Jews of Russia." Meyer London said at a rally "the last persons to oppose granting suffrage . . . should be the foreign-born men who had fled the political oppression of their own countries." Traveling teams of suffrage workers set up where they could attract a crowd and began a "voiceless speech" with placards in Yiddish on a big easel. Torchlight parades brought families onto the streets. Suffrage workers gave yellow caps and yellow lanterns to anyone who would join in. "Children and dogs swarmed under foot, shrieking with joy at the lights and the bands, and it was all so lively and appealing that even tired housewives and young working girls fell in to help carry the banners," recalled one suffrage worker.[36]

The Socialist Party internationally and in New York City had debated at length over the relative importance of woman suffrage campaigning versus effort put into the wider revolution. Historian Mari Jo Buhle sums up this divide saying, "Orthodox Socialists had heretofore treated the woman question as a sentimental fillip upon the main message of the class struggle."[37]

In 1909, the New York Socialist Party voted to begin an aggressive campaign for woman suffrage, opening a small headquarters in Jewish Harlem and expanding into the Lower East Side. Socialists also campaigned in German Yorkville and Italian neighborhoods in Harlem and the Lower East Side. A large number of trade unions beyond the International Ladies' Garment Workers' Union (ILGWU) also came out officially in support in 1915; they included the American Federation of Labor (AFL), the Federation of Labor of New York State, the United Hebrew Trades, the Cigar Makers International Union, and the New York Labor Council.

It is hard to see how any New Yorker could not have been aware that there was a woman suffrage campaign going on. On October 23, the last great parade from Washington Square up Fifth Avenue to 59th Street was so long it ended by moonlight. Despite a bitter wind tearing at their banners, over twenty-five thousand suffragists dressed in yellow, blue, and white marched to the sound of fifty-seven bands. Five thousand men marched with the women. It took three hours for the parade to pass by. Catt thought the crowds watching topped one and a half million. In Madison Square, searchlights, balloons, fireworks, and a symphony orchestra entertained the crowds. The day before the vote suffragists held a twenty-six-hour speaking marathon in Columbus Circle.

On the eve of the 1915 vote, Tammany Hall released its men to vote as they chose, declaring itself neutral on the woman suffrage referendum. All the hoopla, all the hard work and tired feet, and all the politicians lobbied should have made for success, if effort counted. But it did not. The suffrage campaign had failed to reach into the corners of upstate New York and had not racked up enough votes from New York City to balance the upstate opposition. Upstate Republican and Democratic leaders had warned them that the vote would fail in the last days, and it did. Gloom pervaded the women gathered at suffrage headquarters around the state. A total of 553,348 men voted for woman suffrage, but 748,332 voted against. In New York City, no borough provided a majority. Undaunted, and showing her mettle as a leader, Carrie Catt promptly went outside and held a rally to begin the campaign for 1917. She raised $100,000 immediately.

Harriot Blatch reacted with deep and bitter anger. She attacked immigrants and resorted to the kind of elitism that her mother had shown in her turn to "educated suffrage." Harriot Blatch left for Washington, DC, and joined Alice Paul. Blatch's was not the only nativist attack. Some of the ESCC agreed. Lillian Wald, in a letter to the *New York Times*, tried to correct this misapprehension, pointing out that foreign-born voters had been more in favor of suffrage than "Anglo-Saxon naturalized citizens." There were many reasons for failure, but the vote of immigrants was not one of them.

Two years later New York in 1917 finally passed a state constitutional amendment. New York City and particularly the Lower East Side voted for suffrage; upstate did not. The substantial amount of money, greater expertise in campaigning, and renewed vigor in the electioneering upstate helped increase the suffrage vote from that of 1915. A key change was the failure of the antisuffrage women to campaign as hard as they had in 1915 because with the onset of war antisuffrage women turned to war work and the Red Cross. In contrast, suffrage women undertook both war work and suffrage campaigning. New York proved itself the key to the East Coast that Carrie Catt and Harriot Blatch predicted, but in 1917 and not in 1915.

Gloom at failure in 1915 pervaded not just New York but also Massachusetts, Pennsylvania, and New Jersey. The four defeats were a massive blow to the national movement. It was a harsh reminder of the strength of antisuffragist politicians, organized antisuffrage women, the liquor industry, industrial leaders, and the apathy of too many voters. In 1915, it suddenly looked like the suffrage movement was again in the doldrums, which caused a major reassessment of NAWSA leadership.

Each of these three states had different reasons for failure. The four East Coast failures propelled Anna Howard Shaw out of office and Carrie Chapman Catt into office as president of NAWSA. Catt then redirected NAWSA efforts to the federal campaign with a new "Winning Plan." The balance of suffrage work came in Washington, DC, where both Alice Paul and Carrie Catt led their forces for the final five years of the long battle.

NOTES

1. Jacqueline Van Voris, *Carrie Chapman Catt: A Public Life* (New York, NY: Feminist Press, 1996), 129.

2. Caroline Ware, *Why They Marched* (Cambridge, MA: Belknap Press of Harvard University Press, 2019), 209.

3. Christine A. Lunardini, *From Equal Suffrage to Equal Rights: Alice Paul and the National Woman's Party, 1912–1928* (New York: New York University Press, 1986); and Katherine H. Adams and Michael Keene, *Alice Paul and the American Suffrage Campaign* (Urbana: University of Illinois Press, 2008).

4. Rebecca J. Mead, *How the Vote Was Won: Woman Suffrage in the Western United States, 1868–1914* (New York: New York University Press, 2004), 116. Local option was where each town could decide to be "dry" or "wet," meaning that prohibition was a local affair.

5. Suffragists made enormous efforts to erase the characterization of suffragists as masculine, aggressive women who ignored fashion and lacked manners. See Jennifer M. Ross-Nazzal, *Winning the West for Women: The Life of Suffragist Emma Smith DeVoe* (Seattle: University of Washington Press, 2011), 130.

6. May Arkwright Hutton worked as a cook and boarding-house keeper in the mining districts of Idaho, married a locomotive engineer, Levi Hutton, and together they supported miners' organizing. Their wealth was secured by silver mine ownership, particularly the Hercules mines. They moved to Spokane in 1906. She was, therefore, not of the same social standing as the leaders of the Seattle movement. Mead, *How the Vote Was Won*, 106–8.

7. Gayle Ann Gullett, *Becoming Citizens: The Emergence and Development of the California Women's Movement, 1880–1911* (Urbana: University of Illinois Press, 2000), 160.

8. Mead, *How the Vote Was Won*, 20.

9. Mead, *How the Vote Was Won*, 129.

10. Gullett, *Becoming Citizens*, 66–67.

11. In 1907, a suffrage bill had the endorsement of San Francisco's Union Labor Party and the California Federation of Labor. See Susan Englander, "We Want the Ballot for Very Different Reasons," in Robert W. Cherny, Mary Ann Irwin, and Ann Marie Wilson, eds., *California Women and Politics: From the Gold Rush to the Great Depression* (Lincoln: University of Nebraska Press, 2011), 209–36.

12. Susan Englander, *Class Conflict and Class Coalition in the California Woman Suffrage Movement, 1907–1912: The San Francisco Wage Earners' Suffrage League* (Lewiston, NY: Edwin Mellon Press, 1992), 214.

13. Gullett, *Becoming Citizens*, 167.

14. Linda J. Lumsden, *Rampant Women: Suffragists and the Right of Assembly* (Knoxville: University of Tennessee Press, 1997), xix.

15. Grace Wilbur Trout, "Side Lights on Illinois Suffrage History," *Journal of the Illinois State Historical Society* 13, no. 2 (July 1920): 145–79.

16. Harriot Stanton Blatch, *Challenging Years: The Memoirs of Harriot Stanton Blatch* (New York, NY: G.P. Putnam's Sons, 1940), 94.

17. Dan Meharg, "Maud Malone, Suffrage Pioneer Rediscovered," unpublished manuscript (February 2019) in possession of the author.

18. Bettina Boorman Wells is also spelled as Borrman. Ellen Carol DuBois, *Harriot Stanton Blatch and the Winning of Woman Suffrage* (New Haven, CT: Yale University Press, 1999), 101.

19. Meharg, "Maud Malone."

20. Nancy Schrom Dye, *As Equals and As Sisters: Feminism, the Labor Movement, and the Women's Trade Union League of New York* (Columbia: University of Missouri Press, 1980), 40.

21. Nancy Schrom Dye, "Creating a Feminist Alliance: Sisterhood and Class Conflict in the New York Women's Trade Union League, 1903–1914," *Feminist Studies* 2, no. 2/3 (1975): 25.

22. Helen Marot, "A Woman's Strike: An Appreciation of the Shirtwaist Makers of New York," *Proceedings of the Academy of Political Science in the City of New York* 1, no. 1 (October 1910): 119–28.

23. Dye, *As Equals and As Sisters*, 92.

24. Robin Miller Jacoby, "The Women's Trade Union League and American Feminism," *Feminist Studies* 3, no. 1/2 (Autumn 1975): 126–40.

25. Dye, *As Equals and As Sisters*, 45–55, 94.

26. Sylvia D. Hoffert, *Alva Vanderbilt Belmont: Unlikely Champion of Women's Rights* (Bloomington: Indiana University Press, 2012), 78.

27. The Triangle factory was officially the Triangle Waist Factory in 1911, meaning that they made the "shirtwaist" blouses that women wore with a skirt. It is usually referred to as the Triangle Shirtwaist Factory in literature. I use that common usage. See David Von Drehle, *Triangle: The Fire That Changed America* (New York, NY: Grove Press, 2003).

28. DuBois, *Harriot Stanton Blatch*, 120.

29. Ronald Schaffer, "The New York City Woman Suffrage Party, 1909–1919," *New York History* 43, no. 3 (July 1962): 280.

30. Nancy F. Cott, *The Grounding of Modern Feminism* (New Haven, CT: Yale University Press, 1987), 1–5.

31. Susan Goodier and Karen Pastorello, *Women Will Vote: Winning Suffrage in New York State* (Ithaca, NY: Cornell University Press, 2017), 124.

32. Brooke Kroeger, *The Suffragents: How Women Used Men to Get the Vote* (Albany, NY: State University of New York Press, 2017), 13

33. Kroeger, *The Suffragents*, 11; Goodier and Pastorello, *Women Will Vote*, 95.

34. Kroeger, *The Suffragents*, 6.

35. Kroeger, *The Suffragents*, 79–80.

36. See Elinor Lerner, "Jewish Involvement in the New York City Woman Suffrage Movement," *American Jewish History* 70, no. 4 (June 1981): 442–61.

37. Mari Jo Buhle, *Women and American Socialism, 1870–1920* (Urbana: University of Illinois Press, 1981), 240.

CHAPTER 8

THE FINAL TRIUMPH, 1910–1920

"Verily, the way of the reformer is hard."
Carrie Catt to Mary Gray Peck. August 15, 1920[1]

Maud Wood Park was proud of the friendly tag "Front Door Lobby" given to her congressional committee because it implied "above board" tactics by the National American Woman Suffrage Association (NAWSA) members who sat in the House and Senate galleries day after day and who "never used backstairs methods." Park herself, a suffragist since her college years at Radcliffe, had yielded to the pleas of Carrie Chapman Catt and joined the lobbyists in Washington, DC, in December 1916 for the short session of the Sixty-Fourth Congress. Park became the best congressional committee leader NAWSA had and became known as the stable center in a changing cast of women.

Arriving from Boston, Park's first glimpse of the congressional committee offices was of a room overwhelmed by filing cases—each of which she soon learned held bulging portfolios on 531 members of Congress. Alongside basic details on each senator and representative, there were lists of business interests and religious affiliation, together with sketches of his personality and notes on any interactions with suffragists. Here was a huge archive of useful information that reflected the sophistication of NAWSA's lobby in 1916.[2] Not surprisingly, Alice Paul's Congressional Union (CU) offices held the same kind of records.

Front Door NAWSA lobbyists who were not in the galleries spent their days in pairs, trudging the unforgiving marble floors, stopping at the offices of senators and congressmen and knocking politely so that the men inside might take their feet off their desks before the women entered. But the women did not wait for a reply but slipped quickly in before anyone could hasten out a back door—as many were prone to do. Open transoms above office doors made every word spoken in the corridors easily heard by the staff so that suffragists after an interview had to find the nearest "Ladies" dressing room to make notes. Even there they had to be covert about it in case there was an antisuffragist or a staff member in the room. "Never talk with one another about our work" in "elevators, streetcar or corridors," Park was told by old hands like Jennie Roessing from Pennsylvania.

It was a trial of endurance. One of the nearly thirty women who daily knocked on doors commented that she never wanted to hear again the song "I dreamt that I dwelt in marble halls."[3] Even when invited into an office, the meeting often tried their patience, especially when they had to swallow their own irritation by being greeted with abruptness and anger. In these cases, women strove to avoid pushing an antisuffragist to any decision—so that the door was always open for a representative to change his mind. Occasionally, it was easy; Fiorello LaGuardia (later Mayor of New York) said, "'I'm with you; I'm for it; I'm going to vote for it. Now don't bother me.' all in one breath." At night, over dinner at "Suffrage House," which was a "magnificent and uncomfortable" rented mansion on Rhode Island Avenue, lobbyists and out-of-town suffragists staying overnight told tales of these long days, sharing experiences, and at times causing gales of laughter by mimicking the behavior of the men they encountered.

President Woodrow Wilson was set to address a joint session of the House and Senate on opening day, December 5, 1916. As was now his custom, he read his address in person. Maud Wood Park missed this notable event because, as a novice to the arcane ways of Congress, she did not realize that she had to apply long in advance to get a ticket to the galleries for a joint session. On that winter day, President Wilson stood as tall and erect as usual, delivering his annual address, which included discussion of the need for war preparations when five women in the front row of the balcony stood up and one of them, Mabel Vernon, produced a large rolled-up object from under her cloak. Together the women then unfurled a large golden banner on which was emblazoned the message, "Mr. President, What Will You Do for Woman Suffrage?" The room erupted, congressmen strained heads to see, President Wilson stopped talking, recovered, and continued. *The Washington Post* reported the women as sitting perfectly still, "five demure and unruffled women . . . with the cords supporting the fluttering thing clenched in their hands."[4] As police tried to get past CU women on the stairs, a page leaped up and pulled the banner down. A visibly irritated Wilson finished his speech and quickly left. The instant he was gone, congressmen stood up to see who was in the gallery. Alice Paul and the Congressional Union had pulled off another well-planned publicity stunt which would headline in newspapers the next day. Men in the Press Gallery were given copies of an account of the event the moment it was over. President Wilson, with substantial animosity toward the women he thought "militant" in the English suffrage tradition, was further agitated. The newspapers echoed Wilson's judgment and so did seasoned NAWSA leaders who believed the militants' actions to be disastrous to the women's cause.

Though Maud Wood Park missed the unfurling of the suffrage banner, she endured the wrath of senators and congressmen which immediately followed. Soon Park had to listen while members of Congress held forth. In the days that followed, the women were "so constantly blamed for it [the banner incident] that our chairman directed us to make clear in the first words of every interview that we represented the great mass of suffragists, organized in the National American Woman Suffrage Association, who did not approve of the methods used by the small group of militants." As Park later remarked:

Nothing about our work was more unpleasant than the need of explaining that we did not agree as to methods with other women working for the same end. And nothing was more exasperating than the queries that became frequent after later demonstrations: "How can you expect us to vote for you so long as those women go on breaking the law in order to prove that they ought to be allowed to vote for the lawmakers?" or, "Why don't you stop them? Or, "Why don't you women get together? You can't expect us to vote for you if you can't agree among yourselves." We used to point out, as mildly as we could, that men, even within the same party, were not without their differences. But sauce for the goose was rarely accepted as sauce for the gander.[5]

The stunt in Congress and the disruption it caused highlighted the fact that the CU was a well-oiled federal amendment organization. CU members' successful fundraising, their youthful energy and conviction, and their impatience with "educational" respectable methods had brought Alice Paul and Lucy Burns into a head-on conflict with NAWSA leadership. By 1916, NAWSA and the CU held each other in open disdain.

Maud Wood Park's recounting of the trials of NAWSA lobbyists burdened with the flamboyant campaigning of "militants" captures the temper and the depth of the conflict between the two wings of the suffrage movement. NAWSA viewed the women of the CU as especially threatening their successes in the House and Senate. Alice Paul, however, was convinced that "polite" educational methods or state campaigns had proved useless making a federal amendment the only solution. Paul raised large amounts of money and engendered loyalty from wealthy suffragists. The CU had gathered young, energetic suffragists who looked with scorn upon the "dear ladies" of NAWSA.

Between 1913 and 1916, Anna Howard Shaw went from wary to actively opposed to the tactics of the CU. The two suffrage organizations had the same goal during these years, but each believed that the other was deeply wrong in their method of securing a federal amendment and its ratification. The philosophical differences between the CU/NWP and the heir to NAWSA, The League of Women Voters (LWV), continued into the decades after 1920.

Historians have been hard put to decide which side of the suffrage movement had more impact than the other in the passage of the Nineteenth Amendment. The crux of the matter is that whatever the balance of power between NAWSA and the NWP, between them, they pushed Woodrow Wilson to make a stand in favor of a federal amendment. Both sides lobbied Congress to pass the Nineteenth Amendment (Susan B. Anthony Amendment) and send it to the states for ratification. The suffrage movement was divided into two wings that aggressively attacked each other's strategies, got in each other's way while campaigning, and held great animosity for each other, but together they managed to secure votes for American women.

The person at the root of the renewed split was a Quaker from New Jersey. Alice Stokes Paul was born on January 11, 1885, at the family farm, Paulsdale, near Moorestown. Hers was a substantial Quaker family that raised Alice with a belief in the "inner light" and the equality of women before God. Graduating from Swarthmore in 1905, Paul went to

New York to the College Settlement. Social work, she soon concluded, did not have enough impact upon the wider world. Paul returned to university and took up a scholarship at Woodbrooke, a center for Quakerism in Birmingham in the industrial midlands of England. It was not Woodbrooke that made the most impression; rather, it was hearing the great speaker Emmeline Pankhurst, founder of the Women's Social and Political Union (WSPU). Alice Paul dove quickly into militant suffrage work, moving to London.

Alice Paul was unusual within the WSPU. Generally, Quakers, although willing to fight injustice, had not become militant suffragists. The tension between nonviolence and pacifism values taught to Paul contrasted with the increasingly violent militancy of the WSPU and remained a conflict throughout her career. Despite continued personal loyalty to the Pankhursts, Paul did not countenance the destruction of property and followed the path of nonviolent protest in the United States.

Emmeline Pankhurst tutored Paul in the skills of an effective organizer and militant suffragette.[6] Women were blocked from presenting petitions to the British Parliament. When they tried, they were arrested. Around fifty thousand onlookers gathered around the streets of Parliament in the summer of 1909 watching the suffragists' effort to enter the House of Commons to deliver a petition. Mounted police and police on foot barricaded the entrance. Suffragettes threw themselves onto the police cordon, only to be grabbed by the throat and hurtled to the ground. Behind the suffragettes, the crowds pressed in. This was a formula for violence.

The particular nature of Alice Paul's arrest caused mirth and cheers and propelled her into the newspapers. The women were all padded, and when Alice was grabbed by the police, her buttons burst and the padding flew out, as journalist Lawrence Housman wrote, "like the entrails of some wooly monster."[7] While in the police station, Alice Paul met a fellow London School of Economics student, and fellow American, Lucy Burns. The two became close friends.

In November, both Paul and Burns were part of a group disrupting the prime minister at London's Guildhall. Paul was arrested and this time was sentenced to hard labor in Holloway Gaol. In protest, as did all the women of the WSPU when jailed, she went on a hunger strike, whereupon the authorities force-fed her and other strikers. It was not her first arrest, but it was her first experience with force-feeding. No suffragist emerged from force-feeding without permanent damage to her health; Alice Paul suffered for the rest of her life. Her moving account is difficult to read, but it described the experience not only of Alice Paul but of other British suffragettes and American suffragists in 1917. One of the doctors held Paul's head back with a towel around the throat which choked her windpipe, making it hard to breathe. Another forced a tube up one nostril and poured down a mixture of milk and eggs. The tube rarely went into the nostril and down the throat the first time, causing bleeding and damage as the doctors persisted. Alice Paul was force-fed twice a day, in total fifty-five times, while in Holloway.[8] The *New York Times* had headlined the imprisoning of an American, and Alice Paul became infamous. Paul's reputation was already established as she left England.

At twenty-five years of age, Alice Paul boarded the *Haverford* for home on January 6, 1910, as a seasoned campaigner. Less than a week after Paul returned, she started suffrage work again, but in a way that calmed the fears of a group in Philadelphia that she would advocate English militancy. Warding off further criticism, Paul argued that the American system was so different that women should not throw stones, but "organize and create a machine" as men did. When Lucy Burns returned in 1912, they set out together to make an impact on the national suffrage crusade.

From the start, Lucy Burns and Alice Paul presented contrasting personalities. Lucy Burns with her flaming red hair was pretty, taller, a little older than Paul and had an ebullient manner. Lucy Burns was also a good orator, with a musical voice that could hold an audience. Born in Brooklyn to an Irish Catholic family, Burns studied languages at Vassar and Yale and then went to Germany to study in 1906. In 1909, she abandoned study at Oxford to work with the WSPU. Together the women balanced each other's strengths. Alice Paul, tiny and slight, always on the verge of physical collapse, was the leader and brooked no challenges to her decisions, while Lucy Burns was indispensable as the one person who could modify Paul's mind and could revive her spirit. Lucy Burns was the person Alice Paul sent out into the streets to oversee the action.

To mount the 1913 parade, Paul and Burns had recruited a new set of lobbyists to work with them. Alice Paul quickly gathered her new committee: Greenwich village radical, Crystal Eastman, a roommate of Lucy Burns at Vassar, and Mary Ritter Beard who had been in Manchester and was a member of the WSPU and active in New York suffrage. Of a different generation was Dora Kelley Lewis of Philadelphia, a wealthy widow at fifty years old, from a family with substantial social standing and political influence. Lewis would be able to recruit other society women and raise funds. Dora Lewis opened her home to Alice Paul so that she could recuperate illnesses and exhaustion that afflicted her regularly during the endless campaigns between 1913 and 1920. Lewis went to jail and on hunger strike in 1917, the oldest woman to do so . Eastman, Beard, Lewis, Burns and Paul got ready to mount a campaign against Woodrow Wilson's intransigence on the question of woman suffrage.

WOODROW WILSON AND WOMAN SUFFRAGE

By 1916, President Woodrow Wilson was accustomed to being asked for his opinion on a federal woman suffrage amendment, but he never became inured to questions from suffragists who were not cowered by his status as president. Moreover, Wilson's strong personal feelings against women voting were disguised as best he could throughout the 1912 campaign, and as long as he could, once in office. After his inauguration, Wilson first sought to skirt the topic. Initially, if forced to answer, his responses were that his agenda was too full to include woman suffrage, then it became that his hands were tied by the Democratic Party platform, and then he turned to a states' rights rationale. All rang hollow to the suffragists who met with him and were intent on convincing him of the justice of woman suffrage.

The Democratic Party in 1912 won control of both the Senate and the House, as well as the White House. Woodrow Wilson intended to work through his reform agenda, beginning with lowering tariffs. Indeed, Congress passed an impressive set of legislation; to suffragists, this meant that another federal amendment was constitutionally and politically possible. Wilson had won the 1912 election as a progressive, and woman suffrage was part of the progressive agenda. Theodore Roosevelt's, admittedly defeated, Progressive Party had endorsed woman suffrage. Suffragists in 1912 campaigned for Roosevelt, for Wilson, and fewer for William Howard Taft, despite the official stance of NAWSA that its members should remain "non-partisan." Woman suffrage was growing harder to ignore for those sitting in Congress.

As a Southerner who fully absorbed southern beliefs, Woodrow Wilson believed that the family was the basic element of the state. Men stood at the head of the family, with women and children under his care in this private world. Women did not belong in public, campaigning for political and social change. Wilson arrived in Washington with a horror of women who were suffragists. In his twenties, Wilson had written of "the chilled, scandalized feeling that always overcomes me when I see and hear women speak in public"[9] In his early years in office, he often showed his disdain for "unsexed, masculinized females."[10] In 1913, Wilson had no intention of moving ahead on the suffrage question.

ALICE PAUL BEGINS DEPUTATIONS TO THE WHITE HOUSE: 1913

Wilson did not anticipate the force of Alice Paul's determination to change his mind. Delegation after delegation went to the White House. In 1913, in March alone, Alice Paul and four others met with Wilson, and then Elsie Hill, daughter of Congressman Ebenezer Hill, with a delegation of young women from the College Equal Suffrage League went to the White House. In June, it was western women voters. In November, it was seventy-five women from Wilson's home state of New Jersey. The president gave them all as little time as he could without direct rudeness. Wilson initially claimed that he had not considered the question of woman suffrage, which became more and more difficult to say as the deputations kept coming and as each deputation explained why women needed to vote. Wilson steadfastly refused to make any commitments, but as he commented to a friend, "each meeting was more embarrassing than the last."[11]

In June 1914, Wilson became intensely, and unfortunately for him, publicly irritated. A delegation of club women included an outspoken suffragist, journalist, and veteran of the New York campaigns, Rheta Childe Dorr. Dorr asked Wilson pointed questions about the Democratic Party pushing through Wilson's own agenda, although he claimed that he could not add woman suffrage to the docket. Dorr also commented pointedly on the number of women's votes in the West that could be used against the Democrats. Wilson, who rarely lost his usual outward calm, became visibly annoyed, complained about being cross-examined, and walked out of the room. Rheta Childe Dorr described the scene:

A peculiar change took place in President Wilson. His gray eyes turned cold steel, a rigidity of his whole body replaced his former easy and graceful pose, and his jaws became set in a hard and dangerous line. I well understood the terror he inspired in the bravest men of his party.

Because the deputation was made up respectable and politically well-connected women, the press coverage was heavy, and Wilson suffered from his hasty retreat. The *Indianapolis Progressive Star* noted that the president had "'wabbled,' not to say quibbled, in his talk to the women," and the *New York American* noted that the president, when confronted with a group of "ladies" questioning his sincerity, "lost his temper and retired—indeed there was no other retort available to him."[12] Wilson remained unmoved but angry as his dislike of Alice Paul and the CU escalated. By 1915, the president refused to meet with any more delegations of women.

THE SUFFRAGE MOVEMENT SPLITS AGAIN: NAWSA AND THE CU

Anna Howard Shaw's initial doubts about Alice Paul increased over 1913, particularly when the auxiliary organization, the Congressional Union (CU), was founded in April. Paul initially planned to have the CU be an organ for fundraising and work by women who lived in Washington, DC, and in states that already had woman suffrage, but NAWSA board members wondered if Alice Paul was setting up her own separate organization. Demands for letters and petitions from Paul interfered with state work, confusing local clubs as to who was actually in control of national work. In Pennsylvania, Dora Lewis from the CU raised hackles by demanding letters to congressmen from every district leader to be delivered within a week—just as Jennie Roessing was leading a push in the state legislature for an enabling resolution for a state referendum.[13]

Nonetheless, Shaw allowed Alice Paul to organize the NAWSA national convention in Washington in late November 1913. It proved to be the last gasp of a united suffrage front. Paul delivered a speech to the convention tallying the work that had been done by the Congressional Committee and the CU in 1913, beginning with the parade and continuing with deputations to Woodrow Wilson, the "auto" rally in the heat of

July when women converged on Washington and other publicity events. These were the kind of stunts now common in state campaigns, but Paul escalated the scale and impact, making them national news. The convention audience erupted into loud and lasting cheers.

Carrie Catt sat with her hands in her lap. In her opinion, Anna Howard Shaw and NAWSA were in danger of losing control of the movement. Clearly, Catt believed Alice Paul wanted to redirect the whole movement toward a federal amendment alone. Carrie Chapman Catt, at fifty-five, with formidable presence and decades of suffrage experience at home and abroad, rose slowly from her seat once the hurrahs had died down. She began a series of pointed questions. Paul, she implied, had failed to report to headquarters her financial outlays and had not turned over money raised to NAWSA. Unfortunately, for Paul, the amount of money she had raised, and her comments to the convention that NAWSA had failed to raise enough funds for its own needs, raised concerns among NAWSA members. Paul did not actually want to leave NAWSA, with its enormous membership which could be a source of funds, but the next months were ones of fruitless negotiations for Paul, ending in the separation of the CU from NAWSA.

Anna Howard Shaw summoned Alice Paul and Lucy Burns to New York in December 1913. NAWSA board members refused to allow the Congressional Committee and the CU to continue without NAWSA's financial and administrative control. In turn, Paul and Burns rejected any compromise and the split was soon all over the newspapers with comments about women not being able to work together. After one final and contentious meeting in February 1914, with Ruth McCormick describing the CU as "militant clean through," the scene was set for deepening acrimony between the two organizations and the split was complete.

Charismatic, but also autocratic and demanding, Paul aroused enduring loyalty in her followers. In others, she aroused enormous antipathy. Contemporaries described Paul as a dedicated, politically astute leader. Crystal Eastman concluded that Paul "had a passion for service and sacrifice along with the shrewd calculating mind of a born politician."[14] Paul was reserved and often aloof, but she had an uncanny ability to draw women into the cause. Paul presents to history a complex, driven personality, thoroughly engrossed in the cause of the federal amendment, and often overworking herself to the point of collapse. Until the end of the fight, Paul was the central figure in decision-making for the CU and then the National Women's Party (NWP) created in June of 1916 to represent women who could already vote. In March of 1917 the two organizations united under the name the National Woman's Party.

1914: HOLDING THE PARTY IN POWER RESPONSIBLE

Once the separation was a fact, Alice Paul expanded the CU work, but this needed funds. In January 1914, a meeting was held at the imposing house and grounds of the home of Elizabeth Kent, former Congressional Committee chair in 1912 and wife of California Congressman William Kent, thus signaling that the CU was not only the party of young feminists but also the party of the wealthy, monied women who could sustain its coffers. Alva Belmont transferred her loyalties to the CU. Mary Burnham from Philadelphia, heir to the Baldwin Locomotive fortune, gave over $35,000. Paul believed these women, whom she described as "prominent" and "important," could provide entrée to people and power otherwise blocked to them by their lack of political and social connections. Congressional doors opened once women of "wide social influence" were brought in, said Lucy Burns. In June, a new National Advisory Council made up of prominent and wealthy women solidified the central place of elite, monied women in the CU.

Those who were more social justice-minded, including Mary Beard, were not happy with the role of the wealthy in the CU, wanting more focus on both "working and leisured classes." Socialists in the CU had to come to terms with the heavy influence of these wealthy women. Moreover, Alice Paul never made serious efforts to recruit working-class women. Paul insisted to Burns that the CU had only one issue, woman suffrage, and therefore had no opinion on labor issues. As Susan B. Anthony had done, Alice Paul chose to narrow the fight at the expense of other reforms and in this case in favor of the wealthy.

Paul also made the expedient choice of pandering to southern white women. An article in *The Suffragist* titled "The Federal Amendment and the Race Problem" noted that states would be able to control who voted and that "they could retain their white supremacy." The National Association for the Advancement of Colored People (NAACP) formed in 1909 by an interracial group included a rebuke of Alva Belmont in its newspaper, the *Crisis*, criticizing her for not answering a question on black voting, whereupon Belmont replied, "we want the same voting privileges for colored women as are given to colored men." Alice Paul called the accusations of racial exclusion unjust, but privately wrote that she did not "believe in the disfranchisement [sic] of the Negro, but I see no reason why we should not constantly point out that we are working for woman suffrage only and that the question of Negro suffrage is entirely different."[15] Black women remained hidden in Paul's suffrage equation.

In 1914 and 1915, Paul continued using delegations and political stunts to attract national attention to woman suffrage and to pressure both Wilson and Congress into action. As the main strategy, they had served their purpose. Historians Katherine Adams and Michael Keene observe that Paul "had created an unprecedented panoply of nonviolent visual events," and in doing so "courted many forms of nonviolent danger that gained press attention."[16]

Alice Paul explored a new and aggressive political strategy in 1914. The theory upon which this lay was that the party in power was responsible for advancing the progress of the Susan B. Anthony amendment. The goal was to "convince the dominant party, and all other parties, that opposition to suffrage is inexpedient."[17] In her view, politicians wanted to be re-elected, above all. Pleas to persuade them that woman suffrage was a worthy cause were far less effective, to her mind, than threats to their hold on their seat in Congress.

Paul's plan was rooted in her interpretation of British parliamentary politics. In Great Britain, the prime minister was the leader of the House of Commons and the leader of his party in Parliament. He had the power to bring legislation to the floor for discussion and could direct his party to vote for particular legislation. Herbert Asquith, the Liberal Party leader, was determined to block votes for women and had the political power to do so. Woodrow Wilson did not have such powers. Wilson did not have the power to force congressional members to vote for particular legislation. Paul also underestimated the fact that each state existed as a separate power from the federal government. Britain only had one Parliament. Moreover, she underestimated the backlash from suffragists who had stuck to the "non-partisan" position promulgated by Susan B. Anthony. Anna Howard Shaw hastened to tell Woodrow Wilson that NAWSA disavowed this CU policy.

Nonetheless, Paul went ahead with what forces she could muster. If the four million eligible women in the West voted against Democrats, Democrats would change their views, Paul was convinced. "When we have once affected the result of a national election, no party will trifle with suffrage any longer."[18] Campaigns against Democratic politicians were hastily planned with few available organizers and a handful of staff and CU members in each suffrage state.

NAWSA organizers did their best to prevent the CU campaign from having any success. In the end, the CU claimed a hand in twenty-three Democratic losses—Paul saying three defeats were the direct result of CU work. Deep hostility erupted in Congress among members who had survived the election. It made some Congressman almost apoplectic with rage when they had Alice Paul testifying before them. This antagonism was layered upon Wilson's increasing disapproval, making the CU path to lobbying harder and the NAWSA path to congressmen and the president somewhat easier.

WAR IN EUROPE

While Paul's organizers traversed the West, the nation's attention was drawn across the Atlantic to Europe as the news of the war made newspaper headlines. Carrie Chapman Catt was in Britain for a meeting of the International Woman Suffrage Association when the immediate events that precipitated "The Great War" took place. The assassination of the heir to the Austro-Hungarian throne spurred several European military alliances into action, leading to an international war that destroyed a generation of young men, toppled monarchies, precipitated revolution, and redrew national boundaries. The Russian tsar was dethroned and the Bolshevik Revolution began. Great Britain's status as a great power was eroded, if not destroyed, as was its financial leadership. The Ottoman Empire of the Turks was carved up—a consequence that bedevils the Middle East still. From the start of the fighting, President Wilson offered to mediate peace but was generally ignored.[19]

Catt was on the *Kaiser Wilhelm II* bound for New York as armies mobilized. By the time she arrived home, war had broken out. Catt's prompt response was that, "if women had had the vote in all the countries now at war the conflict would have been prevented." Many suffragists were deeply pacifist. One of those was Fanny Garrison Villard, who called Catt the next week with a plan for a peace parade in New York. Catt was caught between two loyalties. She was a strong pacifist, but the woman suffrage cause was in danger of getting linked inextricably with pacifism, which would, she knew, doom the movement. When nearly drawn into a CU organized march for peace in Washington, Catt wrote to Jane Addams, explaining her concerns and wanting Addams to take her place. The result was that Jane Addams became president of the Woman's Peace Party, headquartered in Chicago, and Catt buried her pacifism to carry on the suffrage fight in New York for the 1915 referendum.[20]

Woodrow Wilson urged Americans to be "in fact as well as in name, impartial in thought as well as action." But the facts of global warfare made it difficult to maintain impartiality; the superior power of the British navy made it difficult for Germany to get food and supplies, and leading banker J.P. Morgan supported private loans to the Allies. In 1915, Wilson, concerned that the U.S. economy would be hurt by reduced commerce with combat nations, authorized private loans. Economically, the fortunes of the United States were now closely entwined with the fate of the Allies because many fewer loans were made to Germany. The second challenge came from the use of new technology, the submarine or U-boat, which had to rely upon surprise in using torpedoes to sink ships. Traditional rules of war called for civilian passengers to be allowed to leave belligerent ships before they were fired upon. On May 7, 1915, off the coast of Ireland, a British Cunard Line luxury passenger ship, the *R.M.S. Lusitania*, was sunk without warning by a German submarine. Because the dead included 128 American passengers, American public opinion swayed toward the Allied cause. Germany agreed to Wilson's demand to stop attacking passenger ships but only for a few months.

NAWSA: CARRIE CHAPMAN CATT TAKES THE LEAD

In 1915, Carrie Catt bowed to the wishes of a committee of one hundred women that she once again become president of NAWSA. Catt's first actions reflected her long history of success as an organizer, when for the first months of 1916, she traveled across the country visiting state conventions, conferences, and suffrage meetings in twenty-three states. A new Campaign and Survey Committee supplemented her own meetings.

Catt's comments on what she discovered were not laudatory; NAWSA was a "camel with a hundred humps, each with a blindfolded driver who thought she set the way."[21]

A separate problem facing Catt was the suffrage amendment introduced by John Shafroth and A. Mitchell Palmer (Shafroth-Palmer Amendment), and encouraged by Kate McCormick, which proposed that each state had to hold a referendum if 8 percent of the voters supported woman suffrage in a petition.[22] The existence of two amendments was confusing. NAWSA, led by Catt, reversed NAWSA's position and the Shafroth-Palmer Amendment was withdrawn.

Carrie Catt emerged at this juncture as another in the line of autocratic leaders in suffrage history. Historian Sara Hunter Graham has written critically of the clutching of power in the hands of the Executive Board over policymaking and planning and of Catt's high-handed concentration of power. Graham quoted a friend of Catt pronouncing her an "aristocrat with democratic tendencies." Graham noted also that Catt's regime saw a "growing disregard for internal democracy."[23] Both suffrage organizations, it can be argued, lacked democracy as they both worked for the federal amendment. Though Catt was autocratic, her "Winning Plan" created a unified suffrage machine and an effective political pressure group.

Finished with her investigations, by June 1916, as the convention season for political parties loomed, Catt thought that, given NAWSA's weaknesses, it was vital to secure clear supportive planks on a federal amendment from both major parties. In June, NAWSA women descended on Chicago for the Republican convention. On June 7, women from NAWSA, the CU, and the newly created NWP marched together in surprising cooperation, when the heavens opened with a rainstorm that drenched everyone on the streets. Inside the convention, an antisuffragist was telling the audience that women did not want the vote when the doors of the auditorium opened and hundreds of bedraggled but laughing women flocked in, moving to stand in every empty space, along the walls and in the aisles, encircling the Republican delegates. It was an effective disruption, but even so, the political acumen of Henry Cabot Lodge of Massachusetts blocked the women's advance by choreographing a state's rights rider to the platform plank.

The weather was better in St. Louis on June 14 for the Democrats' gathering, but the results for woman suffrage were not much better. NAWSA put on a good display as six thousand suffragists dressed in white, with yellow sashes and yellow parasols, lined the street from the hotels to the Coliseum so that delegates could choose between a long circuitous walk or to run the gauntlet christened the "Golden Lane." Yet, when it was over, Catt was rendered speechless with anger at the Democratic plank that called for suffrage by state action.

Within thirty minutes of the Democratic convention ending, Catt called an emergency session of the NAWSA executive board. No one argued with the analysis that NAWSA was in crisis. An Emergency Convention was called for Atlantic City in September—everyone hoping that the pleasures of the Jersey Shore would bring out even those exhausted by party conventions. The depth of the predicament went beyond the inability to get support for a federal amendment from two major parties; internal divisions ran in the organization also. In the South, there were those who still supported the Shafroth Amendment, and Kate Gordon remained steadfastly against any federal amendment. Catt had to bring cohesion from this disunion if NAWSA was to survive.

Gathering the Executive Committee to outline her plan before she gave a speech to the whole convention, Catt was blunt. The four 1915 state failures, the confusion and lack of leadership in many states, and the failure of efforts to get party planks added to the calamitous situation. They must turn back to a federal amendment. Those at this closed meeting of the leadership were sworn to secrecy so that the opposition was not aware of the coordination and would not know where to place its next efforts. The women emerged from this meeting knowing it was a new stage of the movement.

"There is no quick, short cut to our liberty," Carrie Catt told the wider convention. "The Federal Amendment means a simultaneous campaign in forty-eight states. It demands organization in every precinct; activity, agitation, education in every corner. It means an appeal to voters only little less general than is required in a referendum. Nothing less than this nationwide, vigilant, unceasing campaigning will win the ratification." With that, she put up a huge map of the country and went through the details of the campaign that was labeled the "Winning Plan."

No longer could states go at their own pace with their own strategies. In states where women did not have the vote and had referenda already organized, they were to go ahead with their planning. States with no referendum planned were to fight for presidential suffrage. In the South, states were to fight for access to primaries as the best option, and at the least for municipal or school suffrage. In other words, each state should work at the state level for the highest level of political access it seemed possible to achieve. Simultaneously, all states were to be ready to respond to calls for pressure upon congressmen and senators. Letters, telegrams, petitions, and visits to party dignitaries and representatives were all options to be called for by the Congressional Committee. Catt's address showed her at her charismatic best, painting a scenario for action that rolled over any opposition, although one southern states' rights woman, probably Kate Gordon, was heard to say, "flattened by a well-oiled steam-roller," in irritation.[24] NAWSA was now a centralized lobby.

The Atlantic City convention was notable for another reason. For the first time, Woodrow Wilson addressed a NAWSA convention, sitting politely through the evening speeches, so that he might be the last to address the audience. Wilson's tone was cordial and complimentary, yet he stopped short of a clearly worded confirmation of his support for the federal amendment. He assured the women that they would win eventually, and therefore, "you can afford a little while to wait." No one in the room wanted to hear such a lukewarm endorsement. Anna Howard Shaw, in response, spoke for all when she turned to the president and said, "we have waited long enough for the vote, we want it now, and we want it to come in your administration."[25] Woodrow Wilson said nothing, just smiled, bowed, and left the auditorium. It was a turning point, but not enough.

1916: WILSON AND WAR PREPARATION

Throughout 1916 Wilson attempted to hold the Germans to their commitment not to attack passenger ships, and at the same time, realizing the increasing difficulty in staying neutral; he sought to increase the strength of the armed forces and American preparedness for war. Wilson, while continuing to make overtures to mediate, realized early in 1916 the need to prepare the United States so in August 1916 the Council of National Defense was created as an advisory body to coordinate industrial and national resources. Catt tried to mitigate the perception that women were opposed to this war preparedness, writing in the *New York Times* in October that women in Europe were doing war work, showing "magnificent loyalty," and that there was no reason to suppose that American women would not do the same. "What European women have done, American women under similar conditions are likely to do."[26] As the November presidential elections came closer, Wilson, aware of divided American opinion toward the war, ran on a policy of staying out of the war. Again, he tried to broker peace. Democrats adopted the slogan "He kept us out of war." Alice Paul's suffragists held banners that said, "He kept us out of suffrage."

Campaigning against Democrats and Wilson's re-election, the CU sent women out West again for the 1916 elections. Twenty-three women took the "Suffrage Special" train and traveled across the country from April to May to raise support for the federal amendment and to oppose Democratic candidates. A small number of organizers then ranged across the western suffrage states. Again, Carrie Catt and NAWSA leaders fumed at the CU/NWP campaigns. Catt wrote to a friend saying that the publicity and "agitation which may seem good to those who do not look deeply into the situation, but in the long run they antagonize more than they win." Simultaneously, the point was made by some newspapers that the women were playing politics as men did—on the basis that, "if you are not for us we are against you, no matter what your politics."[27] Both comments were valid. At least some politicians were noticing that women might form a separate political party.

After the votes were all in, Woodrow Wilson was re-elected. Women voters helped carry Washington state, California, Idaho, Utah, and Arizona for Wilson. Women voters helped elect him, in part, because people felt that Charles Evan Hughes was more likely to take the country into war. Wilson, knowing to whom he owed his re-election, now shifted his stance on the federal amendment. Now, at last, he was willing to work more closely with Catt and NAWSA, if not with Alice Paul. Paul responded to the failure of the CU/NWP by declaring victory, anyway, claiming that woman suffrage had been a crucial issue as never before.

The 1916 campaigns had been more than ever a test of endurance, particularly for Inez Milholland Boissevain (although usually known by her maiden name, Milholland). Loath to travel again, already physically weakened from heavy campaigning, and unknown to her, suffering from aplastic anemia, Milholland spoke day and night, taking trains in the middle of the night, giving a speech in the morning, and traveling again as soon as it was done. Inez Milholland was by now a national figure. The rigors of this travel were too much for her; in Los Angeles in October, in the middle of her speech, having delivered a ringing "President Wilson, how long must this go on? Let me repeat—we are not putting our faith in any man or in any party but in the women voters of the West," she collapsed. It was her last public appearance. Milholland was a romantic figure who seemed to bloom with health, and yet she was struck down at the young age of thirty-one. On November 25, Inez Milholland died in the hospital.[28]

Alice Paul made Inez Milholland into a suffrage martyr. On Christmas Day of 1916, in Statuary Hall in the Capitol Building, a deeply moving memorial service was held, with Maud Younger giving the address; "there [in the West] where the sun goes down in glory in the vast Pacific, her life went out in glory in the shining cause of freedom." Wilson, presented with memorials to Milholland was a trifle more supportive of woman suffrage than usual, but not enough for Paul.

The women returned to Lafayette Square headquarters convinced that they must come up with a new method. On January 10, the day after the deputation to Wilson, twelve women emerged from CU headquarters and marched across Lafayette Square to the White House gates. The women held banners with messages like "Mr President What Will You Do for Woman Suffrage," and, "How Long Must Women Wait for Liberty?" These were the "Silent Sentinels" picketing the White House who garnered attention, both hostile and admiring, and whose picketing resulted in women sent to jail for standing silently on the sidewalk. This tactic, picketing the White House, gained the most attention of all Paul's strategies, resulting in both support and enormous opposition. Picketing became evidence of disloyalty.

As Woodrow Wilson doffed his hat politely to the Silent Sentinels in the early days of picketing, the difficulty of staying out of war escalated. The Germans, increasingly desperate and in need of supplies, now calculated that by resuming unrestricted submarine warfare they could win the war before the United States entered. On February 1, 1917, Germany announced that it would attack all ships, including unarmed American merchant ships that were trying to run the blockade of British ports. Then the British handed over an intercepted message from the German foreign minister to Mexico—the Zimmerman telegram—in which Germany offered the reward of lands lost to the United States in return for Mexico entering the war on the side of the Central Powers.

Wilson delivered his war speech to Congress on April 2, 1917, declaring that the "world must be made safe for democracy." The contradiction that American women were not included in this statement—they were not part of the democracy—was exploited by the Silent Sentinels. The mood of the nation changed rapidly as soon as war was declared, sinking into nativism and war hysteria. Paul's attempts to show that women deserved to participate in this "freedom" and "democracy" hit rocky ground, culminating in the jailing and force-feeding of NWP suffragists.

As the NWP pickets stood valiantly day after day, in shifts, in rain and snow, and miserable cold, Carrie Catt tried to separate NAWSA from the NWP, telling newspapermen, "We feel that our men in Congress should not wait another minute to submit to the legislatures the Federal amendment for woman suffrage. Nevertheless, we are not in the least sympathy with the method that has been used by the White House picketers."[29]

On February 3, 1917, with the threat of war looming, Catt called a meeting of NAWSA leadership to discuss what the position of NAWSA should be with regard to women's war work. A major concern was that suffragists would abandon suffrage organizations to do war work elsewhere—with the Red Cross, for example. Eventually, they drafted a letter to the president that offered the women's services, if needed, saying "we pledge the loyal support of our more than two million members," as well as offering to act as a clearinghouse for women's organizations to coordinate women's war work. At the same time, the NAWSA leadership decided that it would not abandon suffrage agitation. Catt had made a clever political decision, whatever the personal cost. She had delivered substantial public support for the administration when it was most needed, and she and NAWSA could now call in favors. It is significant that the night before the NAWSA meeting she dined at the White House with Woodrow and Edith Galt Wilson.

Alice Paul led her party to a vastly different position. The NWP sent a missive to Wilson, laying out their position. The NWP, believing that it was in the "higher interests of the country," said that they would continue to work for "political liberty." The NWP would not, as an organization, do war work.[30] The NWP stance added to their existing difficulties with Congress.

Congress voted on the war measure on April 6, 1917. Jeannette Rankin, from Montana, the first woman Representative in the House, felt that a woman's voice needed to be heard in the cause of peace; a lifelong pacifist and NAWSA organizer, she faced voting for or against American entry into the war. During the roll call, she answered no, in a voice too low to be heard, and then repeating so that the whole House could hear her "no" firmly and loudly. She was one of only fifty congressmen opposing entry into war and is remembered historically primarily for this brave, but lonely, stand.

SILENT SENTINELS AND OCCOQUAN WORKHOUSE

The country settled into a war footing. The Silent Sentinels continued with only minor scuffles with onlookers who at first were curious, and only toward June became more hostile. In June, arrests began. Because it was not illegal to picket, other offenses were dreamed up. In July, pressure on the justice system escalated so that pickets on July 4 were found guilty and fined. Those arrested refused to pay fines.

On July 14, Bastille Day, sixteen women were arrested for "unlawful assembly" and released on bail. The women, defended by Dudley Malone, a Wilson confidante, Frederick Howe, commissioner of immigration of the Port of New York, and labor leader Frank P. Walsh, appeared in court for a two-day hearing and were then sentenced to sixty days in Occoquan Workhouse. Malone drove to the White House as the women were transported to Occoquan. John Hopkins, chairman of New Jersey's Progressive Party, who had helped finance Wilson's campaign and whose wife was among those arrested, also went to Wilson to urge him to support immediate passage of the suffrage amendment. Wilson prevaricated, eventually refusing to act. Dudley Malone, when faced with Wilson's intransigence, resigned from his position as collector of the Port of New York. Wilson refused to discuss Malone's concerns.

Wilson's next move, with the help of George Creel, in charge of the propaganda machine for the war effort, and with the support of Carrie Chapman Catt, was to squash, or at least repress, the news headlines engendered by the picketing and the violence that was escalating with it. It was a sign of the increasing loss of freedom of the press with the war, which backfired as the news value of the women's protests overcame the pressure on newspapermen to resist Creel's demand to bury the suffrage news on back pages. Wilson's handling of the pickets split his own advisors and caused support for the new amalgamated CU/NWP created in March 1917.

In Occoquan, the women were forced into prison clothing already infested with lice and made to share towels, plates, and soap with women who already had communicable diseases. Conditions for the succession of women sent to jail were appalling. In September, Senator Andrieus Aristedes Jones went to Occoquan to investigate conditions. Returning, obviously moved by the misery and squalid conditions, he called for favorable action on the suffrage bill, which had been stalled for months. The House finally created its own Suffrage Committee. Yet, arrests continued.

With ten other women, Alice Paul went to picket and eventually went to jail, demanding that prisoners in Occoquan be treated as political prisoners, who could wear their own clothes, receive visitors, and be brought books. This was denied. Alice Paul and Dr. Caroline Spencer of Colorado, a fifty-six-year-old with chronic asthma, were sentenced to seven months. Both committed to hunger strikes. Paul told reporters, "I am being imprisoned not because I obstructed traffic, but because I pointed out to President Wilson the fact that he was obstructing the cause of democracy and justice at home, while Americans fight abroad."[31] Alice Paul was taken to the old district jail where conditions were even worse than those at Occoquan.

Paul was separated from other prisoners and sent to a psychiatric unit, presumably to prove that she was deranged. Paul and Rose Winslow were force-fed. On November 15, thirty-one more women were taken to Occoquan and suffered the most brutal treatment of suffragists to that date. Women were dragged by their hair, beaten, and thrown into cells. Dora Lewis hit her head on a wall and collapsed unconscious as others yelled for medical help. Lucy Burns was handcuffed with her arms above her head and left in that position for the night. All the women refused food and did what they could to prevent wardens from doing more harm. The prison superintendent, finally somewhat rattled, asked his bosses if he could concede and give the women political prisoner status. They refused and a detachment of Marines was sent to guard the prison to prevent any communication to or from the inmates. Although Wilson denied knowledge of these events or claimed conditions were fine, behind the scenes he was kept apprised of what was happening.

One of Dudley Malone's lawyers was finally able to get into the prison where he found Alice Paul naked, her clothes having been wrenched off her, wrapped only in a blanket, weak and ill. A week later a U.S. District Court judge ordered all the suffragists to be transferred to the district jail from Occoquan but refused to investigate conditions. Public opinion, nonetheless, swayed to the side of the suffragists as some Democrats began to think that they would lose the next elections over this issue. Women in New York could now vote, and the tide of state campaigns would surely flow across the East Coast. Not knowing when to compromise, Wilson told his aides to claim that the women were lying about jail conditions. Despite his fears of extremism from the suffragists, Judge Waddill of the District Court released the women on November 8. It may have been that Wilson arranged this release.

Months later, in May 1918, a federal appeals court declared the arrests and the jail terms of all the White House picketers unconstitutional. The arrests and extreme treatment remain as one of the more shameful episodes in American history. Historian Linda Lumsden, in writing about Paul's picketing campaigns, concludes that her peaceful and nonviolent efforts "inspired the civil disobedience with which Gandhi led India's fight for independence. Gandhi's influence on Martin Luther King Jr. has been widely noted, yet it is generally unknown that the marches, pickets, symbolic expression, and civil disobedience that formed the core of King's crusade all had precedents in the American suffrage movement."[32]

THE BATTLE IN THE HOUSE AND SENATE

As the NWP picketing and arrests continued, NAWSA kept up its strategy of cultivating amicable relations with Wilson and supporting the war effort, not that anyone in the Wilson Administration knew what to do with all the women who were volunteering for service. Anna Howard Shaw reluctantly agreed to head a newly created Woman's Committee of the Council of National Defense, where her talents were mostly wasted in committees that found it hard to find anything for women to do. Shaw and Catt talked of the fact that neither of them was expected to achieve much. Josephus Daniels, secretary of the Navy, was probably of the same opinion. When Shaw and Catt went to see Daniels, he told them to "take the women off our backs. Here is about a bushel basket full of letters from women asking what they can do. Take it away and tell those women to keep quiet till we get the war going."[33]

The outcome was that Carrie Chapman Catt won the public relations battle over war support. Antisuffragists were incensed but could do little. In January 1917, North Dakota won presidential and municipal suffrage. Wilson wrote an unprecedented letter of congratulations. The White House was now on the side of the NAWSA version of woman suffrage. In February, Ohio voted in presidential suffrage, and the number of electoral votes affected by women increased to 120 of 531. Michigan, Nebraska, and Rhode Island followed in April. As significant as this was, the vote in Arkansas to allow women to vote in primaries was more surprising and a stronger sign of a turning point for the movement. In a one-party state, and a southern state, the primaries were equivalent to presidential suffrage, making this the first breakthrough of the solid South. Then came victory in New York in late 1917. The addition of forty-five electoral votes affected by New York state's women voters moved the pressure dial in Congress perceptibly. The majority of antisuffragists in New York dropped suffrage work as soon as the country went into the war, most of them starting work with the Red Cross.

Antisuffragists shifted the nature of their rhetoric in response to the New York defeat and to signs of suffrage advances. Now the language of the opposition turned to reflect a fear of change combined with war hysteria. Where before woman suffrage had been bad for the family and the structure of society, where before women's interests could be best served by men's voting for them, where before women did not belong in the dirty business of politics, and where before women were more influential as reformers without the vote, now women who were suffragists were simply a threat as unpatriotic radicals, communists, Bolsheviks, or socialists. Feminists and suffragists were bundled together in this logic. Another set of arguments rested on flagrant racism; in the South, it was a question of disenfranchising African Americans; in Massachusetts, it was not enfranchising Catholic women overall, it was about not giving the vote to immigrant women.

Author Kristy Maddux, examining the rhetoric of antisuffragists after 1917, concludes that antis "charged suffragists with treason and subversion, and accused them of being pacifists, which meant they were also Socialists, Bolsheviks, or 'unpatriotic German sympathizers.'"[34] Historians of antisuffragism Jane Camhi and Thomas Jablonsky refer to character assassination of the kind that would grow after the war as part of the "Red Scares" of the early 1920s.

Linked to this shift in rhetoric were the change in leadership and the move from New York in late 1917. The National Association Opposed to Woman Suffrage (NAOWS) had been founded in New York in 1911, and state organizations existed across the country with differing levels of influence. With the new focus on the federal amendment, Alice Hay Wadsworth, wife of New York's Senator James Wadsworth, became national president. In the years that followed, James Wadsworth actually took over the running of the organization and control of its funds. While active, the antisuffrage women's organizations had lost their force after 1917.

The Winning Plan was working. The predicted turning point for woman suffrage had come. From this point on, with 232 electoral votes being influenced by the votes of women, both the Senate and the House were moving, maybe too slowly, toward passage of the Nineteenth Amendment. Catt knew this was happening when an Arkansas representative told a suffragist that he would be "pleased" to vote for the federal amendment.[35]

Eight more states voted for presidential suffrage in 1919. Carrie Catt and Nettie Shuler's account of NAWSA's work portrays a vast army of women directed from NAWSA headquarters. The "parent body . . . directed the great mass of them." In forty-six states, NAWSA women were "functioning as one organ." In New York, the headquarters took up two floors of 171 Madison Avenue. In Washington, DC, at Suffrage House, Maud Wood Park held sway over her troops, numbering twenty-five at times, and backed up by state officers or those who knew particular congressmen or senators, who came when needed. This effective lobbying machine was fueled by endless fundraising.

In late 1917, long-lasting lawsuits over the bequest of Mrs. Frank Leslie to Carrie Chapman Catt were resolved, leaving over one million dollars in Catt's hands to support the suffrage campaigns. Catt created the Leslie Commission, with its own board of advisors, to support educational and campaign work. The Leslie Bureau of Suffrage Education quickly became an effective propaganda arm of NAWSA. In September 1917, Maud Wood Park managed to have formed a House Woman Suffrage Committee, overcoming Edwin Webb's stranglehold of advances with his leadership of the Judiciary Committee where the bill was bottled up. The new committee promptly reported the woman suffrage amendment out favorably, with a House vote scheduled.

On January 10, 1918, Jeannette Rankin of Montana opened the momentous debate in the House. Those in the galleries had an interminable wait as speaker after speaker rose. Through it, all anxious floor leaders tallied votes. The winning margin for the suffragists was reached only by dint of a handful of men who went to extraordinary lengths to be present to vote. Thetus Sims from Tennessee, who walked the halls enduring excruciating pain, refused to have his shoulder set in case the anesthetic prevented him from casting his vote. Henry Barnhardt of Indiana was carried into the chamber on a stretcher. Robert Crosser of Ohio left his hospital sickbed, and James Mann of Illinois also left the hospital precipitously. The most poignant of all these suffrage loyalists was Frederick Hicks of New York who left his suffragist wife's deathbed to vote on her urging. He returned for her funeral.

The debate ended, and in the subsequent roll call, the amendment passed with only one extra vote—274 ayes to 136 noes met the two-thirds requirement. That same day, January 10, British women won the vote, albeit a limited one.[36] The narrowness of the win shows how effective the woman's lobbying had been. As historian Nancy Cott has pointed out, this lobbying work "should be seen as pioneering in the modern mode of exerting political force—that is, interest group politics."[37]

Catt, ready to finish the fight, thought that the Senate would soon follow the House. She ordered a new dress and set to work on the ratification campaign. By April 1918, all the plans for the ratification campaigns were finished, but the Senate failed to cooperate, and Catt's dress lay unworn. A flood of petitions, telegrams, letters, and visits from constituents failed to move the senators.

Catt appealed to Wilson, taking with her an appeal from women of allied nations to show that America was the home of democracy by giving women the vote. Wilson asked for support for the federal amendment, but the Senate, irritated at what it thought was inappropriate pressure, set the vote back. Eventually, a vote in the Senate was scheduled for September 26, 1918. President Wilson responded to Catt's call for help by arriving at the Senate, surrounded by his cabinet, to ask for support in passing the suffrage amendment. It made little, if any, difference. On October 1, 1918, the Senate vote was taken, only to have the amendment lose by two votes.[38]

Then good news came from the states; in 1918, South Dakota, after twenty-eight years of campaigning and seven tries, passed a state referendum. Michigan and Oklahoma also passed full woman suffrage.[39] All these campaigns were undertaken in the face of the great flu epidemic, making travel difficult and sometimes impossible. Still, the votes were not there in the Senate. Wilson wrote letters and spoke to southern Democrats and addressed the Senate in person; "Both of our great national parties are pledged, explicitly pledged, to equality of suffrage for the women of the country . . . its adoption is, in my judgment, clearly necessary to the successful prosecution of the war." Again, no one shifted.

NAWSA could see that one option was to eliminate some of the opposition in the Senate by targeting antisuffrage men in the off-year 1918 elections. Both NWP and NAWSA targeted antisuffrage senators. Two men were toppled—John Weeks of Massachusetts and Willard Saulsbury of Delaware. It was a sign of the pressure that the women's lobby could now muster from suffragists and a warning to opponents. In the midst of this stalemate, the war ended with the armistice declared on November 11, 1918. In December, Woodrow Wilson sailed to negotiate the peace settlements in Paris.

Even with the success of the November elections, another defeat in the Senate in February 1919 meant that the lobbying effort would have to continue when the special session of the Sixty-Sixth Congress began in May 1919. Before that session began, a "Jubilee" convention gathered in St. Louis in March to celebrate fifty years of suffrage organization. Catt introduced her plan for the League of Women Voters (LWV) in the expectation that the vote would soon come. Once the amendment passed, around twenty million women would have had no experience of voting. The LWV would educate women not only about the voting process itself but on politics in general. Women needed a political science course thought Catt as she also imagined that the need for such an organization would disappear within a few years.

VICTORY

On May 19, the Sixty-Sixth Congress opened its special session. The Nineteenth Amendment was introduced on the opening day. The suffrage bill passed the House quickly with an increased positive vote, and the final debate began on June 3 in the Senate, going on for two hot days. Late on June 4, the roll call began. The vote was 65 yes votes and 30 no votes. The Nineteenth Amendment had passed.

The lobbyists, the prosuffrage senators, all the women in the galleries from both NAWSA and NWP, and those supporters in the foyer who could not get in to watch, were all worn out. It had taken a year to win two votes. There was little celebratory spring left in anyone's steps. Maud Younger described the actual vote as a letdown, "because everyone knew what the end would be now. It was all very dull. . . . We walked slowly homeward, talking little, silent a great deal." Exhaustion was the motif, rather than celebration.[40] President Wilson cabled congratulations from Paris and the peace negotiations.

As usual, Catt hardly stopped to think after the Senate vote but sent telegrams to several states where the legislatures were in session and set up a competition for which state would be the first to ratify. No one wanted to let ratification linger on and lose momentum. Illinois, Wisconsin, and Michigan ratified in early June. Kansas, New York, and Ohio followed, then Pennsylvania, the first nonsuffrage state, came through. The western states dragged their feet, to Catt's irritation. Even so, within four months, seventeen states had ratified, half of the number needed—thirty-six was the magic two-thirds majority.[41] In August 1920, the tally had progressed sufficiently that all hopes rested on Tennessee as the likely thirty-sixth state.

THE LAST HURDLE: THE BATTLE FOR TENNESSEE

Both presidential candidates for the 1920 elections officially endorsed ratification, although not always with clarity or with heartfelt language. This became a serious frustration in the last battle state of Tennessee when both James Cox and Warren Harding fudged on the question of whether it was illegal under the Tennessee constitution for legislators to vote for a federal amendment without there being an election beforehand. In Tennessee, in the depth of the summer heat, presidential elections, struggles for power between Republicans and Democrats, the fact that the Louisville and Nashville Railroad had controlled the legislature for generations, liquor industry efforts to defeat the measure, vicious efforts to raise race fears, and a substantial amount of double-dealing where legislators promised support for ratification and then reneged, all combined for one of the most difficult political battles that either NAWSA (now officially the LWV) or the NWP had ever encountered. In the middle of the worst of days of the final legislative votes, a weary Carrie Catt described the situation to Mary Peck:

> Men, lots of them are here. What do they represent? God only knows. We believe they are buying votes. . . . It is hot, muggy, nasty, and this last battle is desperate. We are low in our minds—even if we win we who have been here will never remember it with anything but a shudder. Verily the way of the reformer is hard.[42]

People descended upon Nashville and the Hermitage Hotel where Catt had set up headquarters. From Washington, Alice Paul directed a native Tennessean, Sue Shelton White, although White was desperate for Paul to come to Nashville. Suffragists writing about the campaign recalled times when every legislator they could find was drunk, times when groups of members of the House were disappearing to the eighth floor, and the freely dispensed Jack Daniels' whiskey. Tennessee had been dry for years and voted for the Prohibition Amendment, but, as NAWSA women were told, "in Tennessee whisky and legislation go hand in hand."[43]

The Senate voted in favor. Pressure on members of the House was intense. The speaker of the House, Seth Walker, changed sides. There was talk of bribes, men were called home by sudden "emergencies," lobbyists appeared who were unknown to the Tennessee legislature and to the renowned Sue Shelton White who knew the politics of Tennessee better than anyone.

Antisuffrage forces overflowed the halls and lobby of the Hermitage Hotel. The two powerhouses of the southern suffrage movement, once allies in the cause and now in the camp of the antiratification forces, also arrived in town; Laura Clay and Kate Gordon were also staying at the same hotel. Carrie Catt contended with men listening at the door every day, who then wandered off when confronted. Catt's old friend Harriet Upton found that her telegrams were intercepted on their way to the Western Union desk and handed to the antis.

Antisuffrage women conducted a virulent and impassioned campaign. Central to the call were references to racial equality—a potent warning.

Flyers with dire threats of black voters taking over the state were spread liberally across the state. Antisuffragists brought up "force bills" that were to enforce the Fourteenth and Fifteenth Amendments, but which had never been used in Tennessee, as examples of the expansion of federal power over state's rights that would increase with the enforcement powers of the Nineteenth Amendment. Antisuffragist Charlotte Rowe held forth on this motif and expanded it to fear of radicals, "the Bolsheviks are at your door and seeking the centralization of power. Tennessee has the opportunity to immortalize itself as the savior of the republic."[44]

With another sign of their now finely honed lobbying skills, no NAWSA woman from outside the South was allowed to go near the legislature. Catt stayed in her room as flows of messengers, prosuffrage legislators, and suffragists came and went. During the last days, the tallies of suffrage votes showed men dropping out in alarming numbers. Men who had voted for limited suffrage the year before suddenly reversed their stand.

The floor leader for the prosuffrage forces, Joe Hanover, had his hands full. He was called in the middle of the night by women professing to be "suffs" who wanted to give him vital information—if he would just come to this or that room. Men also called, but with threats. The governor ordered a bodyguard for Hanover. Other prosuffragists were plied with whiskey in the hope that they would be so hungover that they would not appear in the House. Some got phony messages that someone in their family was ill, or a child injured, requiring them to leave Nashville. Eventually, the prosuffrage forces took to knocking on doors every two hours to make sure that no one left town.

Then news came that North Carolina had postponed consideration of ratification. Practically speaking, ratification in North Carolina was dead and Tennessee was the last viable state for a win. Nashville overflowed with people—whole families came from farms, along with workers given the day off to swell the numbers of those with the red roses of the antis. People crowded into every inch of space in the legislative building to be there for the historic battle.

The Tennessee House fight that followed was prolonged and nerve-wracking for both sides. The floor of the House was filled with lobbyists as well as representatives so that the whole scene was one of a raucous throng rather than serious deliberation. The speaker, Seth Walker, one of the apostates who promised suffrage support and then changed his mind, now led the opposition. Democratic presidential candidate James Cox hounded Governor Roberts on the phone because Democrats needed women's votes, as he told Roberts, "the mothers of America want the League of Nations." Standing in Roberts' office was Banks Turner, a thirty-year-old farmer from West Tennessee who had been voting as an anti. Roberts handed the phone over to James Cox to press upon Turner the need for his vote for the Democratic Party platform.

On the last day of debate, Wednesday, Speaker Walker gave over the gavel to someone else, and from the floor, thinking he had the numbers needed, moved to table the amendment. The chamber was rent with shouts, a siren blew from the gallery, and general mayhem broke out. Quiet was eventually restored and the clerk called the roll. Banks Turner voted not to table—Cox must have been effective. The clerk called a tie vote of 48–48, while antis with their own tally clamored that it was 49–47. The speaker had to call the sergeant at arms to reduce the chaos and bring quiet so that roll call could begin again. It was 48–48, and with the tie, tabling the amendment lost. Walker realized that he could muster enough votes to defeat the ratification vote and so supported a vote on the amendment itself. Joe Hanover, the floor leader for the suffragists, was in frenzied motion up and down the aisles. He needed another vote to win and for Banks Turner to stay loyal.

The roll call began again. Harry Burn, a young railroad agent from a small town, knew that his constituents, his mentor in the legislature, and the railroad opposed ratification. He wore the red rose of antisuffrage on his suit lapel. His college-educated mother, on the other hand, was a strong suffragist, and Harry Burn personally was in favor of women voting. He had hoped to avoid such a situation where he was in the position of making or breaking the amendment. Fortuitously for the fortunes of the suffrage lobby, a letter had arrived for him that morning in the Capitol building from his mother. "Dear Son: Hurrah and vote for suffrage and don't keep them in doubt . . . I've been waiting to see how you stood but have not seen anything yet. Don't forget to be a good boy and help Mrs. Catt."[45] Harry Burn voted for suffrage and entered the ranks of heroes of the long suffrage fight. Banks Turner, with Seth Walker leaning threateningly over him, stuck to his support of suffrage. The chamber again exploded with yells, shouts, and general cacophony. Yellow roses from men's lapels were thrown in the air, as women from the galleries threw more petals downwards. In the midst of the mêlée, Seth Walker changed his vote so that he might have the ability to move reconsideration of the vote within the next two days. The final vote was 50 ayes to 46 noes.

The days that followed were full of both high drama and high comedy. Seth Walker and the antisuffrage forces sought more votes. An effort to discredit Harry Burn blew up when newspapers published the whole story of the concocted plan. Burn stood in the House and gave a ringing speech saying that he had changed his vote because he believed in full suffrage as a right, and "I knew that a mother's advice is always safest for her boy to follow and my mother wanted me to vote for ratification."[46] Walker could not muster the needed votes on Friday, and the prosuffrage forces moved to adjourn until Saturday when Walker's time ran out. When Saturday morning came, it was found that, in an attempt to break a quorum and give Walker more time, thirty-eight antisuffragist members had caught trains for Alabama in the middle of the night. The ploy failed, even though other efforts to prove the ratification vote illegal continued. On Tuesday, August 24, Governor Roberts signed the certificate of ratification and sent it off to Washington.

Carrie Catt and Alice Paul both intended to be in Washington when the Secretary of State, Bainbridge Colby, signed the official Proclamation. Neither of them was there because Colby, trying to avoid charges of favoritism, signed the papers from Tennessee when he got them—in the middle of the night. Early on August 26, the Nineteenth Amendment entered the Constitution. It is often forgotten that court challenges to the Nineteenth Amendment from the American Constitutional League, founded after the New York defeat of antisuffragists, continued into 1922 when Justice Louis Brandeis wrote the majority opinion for the U.S. Supreme Court ruling that the Nineteenth Amendment legal. The following Saturday, August 28, all across the country church bells rang at noon to herald a new era of women voters. The Nineteenth Amendment was reality.[47]

Like all the best tales, the saga of woman suffrage has been long and winding. Now it seemed to be over. Maud Wood Park was elected president of the National League of Women Voters with Carrie Catt working alongside her. Alice Paul continued the battle for full equality for women. With Crystal Eastman, she drafted the Equal Rights Amendment, which was introduced in Congress in 1923. Its intent was to guarantee equal rights under the law and prohibit discrimination on account of sex. Politicians worried about the "woman's vote." On November 2, 1920, women across the country voted, a majority for the first time. By the best estimates, those women who voted supported Warren Harding over James Cox.

The next year, on February 21, sculptor Adelaide Johnson's work was presented by the NWP to the U.S. Congress. The sculpture is a conjoined set of three busts: Lucretia Mott, Elizabeth Cady Stanton, and Susan B. Anthony. The unveiling marked another step in the creation of a suffrage myth and the creation of suffrage heroes. Whether women's different values were to have an impact upon politics, or whether women entered politics on an equal footing to men, was the central question for suffragists in 1921. Would women assimilate into the two-party system, or would they form a separate woman's bloc? Would the NWP become a woman's political party contending against the two major parties? The aftermath of the passage of the Nineteenth Amendment, that is the impact of woman's suffrage, has occupied contemporaries and generations of historians and political scientists since 1920. It remains a contested question even today.

NOTES

1. Sara Hunter Graham, *Woman Suffrage and the New Democracy* (New Haven, CT: Yale University Press, 1997), 143.

2. Maud Wood Park, "Front Door Lobby" (unpublished manuscript, 1920), NAWSA Collection, 1–35, www.loc.gov.

3. Park, "Front Door Lobby," 36. "I Dreamt I Dwelt in Marble Halls" or "The Gipsy Girl's Dream" is a popular aria from *The Bohemian Girl*, an 1843 opera by Michael William Balfe, with lyrics by Alfred Bunn.

4. Inez Haynes Gillmore, *The Story of the Woman's Party* (1921; repr., Middletown, DE: n.p, n.d.).

5. Park, "Front Door Lobby," Chapter 1.

6. Members of the WSPU were given the name "suffragettes" initially as a term of scorn, but they adopted the label. Militant suffragists in Britain were called suffragettes, and the term did not apply to American suffragists.

7. J. D. Zahniser and Amelia R. Fry, *Alice Paul: Claiming Power* (Oxford: Oxford University Press, 2014). This is the best work on Alice Paul to date. It draws on extensive oral interviews undertaken by Amelia Fry.

8. Zahniser and Fry, *Alice Paul*, 100.

9. Christine Lunardini and Thomas J. Knock, "Woodrow Wilson and Woman Suffrage: A New Look," *Political Science Quarterly* 95 no. 4 (Winter 1980–1981): 655–71.

10. Lunardini and Knock, "Woodrow Wilson," 656; Linda Ford, *Iron-Jawed Angels: The Suffrage Militancy of the National Woman's Party 1912–1920* (Lanham, MD: University Press of America, 1991), 54.

11. Katherine H. Adams and Michael L. Keene, *Alice Paul and the American Suffrage Campaign* (Urbana: University of Illinois Press, 2008), 129.

12. Adams and Keene, *Alice Paul*, 130–3.

13. Roberta J. Leach, "Jennie Bradley Roessing and the Fight for Woman Suffrage in Pennsylvania," *Western Pennsylvania Historical Magazine* 67, no. 3 (1984): 18–211; Jennie Bradley Roessing, "The Equal Suffrage Campaign in Pennsylvania," *Annals of the American Academy of Political and Social Science* 56 (November 1914): 15–160; and Henrietta Louise Krone, "Dauntless Women: The Story of the Woman Suffrage Movement in Pennsylvania," 1910–1920 (Ph.D, diss. University of Pennsylvania, 1946).

14. Lunardini and Knock, "Woodrow Wilson and Woman Suffrage," 173.

15. Zahniser and Fry, *Alice Paul*, 218.

16. Adams and Keene, *Alice Paul*, 116.

17. Lunardini and Knock, "Woodrow Wilson and Woman Suffrage," 89.

18. Zahniser and Fry, *Alice Paul*, 204.

19. Two alliances emerged from the various treaties linking European powers. The "Allies" were Great Britain, France, and Russia. Japan joined the Allies as did Greece belatedly in June 1917. The "Central Powers" were Germany, Austria-Hungary, and the Ottoman Empire (the Turkish Empire).

20. Jacqueline Van Voris, *Carrie Chapman Catt: A Public Life* (New York: Feminist Press at the City University of New York, 1987), 125.

21. Van Voris, *Carrie Chapman Catt*, 132.

22. The Shafroth-Palmer Amendment of 1914 was put forward as a way to avoid states' rights concerns. If 8 percent of a state's male voters were in favor, a state referendum must be held. It proved confusing to everyone.

23. Graham, *Woman Suffrage*, 150.

24. Van Voris, *Carrie Chapman Catt*, 133.

25. Van Voris, *Carrie Chapman Catt*, 136.

26. Van Voris, *Carrie Chapman Catt*, 137.

27. Adams and Keene, *Alice Paul*, 153–4.

28. Linda J. Lumsden, *Inez: The Life and Times of Inez Milholland* (Bloomington: Indiana University Press, 2016), 152–71. The family refused Alva Belmont's request to hold a large public memorial service.

29. Tina Cassidy, *Mr. President, How Long Must We Wait? Alice Paul, Woodrow Wilson, and the Fight for the Right to Vote* (New York, NY: Simon & Schuster, 2019), 160.

30. Cassidy, *Mr. President*, 146.

31. Cassidy, *Mr. President*, 103.

32. Linda J. Lumsden, *Rampant Women: Suffragists and the Right of Assembly* (Knoxville: University of Tennessee Press, 1997), 143.

33. Van Voris, *Carrie Chapman Catt*, 141.

34. Kristy Maddux, "When Patriots Protest: The Anti-Suffrage Discursive Transformation of 1917," *Rhetoric and Public Affairs* 7, no. 3 (Fall 2004): 283–310. See also, Jane Jerome Camhi, *Women against Women: American Anti-Suffragism, 1880–1920* (Brooklyn, NY: Carlson Publishing, 1994); Thomas J. Jablonsky, *The Home, Heaven, and Mother Party: Female Anti-Suffragists in the United States, 1868–1920* (Brooklyn, NY: Carlson Publishing, 1994); Elna C. Green, *Southern Strategies: Southern Women and the Woman Suffrage Question* (Chapel Hill, NC: University of North Carolina Press, 1997); "Those Opposed: The Antisuffragists in North Carolina, 1900–1920," *North Carolina Historical Review* 67, no. 3. (1990): 315–32; and Susan E. Marshall, *Splintered Sisterhood: Gender and Class in the Campaign against Woman Suffrage* (Madison: University of Wisconsin Press, 1997).

35. Van Voris, *Carrie Chapman Catt*, 147; Carrie Chapman Catt and Nettie Rogers Shuler, *Woman Suffrage and Politics: The Inner Story of the Suffrage Movement* (New York, NY: Charles Scribner's Sons, 1926), 319.

36. Women who were over thirty years of age and were householders, the wives of householders, occupiers of property with an annual rent of five British pounds, or graduates of British universities could vote after 1918. This was only about two-thirds of the female population. The same act, The Representation of the People Act, abolished property and other restrictions for men, meaning that virtually all men over the age of twenty-one could vote. Men in the armed forces could vote if over the age of nineteen. It took until 1928 and the Equal Franchise Act for all women over twenty-one to be able to vote and have the same voting rights as men.

37. Nancy F. Cott, "Across the Great Divide: Women in Politics before and after 1920," in Louise A. Tilly and Patricia Gurin, eds., *Women, Politics and Change* (New York, NY: Russell Sage Foundation, 1990), 153–76; and Susan Ware, *Why They Marched: Untold Stories of the Women Who Fought for the Right to Vote* (Boston, MA: Belknap Press of Harvard University Press, 2019), 255.

38. The vote was sixty-two in favor to thirty-four against.

39. Alexander Keyssar, *The Right to Vote: The Contested History of Democracy in the United States* (New York, NY: Basic Books, 2000), Appendices, Table A.20.

40. Gillmore, *Woman's Party*, 418.

41. The following states ratified the amendment in order of adoption: Illinois, Wisconsin, Michigan, Kansas, Ohio, New York, Pennsylvania, Massachusetts, Texas, Iowa, Missouri, Arkansas, Montana, Nebraska, Minnesota, New Hampshire, Utah, California, Maine, North Dakota, South Dakota, Colorado, Kentucky, Rhode Island, Oregon, Indiana, Wyoming, Nevada, New Jersey, Idaho, Arizona, New Mexico, Oklahoma, West Virginia, Washington, and Tennessee. Delaware, Virginia, Maryland, Alabama, South Carolina, Georgia, Louisiana, and Mississippi rejected the amendment during 1919 and 1920.

42. Elaine Weiss, *The Woman's Hour: The Great Fight to Win the Vote* (New York, NY: Viking Press, 2018), 277.

43. Weiss, *The Woman's Hour*, 228.

44. Weiss, *The Woman's Hour*, 253.

45. Weiss, *The Woman's Hour*, 306.

46. Catt and Shuler, *Woman Suffrage and Politics*, 450. During the debate there were intervals where the galleries resounded with catcalls, whistles, clapping, yelling, and cheering from women. At one point, the sergeant at arms bodily moved representatives back into their seats.

47. Alice Paul had won a publicity coup in naming the suffrage amendment, the Susan B. Anthony Amendment, thus elevating even more the reputation of Anthony as the mother and prime mover of the suffrage movement.

AFTERMATH—NEW VOTERS: WHAT CHANGED?

"We are not wards of the nation but free and equal citizens."

Carrie Catt[1]

"Speaking before a women's club last spring, I told my audience that since many men really did expect a women's battalion of voters to rampage at once, they must be forgiven for saying, after two years, that 'women's entrance into politics made mighty little difference.' What I say is that if one country is annexed by another, its nationality is not changed overnight. Social processes are often very, very slow . . . Wait ten years, and the politicians will one day wake up and say, 'Look who's here!'"

Daisy Harriman[2]

"The Enormous Condescension of Posterity."

E. P. Thompson

Like all the best stories, the tale of woman suffrage has been full of hopes raised and hopes dashed, and populated by a huge cast of characters. Women were denied the basic right to vote, with all the proffered reasons why this should be so piling up over the generations, but none amounting to any logical argument in the minds of any suffragist. With ratification, the final battles were over at last. Women were "free and equal citizens" who could vote. What happened next, what didn't happen, and what continued to happen on either side of 1920 has occupied journalists, pundits, and scholars from many disciplines. What we do know is that the Nineteenth Amendment changed the nature of women's relation to the state. But beyond that, the discussion continues in a good number of well-researched works and with a goodly number of differences of opinion.[3]

Warren Harding's presidential inaugural address in March 1921 hinted at expected contributions women would make to politics. "We may count upon [woman's] intuitions, her refinements, her intelligence, and her influence to exalt the social order."[4] Balancing this lofty expectation was Carrie Catt's warning to New York campaigners in 1915 not to promise too much for the vote. "In a diverse country like the United States, we cannot expect different groups of women to have identical agendas."[5] Harriot Blatch said in 1918 that although suffragists were united in wanting suffrage, "they are not at one in their attitude towards other questions in life."[6] Suffragists had not dwelt on the question of women running for political positions nor had they discussed any joint agenda or woman's voting bloc to be employed once the long battle for suffrage was won. There were hopes and expectations for women's impact on the political world they had fought so long to enter, but few anticipated victory by planning for the future beyond creating the League of Women Voters as an educational organization for women beginning to vote.

Looking back twenty years later, Eleanor Roosevelt, as usual, put forward a level-headed thesis on how women voted: "I think it is fairly obvious that women have voted as individuals and not as a group, in much the same way men do, and that they are influenced by their environment and their experience and background, just as men are."[7] In this light, those suffragists who called for the vote as a question of simple human justice came closest to predicting what happened after 1920.

As the suffrage movement dissolved after 1920, its members split in many directions, but the major division was between those who supported the Equal Rights Amendment (ERA) and those who opposed it. After ratification of the Nineteenth Amendment, Alice Paul and other militant suffragists from the National Woman's Party (NWP) gathered to hammer out a new goal. The result was another constitutional amendment, the ERA, to secure equal legal rights for women.

At the same time, the Supreme Court overturned Washington, DC's, minimum wage law for women. Social feminists feared that legal equality could mean the overturning of all the women-specific laws secured in the progressive era which regulated working conditions. Many NWP women applauded the Court's decision on the grounds that men and women should be treated equally in the marketplace. The social feminist coalition represented by Jane Addams and Florence Kelley in NWP deliberations included the National Women's Trade Union League, the National Consumers League, the Young Women's Christian Association (YWCA), and others who believed the ERA's focus was too narrow in a world where exploitation of women workers was widespread. In the end, Alice Paul went ahead, confident in her belief that race and labor issues would muddy the waters of the one, clear, main goal—legal equity. The upshot was a decades-long division in the women's movement. The ERA was introduced in Congress in 1923 and wended its way through Congress which passed the amendment in 1972. It remains unratified.

In the world of electoral politics, some changes were pretty quickly evident. Women were soon at the polling places as poll watchers and election clerks. The polling places themselves were changed; no longer in barbershops, billiard parlors, or saloons, votes were now cast in public places more suitable for women, such as in fire stations, schools, churches, and town halls.

Much of this atmospheric change remained superficial as men strenuously resisted women's entry into the "smoke-filled" rooms of the inner circles of power in major parties.[8] There were women whose political participation outside of the vote began before 1920 and continued afterward. Daisy Harriman, who began her public life as a New York society woman, moved on to labor reform and then suffrage, and found her métier in a long career in party politics as a Democratic loyalist. Harriman created an organization of women to support Woodrow Wilson's election in 1912, crisscrossing the country stumping for Wilson. For Daisy Harriman and the many others in both the Republican Party and the Democratic Party, public lives in politics were changed by being able to vote, but they were continuing on paths already begun. For all those women who had been voting in those states with woman suffrage before 1920, the Nineteenth Amendment was indeed a historic event, but not a watershed in their political lives.

On the other side of the coin, many women did not want to be tainted by partisan politics, especially those who had spent decades avoiding political partisanship. Party politics was linked to corruption, an intensely masculine culture, alcohol, and rowdiness. For these women, work in organizations that were effective pressure groups was a preferred choice over party politics.

In the aftermath of the Nineteenth Amendment, some commentators expressed disappointment in suffrage as an agent of change—many along the lines of Charles Edward Russell in 1924, who wrote an essay entitled "Is Woman Suffrage a Failure?" which proceeded to explain why it was. Historians, accepting the conventional wisdom built up in the 1920s declared that nothing much happened in political behavior or in electoral politics as a consequence of the Amendment.[9] At the same time, some argued that women were to blame for the dropping turnout at the polls.

Conventional wisdom and fiction intertwined when George Gallup declared in 1940 that women would vote "just as exactly as they were told the night before." A Columbia University survey that found that women "would go to a family member to discuss politics" interpreted this as a signal that women deferred to the male members of the family. One author commented on this leap of logic, saying "the stereotyping achieved in this 'classic' account has rarely been equaled and never surpassed." At least one political scientist disagreed at the time; Charles Merriam wrote in 1929 that it was impossible to conclude that women followed the lead of men in voting, "for in many instances the contrary is true, and the woman may persuade or cajole or intimidate the man."[10]

All this contemporary discussion ignored the large swath of women who were not enfranchised in 1920. The deep divisions of race and ethnicity which excluded some men from voting remained unchanged. Millions of black women continued with the battles not yet won, particularly those in the South. Native Indians, Chinese women, Mexican women whose families had lived in the Southwest for generations, and women who had lost their citizenship because they married a foreign national were also among those who had to continue fighting for their right to vote. Women in the colonial territories acquired in 1898 were not included under the Nineteenth Amendment; they too had to fight on after 1920.

Black women in the South went to register, having held their collective breath during the ratification process.[11] In Baltimore, the black electorate doubled in 1921. In Richmond, Virginia, over twenty-four hundred black women registered, which historian Nancy Hewitt points out was more than 10 percent of the black female population.[12] Hewitt also referred to black women voting in cities across the South, from Greensboro, North Carolina, to Houston, Texas. White election registrars leaped to stop this break in the wall of black disfranchisement. Mississippi and Georgia refused to make the needed changes to their registration laws for women to vote in the 1920 presidential election. In not every southern state was the answer disfranchisement; in North Carolina, for example, "black women voters altered the political style of white supremacy," concludes historian Glenda Gilmore. "White women did not appeal to men to protect them with shotguns as they went to the polls. Instead, they roused white women to outnumber black women—an unfortunate, but legal, method of winning elections."[13]

Overall, Southern black women were the largest group of women blocked from voting after ratification. They had to wait until the passage of the Voting Rights Act in 1965 and blocks on literacy tests and poll taxes before they could vote. Even after 1965, extensive gerrymandering, the adoption of at-large elections, polling stations in areas inaccessible to black voters, and other discriminatory efforts were widespread and effectively "disfranchised" minority women.

Native Americans were officially citizens after the passage of the Indian Citizenship Act of 1924, although the Bureau of Indian Affairs notified its staff that this did not necessarily include the right to vote. Some states kept existing hurdles in place. In 1948, New Mexico and Arizona finally removed barriers to voting and other states followed slowly, with Maine being one of the last to comply, even though its first constitution in 1819 included Native Indians as voters. The barriers against Asian immigrants began to lift with the Magnuson Act of 1943, which repealed the Chinese Exclusion Act of 1882 and made it possible for Chinese immigrant women to become citizens.

Some native-born American women were blocked from voting by their marriage to a foreign alien, which meant they lost citizenship under the provisions of the Expatriation Act of 1907. The Cable Act of 1922 allowed these women to apply for naturalization (if their husbands were eligible), and after 1922, women marrying foreigners who were eligible for citizenship remained American citizens.[14]

Women who lived in the territories acquired in the Spanish American War were not enfranchised in 1920. During the 1930s, in the Philippines, the colonial governor pushed for woman suffrage, but it was not included

in the law code which established self-government in 1935. Filipina suffragists had to start all over again and only succeeded in 1946. In Puerto
Rico, women who could read were added to the polling lists in 1929,
and in 1935 the right to vote was extended to all Puerto Rican women.[15]
Guam had to wait until 1950 for voting rights for both men and women.

While acknowledging those women unable to vote immediately
in 1920, a historical debate has been waged as to the extent to which
1920 marks a dividing line in women's history, and in American history,
for that matter. In 1990, Nancy Cott made a compelling argument for
the Nineteenth Amendment as being one point along a continuum of
women's involvement in the development of liberal democracy, as well as
the long effort to reach equality. In her accounting, 1920 was a "political
watershed" but not the "Great Divide" that some argued it was. Nor was
there any real question of forming a "woman's bloc," which Cott calls an
"interpretive fiction" requiring a willing suspension of disbelief.[16]

The preponderance of evidence points to the Nineteenth Amendment
still being a major achievement. It was secured by a mass movement of
women which was, along with the Civil Rights movement of the 1960s,
one of only two such successful movements in our history. The Nineteenth
Amendment changed the nature of women's citizenship and gave them
a sense of human dignity. However, it was not an end to women's journey for equality, rather, it was a marker on the continuum which reached
beyond 1920. Through organizing for the vote, petitioning and lobbying
legislatures, and engaging in public protest, women had already been political actors and agents; the Nineteenth Amendment made women into
political actors in a formal sense, whose activism and political influence
only increased with time. Woman suffrage was a crucial step toward political equality for women. It was essential as a means of building women's
political power. The centennial of the Nineteenth Amendment's passage
is an appropriate time to look back at the mammoth effort it took to gain
the vote and to consider what that struggle for the vote means for democracy, not only in history but for our own day.

NOTES

1. Jacqueline Van Voris, *Carrie Chapman Catt: A Public Life* (New York, NY:
Feminist Press, 1996), 162.

2. Daisy Hurst Harriman, Florence Jaffray, Carrie Chapman Catt, and National American Woman Suffrage Association Collection, *From Pinafores to Politics* (New York, NY: Henry Holt and Company, 1923), 351, https://www.loc.gov/item/23017479/.

3. Paul Kleppner, "Were Women to Blame? Female Suffrage and Voter Turnout," *Journal of Interdisciplinary History* 12, no. 4 (Spring 1982): 621–43; Sara Alpern and Dale Baum, "Female Ballots: The Impact of the Nineteenth Amendment," *Journal of Interdisciplinary History* 16, no. 1 (Summer 1985): 43–67; Kristi Andersen, *After Suffrage: Women in Partisan and Electoral Politics Before the New Deal* (Chicago, IL: University of Chicago Press, 1996); Kevin J. Corder and Christina Wolbrecht, "Political Context and the Turnout of New Women Voters After Suffrage," *The Journal of Politics* 68, no. 1 (February 2006): 34–39; Nancy F. Cott, "Across the Great Divide: Women in Politics before and After 1920," in Louise A. Tilly and Patricia Gurin, eds., *Women, Politics, and Change* (New York, NY: Russell Sage, 1990), 153–76; Jo Freeman, *A Room at a Time: How Women Entered Party Politics* (Lanham, MD: Rowman & Littlefield, 2000); Felice D. Gordon, *After Winning: The Legacy of the New Jersey Suffragists, 1920–1947* (New Brunswick, NJ: Rutgers University Press, 1986); Nancy A. Hewitt, "From Seneca Falls to Suffrage: Reimagining a 'Master' Narrative in U.S. Women's History," in Nancy A. Hewitt, ed., *No Permanent Waves: Recasting Histories of U.S. Feminism* (Newark, NJ: Rutgers University Press, 2010), 15–38; and Dawn Langan Teele, *Forging the Franchise: The Political Origins of the Women's Vote* (Princeton, NJ: Princeton University Press, 2018).

4. Vanessa B. Beasley, "Engendering Democratic Change: How Three U.S. Presidents Discussed Female Suffrage," *Rhetoric and Public Affairs* 5, no. 1 (Spring 2002): 79–103.

5. Dorothy Cobble, Linda Gordon, and Astrid Henry, ed., *Feminism Unfinished: A Short, Surprising History of American Women's Movements* (New York, NY: W. W. Norton, 2014).

6. Cott, "Across the Great Divide," 157.

7. Keven J. Corder and Christina Wolbrecht, *Counting Women's Ballots: Female Voters from Suffrage through the New Deal* (New York, NY: Cambridge University Press, 2016), 22.

8. Melanie Gustafson, *Women and the Republican Party, 1854–1924* (Urbana: University of Illinois Press, 2001).

9. Quoted in Corder and Wolbrecht, *Counting Women's Ballots*, 20; Carl N. Degler, *At Odds: Women and the Family in America from the Revolution to the Present* (New York, NY: Oxford University Press, 1981); William L. O'Neill, *Everyone Was Brave: The Rise and Fall of Feminism in America* (Chicago, IL: Quadrangle Books, 1971); and William H. Chafe, *The American Woman: Her Changing Social,*

Economic, and Political Roles, 1920–1970 (New York, NY: Oxford University Press, 1972).

10. Corder and Wolbrecht, *Counting Women's Ballots*, 20–21.

11. https://www.justice.gov/crt/history-federal-voting-rights-laws

12. Hewitt, "From Seneca Falls to Suffrage," 31.

13. Glenda Elizabeth Gilmore, *Gender and Jim Crow: Women and the Politics of White Supremacy in North Carolina, 1896–1920* (Chapel Hill: University of North Carolina Press, 2006), 224; Lorraine Gates Schuyler, *The Weight of Their Votes: Southern Women and Political Leverage in the 1920s* (Chapel Hill: University of North Carolina Press, 2006).

14. https://www.archives.gov/files/publications/prologue/2014/spring/citizenship.pdf

15. https://www.nps.gov/articles/puerto-rico-women-s-history.htm

16. Cott, Across the Great Divide," 153–76; Carrie Chapman Catt and Nettie Rogers Shuler, *Woman Suffrage and Politics: The Inner Story of the Suffrage Movement* (Seattle: University of Washington Press, 1970).

BIOGRAPHICAL ESSAYS

A SAMPLE OF THE DIVERSITY OF THE SUFFRAGE MOVEMENT

The short biographies below are intended to show the diversity of the suffrage movement, in contrast to the histories of the movement which concentrate upon the two national organizations and their leadership. Suffragists came from the West, from the South, they were African American, they worked for a living in factories and sweatshops, and some were wealthy philanthropists. These biographies are necessarily short given the demands of space here. They can be filled out by looking for the numerous biographies of these women and others available online. Contrast the lives of these women with the lives of the more well-known leaders – Susan B. Anthony, Elizabeth Cady Stanton, Lucy Stone, Carrie Catt, and Anna Howard Shaw. You will find similarities and differences.

BIOGRAPHIES OF SUFFRAGISTS

The West

Abigail Jane Scott Duniway (October 22, 1834 to October 11, 1915): Suffragist, journalist, and pioneer settler in Oregon.

A young Abigail Scott walked from Illinois across the Oregon trail in 1852. Her family was one of the thousands crossing the mountains that summer, and the Scott family faced death—her mother died of cholera—and hardship, losing their funds in a river accident. As did many women on the frontier, Abigail farmed, taught school, set up a boarding school, and started a millinery shop. She married Benjamin Charles Duniway who had also come from Illinois in August 1853. Influenced by the hardships women endured and the lack of power women had to protect their own income, Duniway moved to Portland and established a weekly woman's rights newspaper. The newspaper was her springboard to a lifetime of campaigning for woman suffrage in the Pacific Northwest and Idaho. She founded the Oregon Equal Suffrage Association in 1873, and was central to the success of woman suffrage campaigning in Washington Territory in 1883 and Idaho in 1896. Duniway was unusual in her virulent opposition to linking woman suffrage and temperance, believing that the Woman's Christian Temperance Union roused the liquor industry to opposition to any suffrage battle. Duniway split with Susan B. Anthony on this issue. After a lifetime in suffrage, Duniway was honored in Chicago at the World's Columbian Exposition in 1893. Abigail Scott Duniway is an example of suffragists who single-handedly raised the question of woman suffrage in the West, put her individual imprint on the suffrage battles, and never came to terms with the respectable turn of the suffrage movement in the 1880s. She died in Portland in 1915.

The South

Kate M. Gordon (July 14, 1861 to August 24, 1932): Suffragist and reformer.

Kate Gordon was a Southern suffragist and municipal reformer, born in New Orleans into a family that moved in fashionable society. Both Kate and her sister June worked on civic reform, but Kate came to believe that only woman suffrage would give women the political power to push through legislation. Finding existing women's clubs too conservative, she founded the ERA club (standing for Equal Rights Association). When Kate Gordon succeeded in improving New Orleans' sewer system, she was invited to address the 1900 annual convention of the National American Woman Suffrage Association (NAWSA). After being appointed correspondence secretary, Gordon persuaded NAWSA to hold their 1903 convention in New Orleans, where southern race rhetoric was overwhelming, and where NAWSA supported a states' rights position on segregation. From 1903 to 1914, Kate Gordon headed the Louisiana State Suffrage Association. When NAWSA moved to action on a federal amendment, which she opposed, Gordon, with funds from Alva Belmont, organized the Southern States Woman Suffrage Conference to oppose any federal amendment. Kate Gordon and Laura Clay from Kentucky went to Tennessee for the ratification campaign, where, abandoning their links with NAWSA, they joined forces with antisuffrage forces to protect a whites' only votes in the South. After 1920, Kate Gordon went back to civic reform, notably to eradicate tuberculosis. She died at age seventy-one in New Orleans.

The Northeast: New York

Leonora O'Reilly (February 16, 1870 to April 3, 1927): Labor organizer, suffragist.

Leonora O'Reilly grew up in poverty in the Lower East Side of New York after the death of her father left her mother penniless. Leonora joined her mother in the garment industry at age seven. Her mother took her to labor meetings, and at age sixteen she joined the Knights of Labor, one of the few labor groups that welcomed women. O'Reilly then organized a Working Women's Society, which caught the notice of philanthropist Josephine Shaw Lowell, who introduced her to other reformers. Eventually, O'Reilly met Lillian Wald of the Henry St. Settlement and was welcomed into the Social Reform Club. O'Reilly bridged the gap between upper-class reformers and working-class women.

While developing her labor and reform connections, Leonora O'Reilly worked ten hours a day in a shirtwaist factory where she organized a local of the United Garment Workers of America and became known as an influential and effective speaker for the cause of working-class women. Wealthy patrons paid for her to take time away from work to expand her education and to rest. O'Reilly emerged from this period as a labor leader, working particularly through the Women's Trade Union League. O'Reilly and Rose Schneiderman became speakers for striking women in the Uprising of the Twenty Thousand and after the Triangle Shirtwaist Fire in March of 1911. O'Reilly was a link between wealthy suffragists in New York and the working-class suffragists of the Lower East Side.

Boston

Josephine St. Pierre Ruffin (August 31, 1842 to March 13, 1924): Suffragist and leader of racial uplift and self-help organizations.

Josephine St. Pierre Ruffin's life exemplifies the life of black women in the late nineteenth century who trod a path through deepening segregation in the North and the hardening of violence and segregation in the South. Born into a wealthy family in Boston and married into another prominent black family, Ruffin had the means to do philanthropic work. Her husband, George, became Boston's first black municipal judge. The double-edged sword of this social and economic status was the need to establish her respectability, education, and ability in a white world determined to ignore class differences in the black community. Ruffin, like other prominent black women, was careful to maintain her respectable and cultivated image.

Married at sixteen to George Lewis Ruffin, the couple moved to England to avoid the tentacles of American racism, returning when civil war looked imminent. Josephine Ruffin raised troops for the fifty-fourth and fifty-fifth Massachusetts regiments and worked for the U.S. Sanitary Commission. She became a journalist using the press as a way to keep black women's clubs in touch with each other. As president of a women's club, the New Era Club, Ruffin was a member of the Massachusetts State Federation of Women's Clubs. Ruffin's presence at the General Federation of Women's Clubs (GFWC) meeting in 1900 precipitated the de facto segregation of the GFWC. Delegates from western states supported Ruffin as she sought to have her credentials accepted as the Executive Board and southerners made efforts to block her from the national meeting. Ruffin refused to give way, forcing a decision. After extensive and acrimonious debate, each club was left to make its own rules for membership.

Josephine Ruffin's public career continued as a social reformer and suffragist, working at times with Lucy Stone and Julia Ward Howe. Understanding that black women could not rely upon others for self-help, Ruffin called for a convention to unite black women's organizations. Women from twenty clubs gathered and established the National Federation of Afro-American Women, which merged with the Colored Women's League in 1896 and became the National Association of Colored Women, whose motto, "Lifting as We Climb," is evidence that African American women believed they must carve their own path to suffrage and community improvement. Ruffin died in Boston in 1924.

The Pacific West: San Francisco

Maud Younger (January 1870 to June 1936): Labor organizer and suffragist.

Maud Younger was one of the wealthy suffragists who provided funds for the cause. She grew up as an heiress who went to Europe every summer, but in 1901, she stopped in New York, intending to spend a few weeks at the College Settlement in Lower East Side to find out more about the lives of impoverished immigrants. Younger stayed for five years, shifting from a society woman to a trade unionist and suffragist. She wrote of her experience working as a waitress in New York in *McClure's Magazine* in 1907 and then returned to San Francisco where she organized a local for waitresses and acquired the nickname of the "millionaire waitress." Young, confident, and a good speaker, Maud Younger was an example of the flamboyant suffragist, determined to make every voting citizen take notice of the suffrage campaign. In 1911, as one of the numerous publicity stunts of the California campaign, Maud drove a team of six horses, with a suffrage float on the wagon behind her, down Market Street in the Labor Day parade. She organized a Wage Earners' Equal Suffrage League which led the working-class women's drive for the vote. With the vote won in California, Younger went back to New York, working with the Women's Trade Union League and then with Alice Paul. Maud Younger became the Congressional Union lobbying counterpart to the NAWSA's Maud Wood Park. With differing notions of what was effective, Younger preferred to put pressure on representatives, while Park focused on engaging men in Congress with a steady stream of visitors and information. Both Park and Younger constructed elaborate index card files on every member of Congress. After ratification, Younger continued to work on protective labor legislation until Alice Paul and the National Woman's Party introduced the Equal Rights Amendment in 1923 when, rather unexpectedly, she abandoned protective labor legislation for equal rights. Maud Younger died in 1936 at her home, Overlook Ranch, in Los Gatos.

PRIMARY DOCUMENTS

1. The Nineteenth Amendment as passed and ratified, 1920

The Nineteenth Amendment recognized women's right to vote on the national level, as well as asserting their right to vote in all state and local elections that had not already expanded the suffrage to them.

Amendment XIX

The right of citizens of the United States to vote shall not be denied or abridged by the United States or by any state on account of sex.

Congress shall have power to enforce this article by appropriate legislation.

Source: Joint Resolution of Congress proposing a constitutional amendment extending the right of suffrage to women, approved June 4, 1919. Ratified Amendments, 1795–1992; General Records of the United States Government; Record Group 11; National Archives.

INTRODUCTION: ABOLITION AND WOMAN'S RIGHTS

Former slave Sojourner Truth was perhaps the most famous black suffragist. She became one of the most popular orators of the mid-nineteenth century, speaking out against slavery and for women's rights. On May 9, 1867, Truth delivered the following address at the first annual meeting of the American Equal Rights Association, formed by many prominent reformers to fight for universal suffrage. In her speech, the first document below, Truth gives her reasons for women needing the vote. The second document shows the divided opinions over supporting votes for black men alone and waiting to secure woman suffrage in another amendment.

2. Sojourner Truth, Address to the American Equal Rights Association (1867)

My friends, I am rejoiced that you are glad, but I don't know how you will feel when I get through. I come from another field—the country of the slave. They have got their liberty—so much good luck to have slavery partly destroyed; not entirely. I want it root and branch destroyed. Then we will all be free indeed. I feel that if I have to answer for the deeds done in my body just as much as a man, I have a right to have just as much as a man. There is a great stir about colored men getting their rights, but not a word about the colored women; and if colored men get their rights, and not colored women theirs, you see the colored men will be masters over the women, and it will be just as bad as it was before. So I am for keeping the thing going while things are stirring; because if we wait till it is still, it will take a great while to get it going again. White women are a great deal smarter, and know more than colored women, while colored women do not know scarcely anything. They go out washing, which is about as high as a colored woman gets, and their men go about idle, strutting up and down; and when the women come home, they ask for their money and take it all, and then scold because there is no food. I want you to consider on that, chil'n. I call you chil'n; you are somebody's chil'n, and I am old enough to be mother of all that is here. I want women to have their rights. In the courts women have no right, no voice; nobody speaks for them. I wish woman to have her voice there among the pettifoggers. If it is not a place fit for women, it is unfit for men to be there.

I am above eighty years old; it is about time for me to be going. I have been forty years a slave and forty years free, and would be here forty years more to have equal rights for all. I suppose I am kept here because something remains for me to do; I suppose I am yet to help to break the chain. I have done a great deal of work; as much as a man, but did not get so much pay. I used to work in the field and bind grain, keeping up with the cradler; but men doing no more, got twice as much pay; so with the German women. They work in the field and do as much work, but do not get the pay. We do as much, we eat as much, we want as much. I suppose I am about the only colored woman that goes about to speak for the rights of the colored women. I want to keep the thing stirring, now that the ice is cracked. What we want is a little money. You men know that you get as much again as women when you write, or for what you do. When we get our rights we shall not have to come to you for money, for then we shall have money enough in our pockets; and may be you will ask us for money. But help us now until we get it. It is a good consolation to know that when we have got this battle once fought we shall not be coming to you any more. You have been having our rights so long, that you think, like a slave-holder, that you own us. I know that it is hard for one who has held the reins for so long to give up; it cuts like a knife. It will feel all the better when it closes up again. I have been in Washington about three years, seeing about these colored people. Now colored men have the right to vote. There ought to be equal rights now more than ever, since colored people have got their freedom. I am going to talk several times while I am here; so now I will do a little singing. I have not heard any singing since I came here.

Source: *New York Tribune* (May 10, 1867), 8.

3. Debates at the American Equal Rights Association Meeting (1869)

STEPHEN FOSTER laid down the principle that when any persons on account of strong objections against them in the minds of some, prevented harmony in a society and efficiency in its operations, those persons should retire from prominent positions in that society. He said he had taken that course when, as agent of the Anti-Slavery Society, he became obnoxious on account of his position on some questions. He objected, to certain nominations made by the committee for various reasons. The first was that the persons nominated had publicly repudiated the principles of the society. One of these was the presiding officer.

Mrs. STANTON: I would like you to say in what respect.

Mr. FOSTER: I will with pleasure; for, ladies and gentlemen, I admire our talented President with all my heart, and love the woman. (Great laughter.) But I believe she has publicly repudiated the principles of the society.

Mrs. STANTON: I would like Mr. Foster to state in what way.

Mr. FOSTER: What are these principles? The equality of men—universal suffrage. These ladies stand at the head of a paper which has adopted as its motto Educated Suffrage. I put myself on this platform as an enemy of educated suffrage, as an enemy of white suffrage, as an enemy of man suffrage, as an enemy of every kind of suffrage except universal suffrage. *The Revolution* lately had an article headed "That Infamous Fifteenth Amendment." It is true it was not written by our President, yet it comes from a person whom she has over and over again publicly indorsed. I am not willing to take George Francis Train on this platform with his ridicule of the negro and opposition to his enfranchisement.

Mrs. MARY A. LIVERMORE: Is it quite generous to bring George Francis Train on this platform when he has retired from *The Revolution* entirely?

Mr. FOSTER: If *The Revolution*, which has so often indorsed George Francis Train, will repudiate him because of his course in respect to the negro's rights, I have nothing further to say. But it does not repudiate him. He goes out; it does not cast him out.

Miss ANTHONY: Of course it does not.

Mr. FOSTER: My friend says yes to what I have said. I thought it was so. I only wanted to tell you why the Massachusetts society can not coalesce with the party here, and why we want these women to retire and leave us to nominate officers who can receive the respect of both parties. The Massachusetts Abolitionists can not co-operate with this society as it is now organized. If you choose to put officers here that ridicule the negro, and pronounce the Amendment infamous, why I must retire; I can not work with you. You can not have my support, and you must not use my name. I can not shoulder the responsibility of electing officers who publicly repudiate the principles of the society.

HENRY B. BLACKWELL said: In regard to the criticisms on our officers, I will agree that many unwise things have been written in *The Revolution* by a gentleman who furnished part of the means by which that paper has been carried on. But that gentleman has withdrawn, and you, who know the real opinions of Miss Anthony and Mrs. Stanton on the question of negro suffrage, do not believe that they mean to create antagonism between the negro and the woman question. If they did disbelieve in negro suffrage, it would be no reason for excluding them. We should no more exclude a person from our platform for disbelieving negro suffrage than a person should be excluded from the anti-slavery platform for disbelieving woman suffrage. But I know that Miss Anthony and Mrs. Stanton believe in the right of the negro to vote. We are united on that point. There is no question of principle between us.

The vote on the report of the Committee on Organization was now taken, and adopted by a large majority.

Mr. DOUGLASS: I came here more as a listener than to speak, and I have listened with a great deal of pleasure to the eloquent address of the Rev. Mr. Frothingham and the splendid address of the President. There is no name greater than that of Elizabeth Cady Stanton in the matter of woman's rights and equal rights, but my sentiments are tinged a little against *The Revolution*.

There was in the address to which I allude the employment of certain names, such as "Sambo," and the gardener, and the bootblack, and the daughters of Jefferson and Washington, and all the rest that I can not coincide with. I have asked what difference there is between the daughters of Jefferson and Washington and other daughters. (Laughter.) I must say that I do not see how any one can pretend that there is the same urgency in giving the ballot to woman as to the negro. With us, the matter is a question of life and death, at least, in fifteen States of the Union. When women, because they are women, are hunted down through the cities of New York and New Orleans; when they are dragged from their houses and hung upon lamp-posts; when their children are torn from their arms, and their brains dashed out upon the pavement; when they are objects of insult and outrage at every turn; when they are in danger of having their homes burnt down over their heads; when their children are not allowed to enter schools; then they will have an urgency to obtain the ballot equal to our own. (Great applause.)

A VOICE: Is that not all true about black women?

Mr. DOUGLASS: Yes, yes, yes; it is true of the black woman, but not because she is a woman, but because she is black. (Applause.) Julia Ward Howe at the conclusion of her great speech delivered at the convention in Boston last year, said: "I am willing that the negro shall get the ballot before me." (Applause.) Woman!

Why, she has 10,000 modes of grappling with her difficulties. I believe that all the virtue of the world can take care of all the evil. I believe that all the intelligence can take care of all the ignorance. (Applause.) I am in favor of woman's suffrage in order that we shall have all the virtue and vice confronted. Let me tell you that when there were few houses in which the black man could have put his head, this woolly head of mine found a refuge in the house of Mrs. Elizabeth Cady Stanton, and if I had been blacker than sixteen midnights, without a single star, it would have been the same. (Applause.)

Miss ANTHONY: The old anti-slavery school say women must stand back and wait until the negroes shall be recognized. But we say, if you will not give the whole loaf of suffrage to the entire people, give it to the most intelligent first. (Applause.) If intelligence, justice, and morality are to have precedence in the Government, let the question of woman be brought up first and that of the negro last. (Applause.) While I was canvassing the State with petitions and had them filled with names for our cause to the Legislature, a man dared to say to me that the freedom of women was all a theory and not a practical thing. (Applause.) When Mr. Douglass mentioned the black man first and the woman last, if he had noticed he would have seen that it was the men that clapped and not the women. There is not the woman born who desires to eat the bread of dependence, no matter whether it be from the hand of father, husband, or brother; for any one who does so eat her bread places herself in the power of the person from whom she takes it. (Applause.) Mr. Douglass talks about the wrongs of the negro; but with all the outrages that he to-day suffers, he would not exchange his sex and take the place of Elizabeth Cady Stanton. (Laughter and applause.)

Mr. DOUGLASS: I want to know if granting you the right of suffrage will change the nature of our sexes? (Great laughter.)

Miss ANTHONY: It will change the pecuniary position of woman; it will place her where she can earn her own bread. (Loud applause.) She will not then be driven to such employments only as man chooses for her.

Mrs. NORTON said that Mr. Douglass's remarks left her to defend the Government from the inferred inability to grapple with the two questions at once. It legislates upon many questions at one and the same time, and it has the power to decide the woman question and the negro question at one and the same time.

(Applause.)

Mrs. LUCY STONE: Mrs. Stanton will, of course, advocate the precedence for her sex, and Mr. Douglass's will strive for the first position for his, and both are perhaps right. If it be true that the government derives its authority from the consent of the governed, we, are safe in trusting that principle to the uttermost. If one has a right to say that you can not read and therefore can not vote, then it may be said that you are a woman and therefore can not vote. We are lost if we turn away from the middle prin- ciple and argue for one class. I was once a teacher among fugitive slaves. There was one old man, and every tooth was gone, his hair was white, and his face was full of wrinkles, yet, day after day and hour after hour, he came up to the school-house and tried with patience to learn to read, and by-and-by, when he had spelled out the first few verses of the first chapter of the Gospel of St. John, he said to me, "Now, I want to learn to write." I tried to make him satisfied with what he had acquired, but the old man said, "Mrs. Stone, somewhere in the wide world I have a son; I have not heard from him in twenty years; if I should hear from him, I want to write to him, so take hold of my hand and teach me." I did, but before he had proceeded in many lessons, the angels came and gathered him up and bore him to his Father. Let no man speak of an educated suffrage. The gentle- man who addressed you claimed that the negroes had the first right to the suffrage, and drew a picture which only his great word-power can do. He again in Massachusetts, when it had cast a majority in favor of Grant and negro suffrage, stood upon the platform and said that woman had better wait for the negro; that is, that both could not be carried, and that the negro had better be the one.

But I freely forgave him because he felt as he spoke. But woman suf- frage is more imperative than his own; and I want to remind the audi- ence that when he says what the Ku-Kluxes did all over the South, the Ku-Kluxes here in the North in the shape of men, take away the children from the mother, and separate them as completely as if done on the block of the auctioneer. Over in New Jersey they have a law which says that any father—he might be the most brutal man that ever existed—any father, it says, whether he be under age or not, may by his last will and testament dispose of the custody of his child, born or to be born, and that such dis- position shall be good against all persons, and that the mother may not recover her child; and that law modified in form exists over every State in the Union except in Kansas. Woman has an ocean of wrongs too deep for any plummet, and the negro, too, has an ocean of wrongs that can not be fathomed. There are two great oceans; in the one is the black man, and in the other is the woman. But I thank God for that XV Amendment, and hope that it will be adopted in every State. I will be thankful in my soul if anybody can get out of the terrible pit. But I believe that the safety of the government would be more promoted by the admission of woman as an element of restoration and harmony than the negro. I believe that the influence of woman will save the country before every other power. (Applause.) I see the signs of the times pointing to this consummation, and I believe that in some parts of the country women will vote for the President of these United States in 1872.

(Applause.)

At the opening of the evening session Henry B. Blackwell presented a series of resolutions. Antoinette Brown Blackwell spoke, and was followed by Olive Logan.

Source: Debates at the American Equal Rights Association Meeting, New York City, May 12–14, 1869. Reprinted in *The History of Woman Suffrage*, Vol. II, edited by Elizabeth Cady Stanton, Susan B. Anthony, and Matilda Joselyn Gage. New York, NY: National American Woman Suffrage Association, 1882, 381–98.

THE NEW DEPARTURE: USING THE FOURTEENTH AMENDMENT TO CLAIM WOMEN'S RIGHT TO VOTE

Political interests and constitutional interpretation collided when suffragists claimed that because they were citizens as defined in the Fourteenth Amendment, they could vote. Virginia Minor's case was appealed upwards to the U.S. Supreme Court in Minor v. Happersett, *and Susan B. Anthony's trial garnered national attention. The logic of the suffragists' argument seems compelling to some historians and scholars alike.*

4. Virginia L. Minor's petition to the circuit court of St. Louis County, Missouri, 1872

Virginia L. Minor and Francis Minor, her husband, Plaintiffs, v. Reese Happersett, Defendant.

The plaintiff, Virginia L. Minor (with whom is joined her husband, Francis Minor, as required by the law of Missouri), states, that under the Constitution and law of Missouri, all persons wishing to vote at any election, must previously have been registered in the manner pointed out by law, this being a condition precedent to the exercise of the elective franchise.

That on the fifteenth day of October, 1872 (one of the days fixed by law for the registration of voters), and long prior thereto, she was a native-born, free white citizen of the United States, and of the State of Missouri, and on the day last mentioned she was over the age of twenty-one years.

That on said day, the plaintiff was a resident of the thirteenth election district of the city and county of St. Louis, in the State of Missouri, and had been residing in said county and election district, for the entire period of twelve months and more, immediately preceding said fifteenth day of October, 1872, and for more than twenty years had been and is a tax-paying, law-abiding citizen of the county and State aforesaid.

That on said last mentioned day, the defendant, having been duly and legally appointed Registrar and entered upon the discharge of the duties thereof at the office of registration, to wit: No. 2004 Market Street, in said city and county of St. Louis, it became and was then and there his duty to register all citizens, resident in said district as aforesaid, entitled to the elective franchise, who might apply to him for that purpose.

The plaintiff further states, that wishing to exercise her privilege as a citizen of the United States, and vote for Electors for President and Vice-President of the United States, and for a Representative in Congress, and for other officers, at the General Election held in November, 1872: While said defendant was so acting as Registrar, on said 15th day of October, 1872, she appeared before him, at his office aforesaid, and then and there offered to take and subscribe the oath to support the Constitution of the United States and of the State of Missouri, as required by the registration law of said State, approved March 10, 1871, and respectfully applied to him to be registered as a lawful voter, which said defendant then and there refused to do.

The plaintiff further states, that the defendant, well knowing that she, as a citizen of the United States and of the State of Missouri, resident as aforesaid, was then and there entitled to all the privileges and immunities of citizenship, chief among which is the elective franchise, and as such, was entitled to be registered, in order to exercise said privilege: yet, unlawfully intending, contriving, and designing to deprive the plaintiff of said franchise or privilege, then and there knowingly, willfully, maliciously, and corruptly refused to place her name upon the list of registered voters, whereby she was deprived of her right to vote.

Defendant stated to plaintiff, that she was not entitled to be registered, or to vote, because she was not a "male" citizen, but a woman! That by the Constitution of Missouri, Art. II., Sec. 18, and by the aforesaid registration law of said State, approved March 10, 1871, it is provided and declared, that only "male citizens" of the United States, etc., are entitled or permitted to vote.

But the plaintiff protests against such decision, and she declares and maintains that said provisions of the Constitution and registration law of Missouri aforesaid, are in conflict with, and repugnant to the Constitution of the United States, which is paramount to State authority; and that they are especially in conflict with the following articles and clauses of said Constitution of the United States, to wit:

Art. I. Sec. 9. Which declares that no Bill of Attainder shall be passed.

Art. I. Sec. 10. No State shall pass any Bill of Attainder, or grant any title of nobility.

Art. IV. Sec. 2. The citizens of each State shall be entitled to all privileges and immunities of citizens in the several States.

Art. IV. Sec. 4. The United States shall guarantee to every State a republican form of government.

Art. VI. This Constitution and the laws of the United States which shall be made in pursuance thereof, shall be the supreme law of the land, anything in the Constitutions or laws of any State to the contrary notwithstanding.

Amendments

Art. V. No person shall be . . . deprived of life, liberty, or property without due process of law.

Art. IX. The enumeration in the Constitution of certain rights, shall not be construed to deny or disparage others retained by the people.

Art. XIV. Sec. 1. All persons born or naturalized in the United States, and subject to the jurisdiction thereof, are citizens of the United States and of the State wherein they reside. No State shall make or enforce any law which shall abridge the privileges or immunities of citizens of the

United States. Nor shall any State deprive any person of life, liberty, or property, without due process of law; nor deny to any person within its jurisdiction, the equal protection of the laws.

The plaintiff states, that by reason of the wrongful act of the defendant as aforesaid, she has been damaged in the sum of ten thousand dollars, for which she prays judgment. . . .

John M. Krum,
Francis Minor, (Att'ys for Plaffs)
John B. Henderson,

Demurrer. In the Circuit Court of St. Louis County: Virginia L. Minor and Francis Minor, her husband, Plaintiffs, versus Reese Happersett.

The defendant, Reese Happersett, demurs to the petition of plaintiffs, and for cause of demurrer defendant states that said petition does not state facts sufficient to constitute a cause of action, for the following reasons:

1. Because said Virginia L. Minor, plaintiff, had no right to vote at the general election held in November, 1872, in said petition referred to.

2. Because said Virginia L. Minor had no right to be registered for voting by said defendant, at the time and in the manner in said petition alleged.

3. Because it was the duty of the defendant to refuse to place said Virginia L. Minor's name upon the list of registered voters in said petition referred to.

All of which appears by said petition.

Smith P. Galt, *Atty for Deft*.

Source: Minor v. Happersett, 88 U.S. (21 Wall.) 162 (1875).

5. The United States of America v. Susan B. Anthony, 1873

United States Circuit Court (Northern District of New York). *The United States of America v. Susan B. Anthony*; Hon. Ward Hunt, Presiding. Appearances: For the United States: Hon. Richard Crowley, U.S. District Attorney; For the Defendant: Hon. Henry R. Selden, John Van Voorhis, Esq.

Tried at Canandaigua, Tuesday and Wednesday, June 17th and 18th, 1873, before Hon. Ward Hunt, and a jury. Jury impaneled at 2:30 p.m.

Mr. Crowley opened the case as follows:

May it please the Court and Gentlemen of the Jury:

On the 5th of November, 1872, there was held in this State, as well as in other States of the Union, a general election for different officers, and among those, for candidates to represent several districts of this State in the Congress of the United States. The defendant, Miss Susan B. Anthony, at the time resided in the city of Rochester, in the country of Monroe, Northern District of New York, and upon the 5th day of November, 1872, she voted for a representative in the Congress of the United States, to represent the 20th Congressional District of the State, and also for a representative at large for the State of New York, to represent the State in the Congress of the United States. At that time she was a woman. I suppose there will be no question about that. The question in this case, if there be a question of fact about it at all, will, in my judgment, be rather a question of law than one of fact. I suppose that there will be no question about fact, substantially, in the case when all of the evidence is out, and it will be for you to decide under the charge of his honor, the Judge, whether or not the defendant committed the offense of voting for a representative in Congress upon that occasion. We think, on the part of the Government, that there is no question about it either one way or the other, neither a question of fact, nor a question of law, and that whatever Miss Anthony's intentions may have been—whether they were good or otherwise—she did not have a right to vote upon that question, and if she did vote without having a lawful right to vote, then there is no question but what she is guilty of violating a law of the United States in that behalf enacted by the Congress of the United States.

We don't claim in the case, gentlemen, that Miss Anthony is of that class of people who go about "repeating." We don't claim that she went from place to place for the purpose of offering her vote. But we do claim that upon the 5th of November, 1872, she voted, and whether she believed that she had a right to vote or not, it being a question of law, that she is within the Statute. Congress in 1870 passed the following statute: (Reads 19th Section of the Act of 1870, page 144, 16th statutes at large.) It is not necessary for me, gentlemen, at this stage of the case, to state all the facts which will be proven on the part of the Government. I shall leave that to be shown by the evidence and by the witnesses, and if any question of law shall arise his Honor will undoubtedly give you instruction as he shall deem proper. Conceded, that on the 5th day of November, 1872, Miss Susan B. Anthony was a woman.

* * *

The Court, after listening to an argument from the District Attorney, denied the motion for a new trial.

The Court: The prisoner will stand up. Has the prisoner anything to say why sentence shall not be pronounced?

Miss Anthony: Yes, your honor, I have many things to say; for in your ordered verdict of guilty, you have trampled underfoot every vital principle of our government. My natural rights, my civil rights, my political rights, are all alike ignored. Robbed of the fundamental privilege of citizenship, I am degraded from the status of a citizen to that of a subject; and not only myself individually, but all of my sex, are, by your honor's verdict, doomed to political subjection under this so-called Republican government.

Judge Hunt: The Court can not listen to a rehearsal of arguments the prisoner's counsel has already consumed three hours in presenting.

Miss Anthony: May it please your honor, I am not arguing the question, but simply stating the reasons why sentence can not, in justice, be pronounced against me. Your denial of my citizen's right to vote is the denial of my right of consent as one of the governed, the denial of my right of representation as one of the taxed, the denial of my right to a trial by a jury of my peers as an offender against law, therefore, the denial of my sacred rights to life, liberty, property, and—

Judge Hunt: The Court can not allow the prisoner to go on.

Miss Anthony: But your honor will not deny me this one and only poor privilege of protest against this high-handed outrage upon my citizen's rights. May it please the Court to remember that since the day of my arrest last November, this is the first time that either myself or any person of my disfranchised class has been allowed a word of defense before judge or jury—

Judge Hunt: The prisoner must sit down. The Court can not allow it.

Miss Anthony: All my prosecutors, from the Eighth Ward corner grocery politician, who entered the complaint, to the United States Marshal,

Commissioner, District Attorney, District Judge, your honor on the bench, not one is my peer, but each and all are my political sovereigns; and had your honor submitted my case to the jury, as was clearly your duty, even then I should have had just cause of protest, for not one of those men was my peer; but, native or foreign, white or black, rich or poor, educated or ignorant, awake or asleep, sober or drunk, each and every man of them was my political superior; hence, in no sense, my peer. Even, under such circumstances, a commoner of England, tried before a jury of lords, would have far less cause to complain than should I, a woman, tried before a jury of men. Even my counsel, the Hon. Henry R. Selden, who has argued my cause so ably, so earnestly, so unanswerably before your honor, is my political sovereign. Precisely as no disfranchised person is entitled to sit upon a jury, and no woman is entitled to the franchise, so, none but a regularly admitted lawyer is allowed to practice in the courts, and no woman can gain admission to the bar—hence, jury, judge, counsel, must all be of the superior class.

Judge Hunt: The Court must insist—the prisoner has been tried according to the established forms of law.

Miss Anthony: Yes, your honor, but by forms of law all made by men, interpreted by men, administered by men, in favor of men, and against women; and hence, your honor's ordered verdict of guilty, against a United States citizen for the exercise of "that citizen's right to vote," simply because that citizen was a woman and not a man. But, yesterday, the same man-made forms of law declared it a crime punishable with $1,000 fine and six months' imprisonment, for you, or me, or any of us, to give a cup of cold water, a crust of bread, or a night's shelter to a panting fugitive as he was tracking his way to Canada. And every man or woman in whose veins coursed a drop of human sympathy violated that wicked law, reckless of consequences, and was justified in so doing. As then the slaves who got their freedom must take it over, or under, or through the unjust forms of law, precisely so now must women, to get their right to a voice in this Government, take it; and I have taken mine, and mean to take it at every opportunity.

Judge Hunt: The Court orders the prisoner to sit down. It will not allow another word.

Miss Anthony: When I was brought before your honor for trial, I hoped for a broad and liberal interpretation of the Constitution and its recent amendments, that should declare all United States citizens under its protecting aegis—that should declare equality of rights the national guarantee of all persons born or naturalized in the United States. But failing to get this justice—failing, even, to get a trial by a jury not of my peers—I ask not leniency at your hands—but rather the full rigors of the law.

Judge Hunt: The Court must insist—(Here the prisoner sat down.)

Judge Hunt: The prisoner will stand up. (Here Miss Anthony rose again.) The sentence of the Court is that you pay a fine of one hundred dollars and the costs of the prosecution.

Miss Anthony: May it please your honor, I shall never pay a dollar of your unjust penalty. All the stock in trade I possess is a $10,000 debt, incurred by publishing my paper—*The Revolution*—four years ago, the sole object of which was to educate all women to do precisely as I have done, rebel against your man-made unjust, unconstitutional forms of law, that tax, fine, imprison, and hang women, while they deny them the right of representation in the Government; and I shall work on with might and main to pay every dollar of that honest debt, but not a penny shall go to this unjust claim. And I shall earnestly and persistently continue to urge all women to the practical recognition of the old revolutionary maxim, that "Resistance to tyranny is obedience to God."

Judge Hunt: Madam, the Court will not order you committed until the fine is paid.

Source: United States v. Susan B. Anthony, 24 Fed. Case No. 14.459 (1873).

NEW ARGUMENTS FOR WOMAN SUFFRAGE: 1890–1913

The following documents reveal new and differing arguments for woman suffrage. Early justifications included the assertion that women should have the vote simply because they were humans and part of those who made up the body politic. By 1900, suffragists had widened their arguments. Belle Kearney uses racial superiority to justify white woman suffrage. Jane Addams reflects the widespread opinion that women voting would improve cities and industrial conditions, and Caroline Lowe shows how working women needed the vote to protect themselves from exploitation.

6. Belle Kearney, "The South and Woman Suffrage," 1903

The address of Miss Belle Kearney, Mississippi's famous orator, was a leading feature of the last evening's program—The South and Woman Suffrage. It began with a comprehensive review of the part the South had had in the development of the nation from its earliest days. "During the seventy-one years reaching from Washington's administration to that of Lincoln," she said, "the United States was practically under the domination of southern thought and leadership." She showed the record southern leaders had made in the wars; she traced the progress of slavery, which began alike in the North and South but proved unnecessary in the former, and told of the enormous struggle for white supremacy which had been placed on the South by the enfranchisement of the negro. "The present suffrage laws in the southern States are only temporary measures for protection," she said. "The enfranchisement of women will have to be effected and an educational and property qualification for the ballot be made to apply without discrimination to both sexes and both races." The address closed as follows:

"The enfranchisement of women would insure immediate and durable white supremacy, honestly attained, for upon unquestioned authority it is stated that in every southern State but one there are more educated women than all the illiterate voters, white and black, native and foreign, combined. As you probably know, of all the women in the South who can read and write, ten out of every eleven are white. When it comes to the proportion of property between the races, that of the white outweighs that of the black immeasurably. The South is slow to grasp the great fact that the enfranchisement of women would settle the race question in politics. The civilization of the North is threatened by the influx of foreigners with their imported customs; by the greed of monopolistic wealth and the unrest among the working classes; by the strength of the liquor traffic and encroachments upon religious belief. Some day the North will be compelled to look to the South for redemption from those evils on account of the purity of its Anglo-Saxon blood, the simplicity of its social and economic structure, the great advance in prohibitory law and the maintenance of the sanctity of its faith, which has been kept inviolate. Just as surely as the North will be forced to turn to the South for the nation's salvation, just so surely will the South be compelled to look to its

Anglo-Saxon women as the medium through which to retain the supremacy of the white race over the African."

Miss Kearney's speech was enthusiastically received and at its end Mrs. Catt said she had been getting many letters from persons hesitating to join the association lest it should admit clubs of colored people. "We recognize States' rights," she said, "and Louisiana has the right to regulate the membership of its own association, but it has not the right to regulate that of Massachusetts or vice versa," and she continued: "We are all of us apt to be arrogant on the score of our Anglo-Saxon blood but we must remember that ages ago the ancestors of the Anglo-Saxons were regarded as so low and embruted that the Romans refused to have them for slaves. The Anglo-Saxon is the dominant race today but things may change. The race that will be dominant through the ages will be the one that proves itself the most worthy. . . . Miss Kearney is right in saying that the race problem is the problem of the whole country and not that of the South alone. The responsibility for it is partly ours but if the North shipped slaves to the South and sold them, remember that the North has sent some money since then into the South to help undo part of the wrong that it did to you and to them. Let us try to get nearer together and to understand each other's ideas on the race question and solve it together."

Source: Belle Kearney. "The South and Woman Suffrage." NAWSA Convention, New Orleans, Louisiana, March 15–25, 1903. Reprinted in *The History of Woman Suffrage*, Vol. V, edited by Ida Husted Harper. New York, NY: National American Woman Suffrage Association, 1922, 82–83.

7. Jane Addams, "The Modern City and the Municipal Franchise for Women," NAWSA Convention, Baltimore, Maryland, February 7–13, 1906

It was at this meeting that Miss Jane Addams of Hull House, Chicago, made the address on The Modern City and the Municipal Franchise for Women, which was thenceforth a part of the standard suffrage literature. Quotations are wholly inadequate.

It has been well said that the modern city is a stronghold of industrialism quite as the feudal city was a stronghold of militarism, but the modern cities fear no enemies and rivals from without and their problems of government are solely internal. Affairs for the most part are going badly in these great new centres, in which the quickly-congregated population has not yet learned to arrange its affairs satisfactorily. Unsanitary housing, poisonous sewage, contaminated water, infant mortality, the spread of contagion, adulterated food, impure milk, smoke-laden air, ill-ventilated factories, dangerous occupations, juvenile crime, unwholesome crowding, prostitution and drunkenness are the enemies which the modern cities must face and overcome, would they survive. Logically their electorate should be made up of those who can bear a valiant part in this arduous contest, those who in the past have at least attempted to care for children, to clean houses, to prepare foods, to isolate the family from moral dangers; those who have traditionally taken care of that side of life which inevitably becomes the subject of municipal consideration and control as soon as the population is congested. To test the elector's fitness to deal with this situation by his ability to bear arms is absurd. These problems must be solved, if they are solved at all, not from the military point of view, not even from the industrial point of view, but from a third, which is rapidly developing in all the great cities of the world—the human-welfare point of view. . .

City housekeeping has failed partly because women, the traditional housekeepers, have not been consulted as to its multiform activities. The men have been carelessly indifferent to much of this civic housekeeping, as they have always been indifferent to the details of the household . . . The very multifariousness and complexity of a city government demand the help of minds accustomed to detail and variety of work, to a sense of obligation for the health and welfare of young children and to a responsibility for the cleanliness and comfort of other people. Because all these things have traditionally been in the hands of women, if they take no part in them now they are not only missing the education which the natural participation in civic life would bring to them but they are losing what they have always had.

Source: Jane Addams, "The Modern City and the Municipal Franchise for Women," NAWSA Convention, Baltimore, Maryland, February 7–13, 1906. Reprinted in *The History of Woman Suffrage*, Vol. V, edited by Ida Husted Harper. New York, NY: National American Woman Suffrage Association, 1922, 178–9.

8. Caroline A. Lowe, Address to NAWSA Convention, Philadelphia, Pennsylvania, November 21–26, 1912

Mrs. Caroline A. Lowe of Kansas City, Mo., spoke in behalf of the 7,000,000 wage-earning women of the United States from the standpoint of one who had earned her living since she was eighteen and declared that to them the need of the ballot was a vital one. She gave heart-breaking proofs of this fact and said:

From the standpoint of wages received we wage earners know it to be almost universal that the men in the industries receive twice the amount granted to us although we may be doing the same work. We work side by side with our brothers; we are children of the same parents, reared in the same homes, educated in the same schools, ride to and fro on the same early morning and late evening cars, work together the same number of hours in the same shops and we have equal need of food, clothing and shelter. But at 21 years of age our brothers are given a powerful weapon for self-defense, a larger means for growth and self-expression. We working women, because we find our sex not a source of strength but a source of weakness and a greater opportunity for exploitation, have even greater need of this weapon which is denied to us. Is there any justice underlying such a condition?

What of the working girl and her employer? Why is the ballot given to him while it is denied to us? Is it for the protection of his property that he may have a voice in the governing of his wealth, of his stocks and bonds and merchandise? The wealth of the working woman is far more precious to the welfare of the State. From nature's raw products the working class can readily replace all of the material wealth owned by the employing class but the wealth of the working woman is the wealth of flesh and blood, of all her physical, mental and spiritual powers. It is not only the wealth of today but that of future generations which is being bartered away so cheaply. Have we no right to a voice in the disposal of our wealth, the greatest that the world possesses, the priceless wealth of its womanhood? Is it not the cruelest injustice that the man whose material wealth is a source of strength and protection to him and of power over us should be given the additional advantage of an even greater weapon which he can use to perpetuate our condition of helpless subjection? . . . The industrial basis of the life of the woman has changed and the political superstructure must be adjusted to conform to it. This industrial change has given to woman a larger horizon, a greater freedom of action in the industrial world. Greater freedom and larger expression are at hand for her in the political life. The time is ripe for the extension of the franchise to women.

Source: Caroline A. Lowe. Address to NAWSA Convention, Philadelphia, Pennsylvania, November 21–26, 1912. Reprinted in *The History of Woman Suffrage,* Vol. V, edited by Ida Husted Harper. New York, NY: National American Woman Suffrage Association, 1922, 350–1.

SUFFRAGISTS CLAIM THE RIGHT TO PUBLIC ASSEMBLY: NEW CAMPAIGN METHODS

State-by-state campaigns for woman suffrage finally triumphed in 1910 after a long series of defeats. In Washington state, California, Illinois, and then across the East Coast, suffragist invented new ways of campaigning for their cause, putting woman suffrage on every corner so that every voter would be aware of their fight. The following documents show the various approaches to campaigning utilized by NAWSA, the Congressional Union, and the National Woman's Party.

9. The New York Campaign, 1915

The story of the growth of the woman suffrage movement in Greater New York is one of the most interesting chapters in the history of this cause, for while it advanced slowly for many years, it rose in 1915 and 1917 to a height never attained elsewhere and culminated in two campaigns that in number of adherents and comprehensive work were never equaled.

The Brooklyn Woman Suffrage Association was formed May 13, 1869, and the New York City Society in 1870. From this time various organizations came into permanent existence until in 1903 there were fifteen devoted to suffrage propaganda. In Manhattan (New York City) and Brooklyn these were bound together by county organizations but in order to unite all the suffragists in cooperative work the Interurban Woman Suffrage Council was formed in 1903 at the Brooklyn home of a pioneer, Mrs. Priscilla D. Hackstaff, with the President of the Kings County Political Equality League, Mrs. Martha Williams, presiding. The Interurban began with a roster of five which gradually increased to twenty affiliated societies, with an associate membership besides of 150 women. Under the able leadership of Mrs. Carrie Chapman Catt, chairman, it established headquarters in the Martha Washington Hotel, New York City, Feb. 15, 1907, with a secretary, Miss Fannie Chafin, in charge, and maintained committees on organization, literature, legislative work, press and lectures; formed clubs, held mass meetings and systematically distributed literature. The Council was the first suffrage organization in New York City to interview Assemblymen and Senators on woman suffrage and it called the first representative convention held in the big metropolis.

The Woman Suffrage Party of Greater New York was launched by this Council at Carnegie Hall, October 29, 1909, modelled after that of the two dominant political parties. Its first convention with 804 delegates and 200 alternates constituted the largest delegate suffrage body ever assembled in New York State. The new party announced that it would have a leader for each of the 63 assembly districts of the city and a captain for each of the 2,127 election districts, these and their assistant officers to be supervised by a borough chairman and other officers in each borough, the entire force to be directed by a city chairman assisted by city officers and a board of directors. Mrs. Catt, with whom the idea of the Party originated, and her co-workers believed that by reaching into every election district to influence its voters, they would bring suffrage close to the people and eventually influence parties and legislators through public opinion.

The population of Greater New York was 4,700,000 and the new party had a task of colossal proportions. It had to appeal to native Americans of all classes and conditions and to thousands of foreign born. It sent its forces to local political conventions; held mass meetings; issued thousands of leaflets in many languages; conducted street meetings, parades, plays, lectures, suffrage schools; gave entertainments and teas; sent appeals to churches and all kinds of organizations and to individual leaders; brought pressure on legislators through their constituents and obtained wide publicity in newspapers and magazines. It succeeded in all its efforts and increased its membership from 20,000 in 1910 to over 500,000 in 1917.

In 1915, at the beginning of the great campaign for a suffrage amendment to the State constitution, which had been submitted by the Legislature, the State was divided into twelve campaign districts. Greater New York was made the first and under the leadership of Miss Mary Garrett

Hay, who since 1912 had served as chairman, the City Woman Suffrage Party plunged into strenuous work, holding conventions, sending out organizers, raising $50,000 as a campaign fund, setting a specific task for each month of 1915 up to Election Day, and forming its own committees with chairmen as follows: Industrial, Miss Leonora O'Reilly; The Woman Voter, Mrs. Thomas B. Wells; Speakers' Bureau, Mrs. Mabel Russell; Congressional, Mrs. Lillian Griffin; the French, Mrs. Anna Ross Weeks; the German, Miss Catherine Dreier; the Press, Mrs. Oreola Williams Haskell; Ways and Means, Mrs. John B. McCutcheon.

The City Party began the intensive work of the campaign in January, 1915, when a swift pace was set for the succeeding months by having 60 district conventions, 170 canvassing suppers, four mass meetings, 27 canvassing conferences and a convention in Carnegie Hall. It was decided to canvass all of the 661,164 registered voters and hundreds of women spent long hours toiling up and down tenement stairs, going from shop to shop, visiting innumerable factories, calling at hundreds of city and suburban homes, covering the rural districts, the big department stores and the immense office buildings with their thousands of occupants. It was estimated that 60 per cent of the enrolled voters received these personal appeals. The membership of the party was increased by 60,535 women secured as members by canvassers.

The following is a brief summing up of the activities of the ten months' campaign.

Voters canvassed (60 per cent of those enrolled)	396,698
Women canvassed	60,535
Voters circularized	826,796
Party membership increased from 151,688 to	212,223
Watchers and pickets furnished for the polls	3,151
Numbers of leaflets printed and distributed	2,883,264
Money expended from the City treasury	$25,579
Number of outdoor meetings	5,225
Number of indoor meetings (district)	660
Number of mass meetings	93
Political meetings addressed by Congressmen, Assemblymen and Constitutional Convention delegates	25

Total number of meetings	6,003
Night speaking in theaters	60
Theater Week (Miner's and Keith's)	2
Speeches and suffrage slides in movie theaters	150
Concerts (indoor, 10, outdoor, 3)	13
Suffrage booths in bazaars	6
Number of Headquarters (Borough 4, Districts, 20)	24
Campaign vans (drawn by horses 6, decorated autos 6, district autos 4), vehicles in constant use	16
Papers served regularly with news (English and foreign)	80
Suffrage editions of papers prepared	2
Special articles on suffrage	150
Sermons preached by request just before election	64

A *Weekly News Bulletin* (for papers and workers) and the *Woman Voter* (a weekly magazine) issued; many unique features like stories, verses, etc.; hundreds of ministers circularized and speakers sent to address congregations; the endorsements of all city officials and of many prominent people and big organizations secured.

In order to accomplish the work indicated by this table a large number of expert canvassers, speakers, executives and clerical workers were required. Mrs. Catt as State Campaign chairman was a great driving force and an inspiration that never failed, and Miss Hay in directing the party forces and raising the money showed remarkable ability. Associated with her were capable officials—Mrs. Margaret Chandler Aldrich, Mrs. Wells, Mrs. Martha Wentworth Suffren, Mrs. Robert McGregor, Mrs. Cornelia K. Hood, Mrs. Marie Jenney Howe, Mrs. Joseph Fitch, Mrs. A. J. Newbury, and the tireless borough chairmen, Mrs. James Lees Laidlaw, Manhattan; Mrs. H. Edward Dreier, Brooklyn; Mrs. Henrietta Speke Seeley, Bronx; Mrs. Alfred J. Eno, Queens, and Mrs. William G. Willcox, Richmond.

The spectacular activities of the campaign caught and held public attention. Various classes of men were complimented by giving them "suffrage days." The appeal to the firemen took the form of an automobile demonstration, open air speaking along the line of march of their annual parade and a ten dollar gold piece given to one of their number who made a daring rescue of a yellow-sashed dummy—a suffrage lady. A circular letter was sent to 800 firemen requesting their help for all suffragists.

"Barbers' Day" produced ten columns of copy in leading New York dailies. Letters were sent in advance to 400 barbers informing them that on a certain day the suffragists would call upon them. The visits were made in autos decorated with barbers' poles and laden with maps and posters to hang up in the shops and then open air meetings were held out in front. Street cleaners on the day of the "White Wings" parade were given souvenirs of tiny brooms and suffrage leaflets and addressed from automobiles. A whole week was given to the street car men who numbered 240,000. Suffrage speeches were given at the car barns and leaflets and a "car barn" poster distributed.

Forty-five banks and trust companies were treated to a "raid" made by suffrage depositors, who gave out literature and held open meetings afterward. Brokers were reached through two days in Wall Street where the suffragists entered in triumphal style, flags flying, bugles playing. Speeches were made, souvenirs distributed and a luncheon held in a "suffrage" restaurant. The second day hundreds of colored balloons were sent up to typify "the suffragists' hopes ascending." Workers in the subway excavations were visited with Irish banners and shamrock fliers; Turkish, Armenian, French, German and Italian restaurants were canvassed as were the laborers on the docks, in vessels and in public markets.

A conspicuous occasion was the Night of the Interurban Council Fires, when on high bluffs in the different boroughs huge bonfires were lighted, fireworks and balloons sent up, while music, speeches and transparencies emphasized the fact that woman's evolution from the campfire of the savage into a new era was commemorated. Twenty-eight parades were a feature of the open air demonstrations. There were besides numbers of torchlight rallies; street dances on the lower East Side; Irish, Syrian, Italian and Polish block parties; outdoor concerts, among them a big one in Madison Square, where a full orchestra played, opera singers sang and eminent orators spoke; open air religious services with the moral and religious aspects of suffrage discussed; a fête held in beautiful Dyckman Glen; flying squadrons of speakers whirling in autos from the Battery to the Bronx; an "interstate meet" on the streets where suffragists of Massachusetts, New Jersey and New York participated. Ninety original features arranged on a big scale with many minor ones brought great publicity to the cause and the suffragists ended their campaign valiantly with sixty speakers talking continuously in Columbus Circle for twenty-six hours.

Source: Reprinted in *The History of Woman Suffrage*, Vol. VI, edited by Ida Husted Harper. New York, NY: National American Woman Suffrage Association, 1922, 459–64.

10. "Women Must Fight, Says Mrs. Belmont: Suffrage Leader, Ready to Sail for World Convention, Praises Militancy," *New York Times*, 1913

Predicts Trouble for Us

If Women Don't Get the Ballot—She Is Taking Cash to Mrs. Pankhurst in London.

Mrs. O. H. P. Belmont, on the eve of a trip abroad to attend the International Woman Suffrage Convention in Budapest, talked yesterday of her firm belief in the militant methods of the English suffragettes, said that conditions would become serious in America if the women after all their hard work for sixty years did not get the vote, and implied that with Charles F. Murphy at the head of Tammany Hall the New York women had an unpromising fight before them.

Mrs. Belmont will sail on the Mauretania on Wednesday morning. She will stop a day in London, taking time to see Mrs. Pankhurst and give her the check for several hundred pounds she promised her at the time of the recent suffragette meeting in London, when $75,000 was raised. She will spend some time in Paris, where she will be with Christabel Pankhurst and "learn something of militant methods," as she said with a smile. The Duchess of Marlborough expects to accompany Mrs. Belmont to Budapest, where the convention will open on June 15.

"I have not been abroad for four years," said Mrs. Belmont yesterday. "There has been so much suffrage work to attend to that I have not had time and now I need the rest, for there will be a great deal of work when I come back if we do what we should to win the vote in 1915. If the women do not win then, conditions will be very serious. The women here have been working for sixty years, while the women of England have been working for forty-five years. They will not be contented to go on in the same way forever. The English women will get the vote now before we do, and that will be a disgrace.

"It will all be due to the English militant methods. The women would never have had anything if they had gone on in the old way. People here do not know it, but Mrs. Pankhurst was told by Arthur Balfour and other big men that these were the methods that she must pursue. Men have never won their freedom without shedding blood, and the women will not get theirs without fighting. They have said that they would not hurt any one but themselves, and that is what they have done. It is not pleasant to go out and smash windows. You wouldn't like it and I would not like to, but it is the only thing to be done. See what the men are doing in Belgium, but that is all right because men are doing it. They are right and so are the women.

"Women fought in the French Revolution and in the Reformation. But then they were fighting for the liberty of men, and it was all right. There is a monument to a woman of the Revolution on the Hudson. Her husband was killed and she took his place and fired the cannon, but then that was fighting for the liberty of men. I don't know what our women will do when the time comes, but I should be ashamed of them if they were not as brave as the English women.

"Here we have the liquor interests and the worst politicians against us. Murphy will have nothing to do with us. All the Republican organizations have allowed us to hold meetings in their clubhouses, and I wrote and asked Mr. Murphy to grant us the use of Tammany Hall, but he refused. We shall have the better men with us, but in New York we shall have a hard fight, especially if Murphy continues in power.

"I believe the vote will come to New York through the Federal Government. With Alaska we now have the entire Pacific Coast. There are nine Western States that will come in in November, and others a little later. When the greater number of the Western States have enfranchised their women and send representations the Federal Government can then force the enfranchisement of women upon the Eastern States. That will be a humiliating thing to do, but it may be the only way in which we will get the vote.

"I am saving the sayings of well-known men in regard to suffrage, and some day I shall publish them in a book, and they will not be proud of them. I wrote to Senator Clark and asked him to take a box at the Metropolitan Opera House on the night of the pageant, and he wrote me a letter of six pages to say that after my expression of sympathy with the suffragettes of England he could not think of doing so. I am saving that letter for my book, and I have many others.

"The Budapest Convention will be of great interest. Every Nation will be represented, and for the first time the Chinese women will come as delegates. They have enfranchised the women in Hungary, but only the women of wealth, and the Socialists are opposing it, asking for the full franchise for all men and women. The authorities are anxious to have us meet in Budapest, and there has been feeling in Vienna because the convention is not to be held there. Hungary was chosen for the convention because it makes it simpler for the women of the Orient to reach there."

Mrs. Belmont is a delegate from the United States to the convention. She has taken a house for the months of July and August on the French coast and will return in September. Her New York lunchroom will be closed during the Summer, as usual, but the offices will be open, and the work of suffrage will continue. During her absence Mrs. Belmont will have a large corps of suffrage organizers working in different parts of the country.

Source: "Women Must Fight, Says Mrs. Belmont: Suffrage Leader, Ready to Sail for World Convention, Praises Militancy," *New York Times*, April 22, 1913.

11. "Mrs. Brannan Tells of Jail Treatment: Asserts That Women Pickets Were Roughly Handled at Occoquan. Demands Removal of Flag. Believes That Attempt Was Made to Break Prisoners Spirit by Torture of Fear," *New York Times*, 1917

Mrs. Eunice Dana Brannan, wife of John Winters Brannan, President of Bellevue and Allied Hospitals, sent out last night, through the National Woman's Party, of which she is acting Chairman for this State, a signed account of her experiences in Occoquan prison, where she was confined for her picketing activities. Mrs. Brannan was brought back to this city a few days ago by her husband, after she had been made ill, it was said, by her treatment in the prison. Mrs. Brannan attacked the administration of the prison; demanded that the American flag no longer should fly over it, and asserted that the pickets had been confined under trumped-up charges of obstructing traffic, when, in reality, they could have obtained their release at any time by promising to stop picketing.

Mrs. Brannan said that she and her companions had been cruelly treated, and that last July, when sixteen pickets had first been committed to the workhouse, the plan had been "to break us down by inflicting extraordinary humiliation upon us." This, Mrs. Brannan added, had failed to stop the picketing, and then, she alleges, "the plan of terrorizing us was conceived and carried out to a degree that has not yet been told."

Continuing Mrs. Brannan said: "The plan last July, when sixteen of us were first committed to the workhouse, was plainly to break us down by inflicting extraordinary humiliations upon us."

Mrs. Brannan added that she and her companions were deprived of every decency of personal life such as combs and tooth brushes, and that only one piece of soap was allowed to all the inmates of the dormitory. The head matron, she said, had emphasized the danger of communicable diseases.

"The plan of humiliation failed to stop our peaceful legal picketing." Mrs. Brannan added, "On Nov. 10 forty-one women of the National Woman's Party picketed the White House gates. Then the plan of terrorizing us was conceived and carried out to a degree that has not yet been told. The scene that took place in the reception room of the workhouse on the night of Nov. 14 was of incredibly infamous cruelty. Nothing that we know of German frightfulness short of murdering and maiming noncombatants could exceed the brutality that was used toward us.

I saw three men seize Miss Burns, twisting her arms behind her, and then two other men grasp her shoulders. There were six to ten guards in the room and many others collected on the porch—forty to fifty in all. These all rushed in. Instantly the room was in havoc. The guards fell upon us. I saw Miss Lincoln, a slight young girl, thrown to the floor. Mrs. Nolan, a delicate old lady of 73, was mastered by two men. The furniture was overturned and the room was a scene of havoc. The whole group of women were thrown, dragged and hurled out of the office, down the steps and across the road and field to the Administration Building, where another group of bullies was waiting for us. The women were thrown down roughly on benches. I was thrown with four others in a cell with a narrow bed and dirty blankets. The chair was immediately taken out.

The cell door opposite was opened for a moment. I saw Miss Lincoln and spoke across to her. 'Are you all right?' Instantly the guard appeared. 'Stop that,' he yelled at me: 'not another word from your mouth or I will handcuff you and gag you and put you in a straitjacket if you say another word.' Not a woman attendant was in sight. We were absolutely in the power of a gang of prison thugs. It was a night of most extreme terror. The guards clanged the barred doors and opened them upon us at their will, gave us or denied us water, jeered at me when I asked for a pillow or more water. No food of any kind was offered to us. There is no question that this time our jailors made the attempt to break us down by the mental torture of fear.

I noticed one of the guards had a billy in his hands. There were idle matrons in the dormatories that might readily have been sent to the prison to look after us and ensure decent respect for us as women.

At 11 o'clock Thursday our group came out fainting and ill—in a state of exhaustion and shock and indescribable stunning of every faculty. Added to this was my anxiety as to the fate of my companions.

On this same day half swooning. I fell upon my knees in the doctor's office, where I had gone to ask to be allowed to lie down. I was in terror of another attack by the guards every moment. I could not sleep for fears."

Mrs. Brannan took a walk on Friday in the woods near the prison while, she says, an attempt was made to terrorize the women with bloodhounds.

"On our way back." Mrs. Brannan continued, "we heard the baying of hounds in the woods very near us. The matron said: 'You must hurry up,' the bloodhounds are lose.' Miss Findissen asked: 'Would they attack us?' 'That's just what they would do,' she answered, and hurried us on faster. The baying grow louder and nearer at times and then more distinct as the dogs rushed back and forth. They were very close to us when we finally reached the sewing room."

"An hour after this," she added, "our counsel. Mr. O'Brien, was able to effect an entrance to our prison and to see us alone—the first blessed evidence that our friends could at last reach and protect us."

In conclusion, Mrs. Brannan said:

"If proof is needed that the Administration is behind the attempt to suppress our campaign for the Federal suffrage amendment, it can be found in the following fact. When Mrs. Morey and three others were giving their names at the desk Whittaker said to them. 'If you will promise not to picket again, I will release you at once. I will take back to Washington in my own car you need not pay your fines.' Yet people say we were arrested for obstructing traffic!"

Source: "Mrs. Brannan Tells of Jail Treatment: Asserts That Women Pickets Were Roughly Handled at Occoquan. Demands Removal of Flag. Believes That Attempt Was Made to Break Prisoners Spirit by Torture of Fear," *New York Times*, November 29, 1917.

12. "Pickets Are Praised: Dudley Field Malone Talks to Mass Meeting in Their Honor," Special to the *New York Times*, 1917

PICKETS ARE PRAISED

Dudley Field Malone Talks to Mass Meeting in Their Honor.

Special to The New York Times.

WASHINGTON, Dec. 9.—At a mass meeting at the Belasco Theatre this afternoon in honor of militant suffragists—members of the National Woman's Party who served terms of imprisonment in the workhouse at Occoquan, Va., for picketing the White House—Dudley Field Malone said:

"In last August my good friend the Attorney General, Mr. Gregory, told me in the presence of witnesses that whenever it should be necessary to suppress political propaganda advocated by women the thing to do was to make the women look ridiculous, and he advocated the sprinkling of woman suffragists with a hose when they went to picket for the Federal amendment. Yet in the shadow of impending events of November the same Mr. Gregory wrote an urgent letter to the men of New York begging them to vote for woman suffrage. But there is nothing more admirable than a sudden convert."

The theatre was packed and a large force of police was on hand to preserve order. Mrs. O. H. P. Belmont of New York presided. To carry on the campaign for the suffrage amendment to the Federal Constitution $86,326.34 was collected. The crowd was enthusiastic, and when ninety-seven pickets who had served time in the workhouse paraded around the theatre, carrying suffrage banners, the crowd made a great demonstration. Mrs. William Kent of California, wife of an ex-Congressman who is a member of the Federal Trade Commission, presented to each of the released pickets pins made in the design of cell doors.

When pledges were called for Mrs. Belmont gave $1,000 "in honor of Alice Paul." Mrs. Howard Gould gave $5,000 in honor of Mr. Malone, "the first and so far the only man to put the freedom of American women before all other interests." Mrs. J. A. H. Hopkins of New Jersey pledged $2,000. Two women who had been prisoners at Occoquan gave 50 cents and 30 cents, respectively. State pledges were: Virginia, $15.000; New York, $20,000: Pennsylvania, $10,000; District of Columbia, $6,000: Maryland, $5,000; California, $3,000; Connecticut, $3,000; Minnesota, $2,000; New Jersey, $2,000; Massachusetts, $1,000; Illinois, $600; Utah, $300; Maine, Delaware, Colorado, Louisville, KY, and Newark, NJ, $100 each. Florida gave $150, and Panama $5.

Source: "Pickets Are Praised: Dudley Field Malone Talks to Mass Meeting in Their Honor," Special to the *New York Times, New York Times*, December 10, 1917.

Appendix: Suffrage Timetable

COUNTRIES IN WHICH WOMEN COULD VOTE BEFORE THE UNITED STATES:

New Zealand	1893	Scotland	1918
Australia	1902	Austria	1918
Finland	1906	Czechoslovakia	1918
Norway	1907	Hungary	1918
Denmark	1915	Holland	1919
Mexico	1917	British East Africa	1919
Russia	1917	Luxemburg	1919
Ireland	1918	Uruguay	1919
Wales	1918	Belgium	1919
Canada	1918	Rhodesia	1919
Germany	1918	Iceland	1919
England	1918	Sweden	1919
Poland	1918	United States	1920

SELECTED
BIBLIOGRAPHY

Adams, Jad. *Women and the Vote: A World History*. Oxford: Oxford University Press, 2016.

Adams, Katherine H., and Michael L. Keene. *Alice Paul and the American Suffrage Campaign*. Urbana: University of Illinois Press, 2008.

Alpern, Sara, and Dale Baum. "Female Ballots: The Impact of the Nineteenth Amendment." *Journal of Interdisciplinary History* 16, no. 1 (Summer 1985): 43–67.

Andersen, Kristi. *After Suffrage: Women in Partisan and Electoral Politics before the New Deal*. American Politics and Political Economy. Chicago, IL: University of Chicago, 1996.

Andolsen, Barbara Hilkert. *"Daughters of Jefferson, Daughters of Bootblacks": Racism and American Feminism*. Macon, GA: Mercer University Press, 1986.

Baker, Jean H. *Votes for Women: The Struggle for Suffrage Revisited*. New York, NY: Oxford University Press, 2002.

Banaszak, Lee Ann. *Why Movements Succeed or Fail: Opportunity, Culture and the Struggle for Women Suffrage*. Princeton, NJ: Princeton University Press, 1996.

Barry, Kathleen. *Susan B. Anthony: A Biography of a Singular Feminist*. New York, NY: Ballantine Books, 1990.

Beeton, Beverly. *Women Vote in the West: The Woman Suffrage Movement, 1869–1896*. New York, NY: Garland, 1986.

Blatch, Harriot Stanton, and Alma Lutz. *Challenging Years: The Memoirs of Harriot Stanton Blatch*. New York, NY: Putnam's, 1940.

Bolt, Christine. *The Women's Movements in the United States and Britain from the 1790s to the 1920s.* Amherst: University of Massachusetts Press, 1993.

Bordin, Ruth. *Frances Willard: A Biography.* Chapel Hill: University of North Carolina Press, 1986.

Bordin, Ruth Birgitta Anderson. *Woman and Temperance: The Quest for Power and Liberty, 1873–1900.* New Brunswick, NJ: Rutgers University Press, 1981.

Boydston, Jeanne, Mary Kelley, and Anne Throne Margolis. *The Limits of Sisterhood: The Beecher Sisters on Women's Rights and Woman's Sphere.* Gender and American Culture. Chapel Hill: University of North Carolina Press, 1988.

Boylan, Anne M. *The Origins of Women's Activism.* Chapel Hill: University of North Carolina Press, 2002.

Brammer, Leila R. *Excluded from Suffrage History: Matilda Joslyn Gage, Nineteenth-Century American Feminist.* Westport, CT: Greenwood Press, 2000.

Brown, Elsa Barkley. "'What Has Happened Here': The Politics of Difference in Women's History and Feminist Politics." *Feminist Studies* 18, no. 2 (Summer 1992): 295–312.

Brown, Elsa Barkley, Darlene Clark Hine, and Rosalyn Terborg-Penn. *Black Women in America.* Brooklyn, NY: Carlson Publishing, 1993.

Buechler, Steven M. *The Transformation of the Woman Suffrage Movement: The Case of Illinois, 1850–1920.* New Brunswick, NJ: Rutgers University Press, 1986.

Buhle, Mari Jo. *Women and American Socialism, 1870–1920.* Urbana: University of Illinois Press, 1981.

Buhle, Mari Jo, and Paul Buhle, eds. *The Concise History of Woman Suffrage: Selections from the Classic Work of Stanton, Anthony, Gage, and Harper.* Urbana: University of Illinois Press, 1978.

Camhi, Jane Jerome. *Women against Women: American Anti-Suffragism, 1880–1920.* Brooklyn, NY: Carlson Publishing, 1994.

Cassidy, Tina. *Mr. President, How Long Must We Wait? Alice Paul, Woodrow Wilson, and the Fight for the Right to Vote.* New York, NY: Simon and Schuster, 2019.

Chapman, Mary, and Angela Mills. *Treacherous Texts: U.S. Suffrage Literature, 1846–1946*. New Brunswick, NJ: Rutgers University Press, 2011.

Cooney, Robert. *Winning the Vote: The Triumph of the American Woman Suffrage Movement*. Santa Cruz, CA: American Graphic Press, 2005.

Corder, J. Kevin, and Christina Wolbrecht. *Counting Women's Ballots: Female Voters from Suffrage through the New Deal*. New York, NY: Cambridge University Press, 2016.

Cott, Nancy F. "Feminist Politics in the 1920s: The National Woman's Party." *Journal of American History* 71, no. 1 (June 1984): 43–68.

Cott, Nancy F. *The Grounding of Modern Feminism*. New Haven, CT: Yale University Press, 1987.

DuBois, Ellen Carol. *Feminism and Suffrage: The Emergence of an Independent Women's Movement in America, 1848–1869*. Ithaca, NY: Cornell University Press, 1999.

DuBois, Ellen Carol. *Harriot Stanton Blatch and the Winning of Woman Suffrage*. New Haven, CT: Yale University Press, 1999.

DuBois, Ellen Carol. *Woman Suffrage and Women's Rights*. New York: New York University Press, 1998.

Dudden, Faye E. *Fighting Chance: The Struggle over Woman Suffrage and Black Suffrage in Reconstruction America*. New York, NY: Oxford University Press, 2011.

Dye, Nancy Schrom. *As Equals and as Sisters: Feminism, the Labor Movement, and the Women's Trade Union League of New York*. Columbia: University of Missouri Press, 1980.

Edwards, G. Thomas. *Sowing Good Seeds: The Northwest Suffrage Campaigns of Susan B. Anthony*. Portland: Oregon Historical Society Press, 1990.

Edwards, Laura F. *Gendered Strife & Confusion: The Political Culture of Reconstruction*. Urbana: University of Illinois Press, 1997.

Edwards, Rebecca. *Angels in the Machinery: Gender in American Party Politics from the Civil War to the Progressive Era*. New York, NY: Oxford University Press, 1997.

Egge, Sara. *Woman Suffrage and Citizenship in the Midwest, 1870–1920*. Iowa City: University of Iowa Press, 2018.

Farrell, Grace. *Lillie Devereux Blake: Retracing a Life Erased.* Amherst: University of Massachusetts Press, 2002.

Faulkner, Carol. *Lucretia Mott's Heresy: Abolition and Women's Rights in Nineteenth-Century America.* Philadelphia: University of Pennsylvania Press, 2011.

Finnegan, Margaret Mary. *Selling Suffrage: Consumer Culture & Votes for Women.* New York, NY: Columbia University Press, 1999.

Flexner, Eleanor. *Century of Struggle; the Woman's Rights Movement in the United States.* New York, NY: Atheneum, 1972.

Foner, Philip S., ed. *Frederick Douglas on Women's Rights.* New York, NY: Da Capo Press, 1992.

Ford, Linda. *Iron-Jawed Angels: The Suffrage Militancy of the National Woman's Party, 1912–1920.* Lanham, MD: University Press of America, 1991.

Fowler, Robert Booth. *Carrie Catt: Feminist Politician.* Boston, MA: Northeastern University Press, 1986.

Franzen, Trisha. *Anna Howard Shaw: The Work of Woman Suffrage.* Urbana: University of Illinois Press, 2014.

Free, Laura E. *Suffrage Reconstructed: Gender, Race, and Voting Rights in the Civil War Era.* Ithaca, NY: Cornell University Press, 2015.

Freeman, Jo. *A Room at a Time: How Women Entered Party Politics.* Lanham, MD: Rowman & Littlefield, 2000.

Frost-Knappman, Elizabeth, and Kathryn Cullen-DuPont. *Women's Suffrage in America.* Updated ed. New York, NY: Facts on File, 2005.

Fuller, Paul E. *Laura Clay and the Woman's Rights Movement.* Lexington: University Press of Kentucky, 1975.

Giddings, Paula. *When and Where I Enter: The Impact of Black Women on Race and Sex in America.* New York, NY: William Morrow, 1984.

Giesberg, Judith Ann. *Army at Home: Women and the Civil War on the Northern Home Front.* Chapel Hill: University of North Carolina Press, 2009.

Gilmore, Glenda Elizabeth. *Gender and Jim Crow: Women and the Politics of White Supremacy in North Carolina, 1896–1920.* Chapel Hill: University of North Carolina Press, 2006.

Ginzberg, Lori D. *Elizabeth Cady Stanton: An American Life.* New York, NY: Hill and Wang, 2009.

Ginzberg, Lori D. *Untidy Origins: A Story of Woman's Rights in Antebellum New York.* Chapel Hill: University of North Carolina Press, 2005.

Goldberg, Michael L. *An Army of Women: Gender and Politics in Gilded Age Kansas.* Baltimore, MD: Johns Hopkins University Press, 1997.

Goodier, Susan. *No Votes for Women: The New York State Anti-Suffrage Movement.* Urbana: University of Illinois Press, 2013.

Goodier, Susan, and Karen Pastorello. *Women Will Vote: Winning Suffrage in New York State.* Ithaca, NY: Cornell University Press, 2017.

Gordon, Ann D., ed. *African American Women and the Vote, 1837–1965.* Amherst: University of Massachusetts Press, 1997.

Gordon, Ann D., ed. *The Selected Papers of Elizabeth Cady Stanton and Susan B. Anthony.* 6 vols. New Brunswick, NJ: Rutgers University Press, 1997–2013.

Gordon, Ann D. *The Trial of Susan B. Anthony.* Washington, DC: Federal Judicial Center, 2005.

Gordon, Felice D. *After Winning: The Legacy of the New Jersey Suffragists, 1920–1947.* New Brunswick, NJ: Rutgers University Press, 1986.

Gordon, Sarah Barringer. "'The Liberty of Self-Degradation': Polygamy, Woman Suffrage, and Consent in Nineteenth-Century America." *Journal of American History* 83, no. 3 (1996): 815–47.

Green, Elna C. *Southern Strategies: Southern Women and the Woman Suffrage Question.* Chapel Hill: University of North Carolina Press, 1997.

Griffith, Elisabeth. *In Her Own Right: The Life of Elizabeth Cady Stanton.* New York, NY: Oxford University Press, 1984.

Gustafson, Melanie S. *Women and the Republican Party, 1854–1924.* Urbana: University of Illinois Press, 2001.

Gustafson, Melanie S., Kristie Miller, and Elisabeth Israels Perry. *We Have Come to Stay: American Women and Political Parties, 1880–1960.* Albuquerque: University of New Mexico Press, 1999.

Harley, Sharon, and Rosalyn Terborg-Penn. *The Afro-American Woman: Struggles and Images.* Baltimore, MD: Black Classic Press, 1997.

Harrison, Patricia Greenwood. *Connecting Links: The British and American Woman Suffrage Movements, 1900–1914*. Westport, CT: Greenwood Press, 2000.

Hendricks, Wanda A. *Gender, Race, and Politics in the Midwest: Black Club Women in Illinois*. Bloomington: Indiana University Press, 1998.

Hersh, Blanche Glassman. *The Slavery of Sex: Feminist-Abolitionists in America*. Urbana: University of Illinois Press, 1978.

Hewitt, Nancy A. "Feminist Friends: Agrarian Quakers and the Emergence of Woman's Rights in America." *Feminist Studies* 12, no. 1 (Spring 1986): 27–49.

Hewitt, Nancy A. "From Seneca Falls to Suffrage: Reimagining a 'Master' Narrative in U.S. Women's History." In *No Permanent Waves: Recasting Histories of U.S. Feminism*, edited by Nancy A. Hewitt. New Brunswick, NJ: Rutgers University Press, 2010.

Hewitt, Nancy A. *Women's Activism and Social Change: Rochester, New York, 1822–1872*. Ithaca, NY: Cornell University Press, 1984.

Hewitt, Nancy A., and Suzanne Lebsock. *Visible Women: New Essays on American Activism*. Women in American History. Urbana: University of Illinois Press, 1993.

Higginbotham, Evelyn Brooks. *Righteous Discontent: The Women's Movement in the Black Baptist Church, 1880–1920*. Cambridge, MA: Harvard University Press, 1994.

Hine, Darlene Clark, Elsa Barkley Brown, and Rosalyn Terborg-Penn, eds. *Black Women in America: An Historical Encyclopedia*. 2 vols. Bloomington: Indiana University Press, 1994.

Hoffert, Sylvia D. *Alva Vanderbilt Belmont: Unlikely Champion of Women's Rights*. Bloomington: Indiana University Press, 2012.

Hoffert, Sylvia D. *Jane Grey Swisshelm: An Unconventional Life. 1815–1884*. Chapel Hill: University of North Carolina Press, 2004.

Hoffert, Sylvia D. *When Hens Crow: The Woman's Rights Movement in Antebellum America*. Bloomington: Indiana University Press, 1995.

Isenberg, Nancy. *Sex and Citizenship in Antebellum America*. Gender and American Culture. Chapel Hill: University of North Carolina Press, 1998.

James, Edward L., Janet Wilson James, and Paul S. Boyer., eds. *Notable American Women: A Biographical Dictionary*. Vols. 1–3. Cambridge, MA: Belknap Press of Harvard University Press, 1971.

Jeffrey, Julie Roy. *The Great Silent Army of Abolitionism: Ordinary Women in the Antislavery Movement*. Chapel Hill: University of North Carolina Press, 1998.

Johnson, Joan Marie. *Southern Ladies, New Women: Race, Religion, and Clubwomen in South Carolina, 1890–1930*. Gainesville: University Press of Florida, 2004.

Jones, Martha S. *All Bound Up Together: The Woman Question in African American Public Culture, 1830–1900*. Chapel Hill: University of North Carolina Press, 2007.

Kerber, Linda K. *Women of the Republic: Intellect and Ideology in Revolutionary America*. Chapel Hill: University of North Carolina Press, 1980.

Keyssar, Alexander. *The Right to Vote: The Contested History of Democracy in the United States*. New York, NY: Basic Books, 2000.

Klapper, Melissa R. *Ballots, Babies, and Banners of Peace: American Jewish Women's Activism, 1890–1940*. New York: New York University Press, 2013.

Kraditer, Aileen S. *The Ideas of the Woman Suffrage Movement: 1890–1920*. New York, NY: W. W. Norton, 1981.

Kroeger, Brooke. *The Suffragents: How Women Used Men to Get the Vote*. Albany: State University of New York Press, 2017.

Lasser, Carol, and Marlene Merrill, eds. *Friends and Sisters: Letters between Lucy Stone and Antoinette Brown Blackwell, 1846–93*. Urbana: University of Illinois Press, 1987.

Lasser, Carol, and Stacey M. Robertson. *Antebellum Women: Private, Public, Partisan*. Lanham, MD: Rowman & Littlefield, 2010.

Lerner, Gerda. *The Grimké Sisters from South Carolina: Pioneers for Women's Rights and Abolition*. Revised and expanded ed. Chapel Hill: University of North Carolina Press, 2004.

Lumsden, Linda J. *Inez: The Life and Times of Inez Milholland*. Bloomington: Indiana University Press, 2004.

Lumsden, Linda J. *Rampant Women: Suffragists and the Right of Assembly*. Knoxville: University of Tennessee Press, 1997.

Lunardini, Christine A. *Alice Paul: Equality for Women. Lives of American Women*. Philadelphia, PA: Westview Press, 2013.

Lunardini, Christine A., and Thomas J. Knock. "Woodrow Wilson and Woman Suffrage: A New Look." *Political Science Quarterly* 95, no. 4 (Winter 1980–1981): 655–71.

Marilley, Suzanne M. *Woman Suffrage and the Origins of Liberal Feminism in the United States, 1820–1920*. Cambridge, MA: Harvard University Press, 1996.

Marshall, Susan E. *Splintered Sisterhood: Gender and Class in the Campaign against Woman Suffrage*. Madison: University of Wisconsin Press, 1997.

McCammon, Holly J. "Stirring Up Suffrage Sentiment: The Formation of the State Woman Suffrage Organizations, 1866–1914." *Social Forces* 80, no. 2 (2001): 449–80.

McCarthy, Tara M. *Respectability and Reform: Irish American Women's Activism. 1880–1920*. Syracuse, NY: Syracuse University Press, 2018.

McConnaughy, Corrine M. *The Woman Suffrage Movement in America: A Reassessment*. New York, NY: Cambridge University, 2013.

McMillen, Sally G. *Lucy Stone: An Unapologetic Life*. New York, NY: Oxford University Press, 2015.

Murphy, Teresa Anne. *Citizenship and the Origins of Women's History in the United States*. Democracy, Citizenship, and Constitutionalism. Philadelphia: University of Pennsylvania Press, 2013.

Newman, Louise Michele. *White Women's Rights: The Racial Origins of Feminism in the United States*. New York, NY: Oxford University Press, 1999.

Nichols, Carole. *Votes and More for Women: Suffrage and After in Connecticut*. New York, NY: Haworth Press, 1983.

Norgren, Jill. *Belva Lockwood: The Woman Who Would Be President*. New York: New York University Press, 2007.

Opdyke, Sandra. *When Women Won the Vote: The Final Decade, 1910–1920*. New York, NY: Routledge, 2020.

Painter, Nell Irvin. *Sojourner Truth: A Life, a Symbol*. New York, NY: W. W. Norton, 2007.

Park, Maude Wood. *Front Door Lobby*. Edited by Edna Lamprey Stantial. Boston, MA: Beacon Press, 1960.

Parker, Alison M. *Articulating Rights: Nineteenth-Century American Women on Race, Reform, and the State*. DeKalb: Northern Illinois University Press, 2010.

Parker, Alison M., and Stephanie Cole, eds. *Women and the Unstable State in Nineteenth-Century America*. College Station: Texas A & M University Press, 2000.

Penney, Sherry H., and James D. Livingston. *A Very Dangerous Woman: Martha Wright and Women's Rights*. Amherst: University of Massachusetts Press, 2004.

Pierson, Michael D. *Free Hearts and Free Homes: Gender and American Antislavery Politics*. Chapel Hill: University of North Carolina Press, 2003.

Robertson, Stacey M. *Betsy Mix Cowles: Champion of Equality*. New York, NY: Rutledge, 2013.

Rogoff, Leonard. *Gertrude Weil: Jewish Progressive in the New South*. Chapel Hill: University of North Carolina Press, 2017.

Ross-Nazzal, Jennifer M. *Winning the West for Women: The Life of Suffragist Emma Smith DeVoe*. Seattle: University of Washington Press, 2011.

Schechter, Patricia Ann. *Ida B. Wells-Barnett and American Reform, 1880–1930*. Chapel Hill: University of North Carolina Press, 2001.

Schuyler, Lorraine Gates. *The Weight of their Votes*. Chapel Hill: University of North Carolina Press, 2008.

Scott, Anne Firor. *Natural Allies: Women's Associations in American History*. Urbana: University of Illinois Press, 1991.

Scott, Anne Firor. *The Southern Lady: From Pedestal to Politics, 1830–1930*. Chicago, IL: University of Chicago Press, 1970.

Scott, Anne Firor, and Andrew M. Scott. *One Half the People: The Fight for Woman Suffrage*. Urbana: University of Illinois Press, 1982.

Showalter, Elaine. *The Civil Wars of Julia Ward Howe: A Biography*. New York, NY: Simon and Schuster, 2016.

Sicherman, Barbara, and Carol Hurd Green, eds. *Notable American Women: The Modern Period*. Cambridge, MA: Harvard University Press, 1980.

Sklar, Kathryn Kish. *Catharine Beecher: A Study in American Domesticity*. New Haven, CT: Yale University Press, 1973.

Smith, Norma. *Jeannette Rankin, America's Conscience*. Helena: Montana Historical Society Press, 2002.

Sneider, Allison L. *Suffragists in an Imperial Age: U.S. Expansion and the Woman Question, 1870–1929*. New York, NY: Oxford University Press, 2008.

Solomon, Martha M. *A Voice of their Own: The Woman Suffrage Press: 1840–1910*. Tuscaloosa: University of Alabama Press, 1991.

Southard, Belinda A. Stillion. *Militant Citizenship: Rhetorical Strategies of the National Woman's Party, 1913–1920*. College Station: Texas A & M University Press, 2011.

Stansell, Christine. *American Moderns: Bohemian New York and the Creation of a New Century*. New York, NY: Henry Holt, 2001.

Stanton, Elizabeth Cady. *Eighty Years and More (1815–1897 Reminiscences of Elizabeth Cady Stanton)*. 1898. Repr. New York, NY: Schocken Books, 1971.

Stanton, Elizabeth Cady, and Susan B. Anthony. *The Elizabeth Cady Stanton-Susan B. Anthony Reader: Correspondence, Writings, Speeches*. Edited by Ellen Carol DuBois. Boston, MA: Northeastern University Press, 1992.

Stanton, Elizabeth Cady, and Susan B. Anthony, and Matilda Joslyn Gage, and Ida Husted Harper, eds. *The History of Woman Suffrage*. 6 vols. 1881–1992. Reprint ed. Salem, NH: Ayer, 1985.

Sterling, Dorothy. *Ahead of Her Time: Abby Kelley and the Politics of Anti-Slavery*. New York, NY: W.W. Norton, 1991.

Sterling, Dorothy. *We Are Your Sisters: Black Women in the Nineteenth Century*. New York, NY: W.W. Norton, 1984.

Stevens, Doris and Marjorie Julian Spruill. *Jailed for Freedom: The Story of the Militant American Suffragist Movement*. Chicago, IL: R.R. Donnelley & Sons, 2008.

Teele, Dawn Langan. *Forging the Franchise: The Political Origins of the Women's Vote*. Princeton, NJ: Princeton University Press, 2018.

Terborg-Penn, Rosalyn. *African American Women in the Struggle for the Vote, 1850–1920*. Blacks in the Diaspora. Bloomington: Indiana University Press, 1998.

Tetrault, Lisa. "The Incorporation of American Feminism: Suffragists and the Postbellum Lyceum." *Journal of American History* 96, no. 4 (2010): 1027–56.

Tetrault, Lisa. *The Myth of Seneca Falls: Memory and the Women's Suffrage Movement, 1848–1898*. Chapel Hill, NC: University of North Carolina Press, 2014.

Tyrrell, Ian R. *Woman's World Empire: The Woman's Christian Temperance Union in International Perspective, 1880–1930*. Chapel Hill: University of North Carolina Press, 1991.

VanBurkleo, Sandra F. *Gender Remade: Citizenship, Suffrage, and Public Power in the New Northwest, 1879–1912*. New York, NY: Cambridge University Press, 2015.

Varon, Elizabeth R. *We Mean to Be Counted: White Women & Politics in Antebellum Virginia*. Chapel Hill: University of North Carolina Press, 1998.

Venet, Wendy Hamand. *A Strong-Minded Woman: The Life of Mary Livermore*. Amherst: University of Massachusetts Press, 2005.

Vucic, Karen Dixon. *The Girls Next Door: Bringing the Home Front to the Front Lines*. Cambridge, MA: Harvard University Press, 2019.

Ware, Susan. *Why They Marched: Untold Stories of the Women Who Fought for the Right to Vote*. Cambridge, MA: Belknap Press of Harvard University Press, 2019.

Washington, Margaret. *Neither Ballots nor Bullets: Women Abolitionists and the Civil War*. Charlottesville: University Press of Virginia, 1991.

Washington, Margaret. *Sojourner Truth's America*. Urbana: University of Illinois Press, 2011.

Wellman, Judith. *The Road to Seneca Falls: Elizabeth Cady Stanton and the First Woman's Rights Convention*. Urbana: University of Illinois Press, 2004.

Wheeler, Marjorie Spruill. *New Women of the New South: The Leaders of the Woman Suffrage Movement in the Southern States*. New York, NY: Oxford University Press, 1993.

Wheeler, Marjorie Spruill. *One Woman, One Vote: Rediscovering the Woman Suffrage Movement*. Troutdale, OR: NewSage Press, 1995.

Wheeler, Marjorie Spruill. *Votes for Women!: The Woman Suffrage Movement in Tennessee, the South, and the Nation*. Knoxville, TN: University of Tennessee Press, 1995.

White, Deborah Gray. *Too Heavy a Load: Black Women in Defense of Themselves, 1894–1994*. New York, NY: W. W. Norton, 1999.

Yee, Shirley J. *Black Women Abolitionists: A Study in Activism, 1828–1860*. Knoxville: University of Tennessee Press, 1993.

Zahniser, Jill Diane, and Amelia R. Fry. *Alice Paul: Claiming Power*. New York, NY: Oxford University Press, 2014.

ONLINE RESOURCES

HistoryNet. https://www.historynet.com/susan-b-anthony.

Library of Congress: For Teachers, Votes for Women. http://www.loc.gov/teachers/classroommaterials/connections/votes-women/.

Library of Congress: National Woman Suffrage Collection. https://www.loc.gov/collections/national-american-woman-suffrage-association/about-this-collection/.

Library of Congress: Prints and Photographs, Votes for Women. https://www.loc.gov/rr/print/list/076_vfw.html.

National Park Service; Women's History. https://www.nps.gov/subjects/womenshistory/struggle-for-suffrage.htm.

National Women's History Museum. https://www.womenshistory.org/.

Women and Social Movements in the United States, 1600–2000. https://womhist.alexanderstreet.com/.

INDEX

About the Author

Marion W. Roydhouse, PhD, is emerita professor of history and founding director of the Center for Teaching Innovation and Nexus Learning at Thomas Jefferson University, Philadelphia, PA. Her published work includes the book *Women of Industry and Reform: Shaping the History of Pennsylvania, 1865–1940* and the articles "Bridging Chasms: Community and the Southern YWCA"; "Big Enough to Tell the Weeds from the Beans: The Impact of Industrial Life on Women in the South"; and "Partners in Progress: The Affiliated Schools for Women Workers." With experience in both secondary education and higher education, she chaired the Test Development Committee for American History and Social Studies Achievement Tests, was a reader for AP American History, and participated in grant projects on teaching history and as a consultant on writing across the curriculum in the K–12 system. She led grants in higher education, including grants from NEH, FIPSE, and an integrative learning grant from the Association of American Colleges and Universities (AAC&U) and the Carnegie Foundation for Advancement of Teaching.